Basic Legal Forms
for Business

Other books by the author

Operational Cash Flow Management and Control (Prentice-Hall, 1982)

The Property Maintenance Logbook (with William Chargar; Prentice-Hall, 1985)

Balance Sheet Management (Wiley, 1987)

The Right Price for Your Business (Wiley, 1988)

Basic Legal Forms
for Business

Morris A. Nunes

John Wiley & Sons, Inc.
New York • Chichester • Brisbane • Toronto • Singapore

To my wife, Janie . . .

"The Love that moves the sun and the other stars."

Dante

USING THIS BOOK

This book contains business forms prepared in a format which is readily convertible to personal use. Readers should feel free to reproduce or retype these forms for their personal use or for the use of their offices. These forms should not be used without having read the text in the book which accompanies the forms, nor should they be used without the user's absolute certainty that they have been changed to reflect the specific agreements of the user's business transaction. Thoughtless use of these forms may lead to agreements that do not reflect the wishes of the user or the party with whom the user is doing business. These forms are not to be resold.

Library of Congress Cataloging-in-Publication Data

Nunes, Morris A.
    Basic legal forms for business / Morris A. Nunes.
      p.   cm.
    Includes index.
    ISBN 0-471-59279-X (pbk.)
    1. Corporation law—United States—Forms.   2. Business
enterprises—United States—Forms.   I. Title.
KF 1411.N86 1993
346.73'066'0269—dc20   92-33345
[347.306660269]

Printed in the United States of America

10 9 8 7 6 5 4 3 2 1

Using the Diskette

DISK INSTRUCTIONS

The enclosed disk contains the text for 100 forms from this book. The data file names are listed in parentheses in the Table of Contents starting on page xi. A complete listing of the disk contents can also be found in a file called FILES.TXT.

Each form is saved in a separate data file on the disk. The data files are named using a simple formula of the Module number and form number. Therefore, file IX-02.TXT is the second file in Module IX, which is called *Invention of Confidentiality Agreement* and can be found on page 181 of the book. If there is no file name listed next to a particular form in the Table of Contents, then the form is not included on this disk.

System Requirements

This disk requires an IBM-PC or compatible computer with DOS Version 2.0 or later. The files can be used in both DOS and Windows environments using your own word processing software.

Getting Started

The files on this disk are in ASCII format. ASCII format is a standard text format for DOS computers. Using this format, a number of different users with different word processing programs can read the disks. Once the forms are loaded into your word processor, you can customize them to suit your individual needs. Some common word processing programs that can read ASCII format include WordPerfect, WordStar, Microsoft Word, both the DOS and Windows versions.

Before using this disk, we strongly recommend that you make a backup copy of the original. Making a backup copy will allow you to have a clean set of forms in case you accidentally change a file or delete a file. Remember, however, that a backup copy is for your own personal use only. Any other use of the backup disk violates copyright law.

You can make a backup copy of this disk by following the instructions in your DOS manual for using the DISKCOPY program. Alternately, you can copy the contents of this disk onto a hard disk for easy access. Refer to your DOS manual for instructions on creating a subdirectory on your hard disk and using the COPY command.

Using the Data Files

The enclosed data files are very easy to use on your word processing program. You merely have to follow these general steps, pressing the correct keys for your particular word processing program.

	General Instructions	WordPerfect Instructions	Word for Windows Instructions
Step 1	Load the program as normal	At the DOS prompt, type WP	At the Windows Program Manager, double click on the icon for Word for Windows
Step 2	Select the option for retrieving a document	Press SHIFT [F10]	Select Open from the File Menu
Step 3	Type in the appropriate file name	Type the drive letter and file name	Select to list Text Files from the List File Type window. Click on the name of the file to open. Click OK.

After these simple steps, most programs will load the files. If you have any difficulty, consult the manual to accompany your word processing program. You should look for instructions on *Importing ASCII Text Files.*

Notes About the Data Files

Due to the limits of ASCII format, the data files on this disk do not contain any special fonts or formats (like italics, bold, underline). Therefore, important information has been put in capital letters.

For ease of use in your word processing program, forms that are likely to be heavily edited have places for you to insert pertinent information. These "place markers" are in capital letters and surrounded by square brackets to differentiate them from regular text. For instance, in III-02.TXT, which contains a *Letter of Approval of Credit Application* form letter, you can see the following:

" . . . Payment terms are [PERCENT]% within [NUMBER] days . . ."

You can merely replace the place markers for [PERCENT] and [NUMBER] with the appropriate figures when you edit the letter.

Acknowledgments

My sincerest thanks to all those who aided me in putting this book together . . .

these Contributors who provided forms and other assistance:

American Trucking Associations (Alexandria, VA)
Priscilla Bornmann, Attorney (Alexandria, VA)
Jim Early, President, Capital Technigraphics Corporation (Springfield, VA)
Robert L. Fredericks, Jr., Attorney (Annandale, VA)
Joseph Gargiulo, President, Stuart-Dean Company of Virginia (Alexandria, VA)
John L. Grasser, Media Affairs Director, National Coal Association (Washington, D.C.)
Patrick Grassy, President, International Housewares Corporation (Housatonic, MA)
Jay Haddock, Vice President, Potomac Hotel Group (Rosslyn, VA)
Anthony R. Jakubicek, Director of Operations, American Warehouseman's Association (Chicago, IL)
John F. Lenihan, Controller, International Housewares Corporation (Housatonic, MA)
Joan Simmons, President, Modern Transportation Services, Inc. (Woodbridge, VA)
Signet Bank of Virginia

and special thanks to

John Holbrook, President, Associated Graphics (Franconia, VA), who provided many generic forms and spent literally hours offering suggestions and advice

also, my staff members who provided assistance:

Connie Badger, who provided various logistical support
Ann DeTorres, who spent endless hours at the keyboard
Stephen C. Jones, who made many of the contacts and helped obtain many of the generic forms

and, as always, my wife, Janie, and my young son, Ryan, whose support, understanding, and cooperation were vital.

About the Author

Morris A. Nunes is an attorney and financial consultant in suburban Washington, D.C. He is counsel to many small businesses and their owners and serves on the board of directors for several client companies.

A graduate of the University of Pennsylvania and its Wharton School of Business, he holds degrees in finance and accounting. He spent several years in controllership positions before obtaining a law degree from Georgetown University.

Mr. Nunes is admitted to the Virginia, District of Columbia, and federal bars and is licensed to practice before several appellate courts, including the U.S. Tax Court and the U.S. Supreme Court. In addition, he belongs to the American Society of Appraisers (Business Division) and has his own appraisal firm, Net Worth, Inc. He also serves as a commercial arbitrator for the American Arbitration Association and has appeared as an expert witness on business and legal matters before several courts.

This is his fifth book, and he has written articles on legal and financial subjects for the American Management Association's *Management Review, Public Utilities Fortnightly, Business Magazine,* and many other publications. He has also written microcomputer financial analysis programs published by Hewlett-Packard.

Mr. Nunes has taught finance and tax courses in college and continuing education programs, and he teaches legal issues for the Northern Virginia Association of Realtors. He also frequently speaks to business and professional groups. He formerly hosted a weekly cable television show, *General Counsel,* on legal subjects and holds a patent on a food storage invention.

An avid racquet sportsman, he lives with his wife of 19 years, Janie, and their son, Ryan, in northern Virginia.

Contents

Using the Diskette   v

Introduction   1

MODULE I: Collections   7

Introduction   7
Module Forms
    Invoice for Sale of Goods (I-01.TXT)   14
    Invoice for Sale of Services (I-02.TXT)   15
    Statement of Account (I-03.TXT)   16
    Demand for Payment (I-04.TXT)   17
    Final Demand for Payment (I-05.TXT)   18
    Appointment of Collection Agent (I-06.TXT)   19
    Assignment of Account for Collection (I-07.TXT)   20
    Notice of Account Assignment (I-08.TXT)   21
    Bankruptcy Court Proof of Claim (I-09.TXT)   22
    Bankruptcy Court Reaffirmation of Debt   23

MODULE II: Contract Formation and Administration   24

Introduction   24
Module Forms
    Letter of Intent (cover sheet) (II-01.TXT)   31
    Individual Acknowledgment (II-02.TXT)   32
    Attorney-in-Fact Acknowledgment (II-03.TXT)   33
    Partner's Acknowledgment (II-04.TXT)   34
    Corporate Acknowledgment (II-05.TXT)   35
    Power of Attorney (II-06.TXT)   36
    Modification Agreement (II-07.TXT)   37
    Assignment of Contract (II-08.TXT)   38

Early Termination and Mutual Release of Contract (II-09.TXT)   39
Notice of Breach (II-10.TXT)   40
Agreement to Binding Arbitration (II-11.TXT)   41

MODULE III: Credit Extension   **42**

Introduction   **42**
Module Forms

Business Credit Application (III-01.TXT)   47
Loan Application (for consumers)   49
Personal Financial Statement   51
Letter of Approval of Credit Application (III-02.TXT)   53
Letter of Rejection of Credit Application (III-03.TXT)   54
Notice of Change in Credit Terms (III-04.TXT)   55
Termination of Credit Line (III-05.TXT)   56

MODULE IV: Employment   **57**

Introduction   **57**
Module Forms

Employment Application (IV-01.TXT)   64
Letter Requesting Employment Verification (IV-02.TXT)   66
Authorization for Medical Examination and Testing (IV-03.TXT)   67
Physical Examination Form   68
Request for Medical Records (IV-04.TXT)   70
Employment Eligibility Verification (Form I-9)   71
Employment Contract (IV-05.TXT)   73
Employee's Covenants (IV-06.TXT)   75
Employee Confidentiality Certification (IV-07.TXT)   77
Receipt for Samples and Documents (IV-08.TXT)   78
Employee Weekly Time Sheet (IV-09.TXT)   79
Expense Voucher (IV-10.TXT)   80

MODULE V: Leases   **81**

Introduction   **81**
Module Forms

Equipment Lease   86
Lease (for real estate) (V-01.TXT)   88
Guaranty of Realty Lease (V-02.TXT)   92
Memorandum of Lease (V-03.TXT)   93
Assignment of Equipment Lease by Lessor (V-04.TXT)   95
Assignment of Equipment Lease by Lessee (V-05.TXT)   96
Assignment of Realty Lease by Lessor (V-06.TXT)   97
Assignment of Realty Lease by Lessee (V-07.TXT)   98

MODULE VI: Loans and Security   **99**

Introduction   **99**
Module Forms

Truth in Lending Disclosure (VI-01.TXT)   107
Promissory Note (simple) (VI-02.TXT)   109

Commercial Loan Note   110
Consumer Loan Note (Instalment)   112
Promissory Note of Employee (VI-03.TXT)   114
Confess Judgment Promissory Note (VI-04.TXT)   115
Borrower's Waiver of Right of Rescission (VI-05.TXT)   117
Notice to Cosigner (VI-06.TXT)   118
Consumer Security Agreement   119
Guaranty (commercial) (VI-07.TXT)   122
Loan and Security Agreement (VI-08.TXT)   125
Deed of Trust (VI-09.TXT)   135
Financing Statement (UCC) (VI-10.TXT)   137
Receipt for Collateral (VI-11.TXT)   138
Collateral Substitution Agreement (VI-12.TXT)   139
Warehousing Agreement (VI-13.TXT, VI-14.TXT, VI-15.TXT)   140
Non-Negotiable Warehouse Receipt   147

MODULE VII: Payments and Releases   **149**

Introduction   **149**

Module Forms

Waiver and Assumption of Risk (VII-01.TXT)   155
Receipt for Deposit (VII-02.TXT)   156
Receipt for Payment (VII-03.TXT)   157
Payment Advice (VII-04.TXT)   158
Release of Claims (VII-05.TXT)   159
Release of Note (VII-06.TXT)   160
Release of UCC Financing Statement (VII-07.TXT)   161
Certificate of Satisfaction (VII-08.TXT)   162
Waiver and Release of Liens (VII-09.TXT)   163
Mutual Release (VII-10.TXT)   164

MODULE VIII: Safety   **165**

Introduction   **165**

Module Forms

Employee Injury Report and Investigation Form   169
Preliminary Report of Accident or Loss   170
Security Incident Report (VIII-01.TXT)   171
Insurance Incident Report (VIII-02.TXT)   172
Report of OSHA Inspection   173

MODULE IX: Sale of Business Assets   **175**

Introduction   **175**

Module Forms

Potential Acquirer's Covenant of Confidentiality (IX-01.TXT)   180
Invention Confidentiality Agreement (IX-02.TXT)   181
Business Sale Agreement (IX-03.TXT)   182
Bulk Transfers Notice (IX-04.TXT)   185
Bulk Transfer Tax Authorities Notice (IX-05.TXT)   187
Bulk Transfer Affidavit (IX-06.TXT)   188
Bulk Sales Compliance Affidavit (IX-07.TXT)   189

Affidavit of Title (IX-08.TXT) 190
Bill of Sale (IX-09.TXT) 192

MODULE X: Sale of Goods and Services **193**

Introduction **193**
Module Forms

Catalogue Disclaimer (X-01.TXT) 200
Federal Bidder's Mailing List Application 201
Request for Quotation (X-02.TXT) 204
Quotation (X-03.TXT, X-04.TXT) 206
Purchase Order (X-05.TXT, X-06.TXT) 208
Order Acknowledgment (X-07.TXT, X-08.TXT) 210
Blanket Purchase Order Requisition (X-09.TXT) 212
Consignment Agreement (X-10.TXT) 213
Maintenance Agreement (X-11.TXT) 215
Services Agreement (X-12.TXT) 217
Contract for Sale of Goods (X-13.TXT) 219
Notice of Warranty Claim (X-14.TXT) 221
Disclaimer of Warranty (X-15.TXT) 222

MODULE XI: Shipment and Delivery **223**

Introduction **223**
Module Forms

Straight Bill of Lading 229
Packing Slip (XI-01.TXT) 230
Delivery Receipt (XI-02.TXT) 231
Notice of Rejection (XI-03.TXT) 232
Claim for Damage (XI-04.TXT) 233
Notice of Return of Goods (XI-05.TXT) 234
Receipt and Conditional Credit (XI-06.TXT) 235
Receipt for Completed Services (XI-07.TXT) 236

INDEX **237**

Introduction

Every day, all over the country, indeed all over the globe, business people exchange millions of legal documents. Most of these are not reviewed by a lawyer. Often they are not read fully by the correspondents themselves. To a great extent (and speaking as a practicing attorney), that's how it should be! Any businessperson who had to read the full text of every purchase order, every invoice, every acknowledgment, every payment advice (let alone have each reviewed by a lawyer), would have little time to perform his or her job effectively. An efficient businessperson's involvement should be limited to *understanding* the purpose of each document, its pitfalls and benefits, and when and how it should be used.

IS THIS BOOK FOR YOU?

Try this simple test:

Envision one of your company's purchase order forms, but don't read one. (If your company doesn't have a purchase order form, you've already flunked the test.) Now answer these five simple questions with "yes," "no," or "don't know."

1. Does the purchase order allow you to cancel if the goods are not shipped or the services are not performed within a specific time?
2. Does the purchase order reserve all warranties?
3. Does the purchase order prevent the seller from tacking on hidden charges, such as packing, handling, shipping, order processing, or other unexpected expense?
4. Does the purchase order preserve your right to return damaged goods, goods ordered by mistake, and goods not exactly to specifications?

5. Does the purchase order give you the right to reject deliveries if the deliveries do not meet stated schedule requirements (e.g., between 8 A.M. and 4 P.M.., Monday through Thursday only) and stated packaging requirements (e.g., standard pallets of two dozen cartons per pallet)?

Now pull out one of your purchase order forms and see if you gave the correct answers. If you answered "no" or "don't know" to any of the questions, you failed the test. In business, the penalty for failing may be thousands of dollars in losses and lawsuits, credit problems, bankruptcy, and countless hours of wasted effort. Personally it can mean loss of your job or your business and perhaps enormous embarrassment if you are, say, forced to confess error in a crowded courtroom.

The transcript could read something like this:

CROSS-EXAMINING ATTORNEY: Now then, Mr. Doe, when Sample delivered the cartons at your dock, you say you rejected them because they were not palletized two dozen to a skid. Is that right?

THE WITNESS: Yes, that's right.

CROSS-EXAMINING ATTORNEY: But you had no right to do that, did you?

THE WITNESS: Sure I did. Everybody in the industry knows we always take delivery of two dozen per pallet.

CROSS-EXAMINING ATTORNEY: I see. You say "always." How long have you been ordering these materials, Mr. Doe?

THE WITNESS: I've been in this job just under seven years.

CROSS-EXAMINING ATTORNEY: Did you read Sample's brochure, previously shown to you as plaintiff's exhibit A, where it said Sample ships *three* dozen per pallet?

THE WITNESS: Um . . . that must have been in small type. I didn't see it, that I remember. Anyway, when I called the order in they didn't say anything about it.

CROSS-EXAMINING ATTORNEY: Neither did you, right?

THE WITNESS: I'm not sure.

CROSS-EXAMINING ATTORNEY: Did you read the order acknowledgment you received from Ace?

THE WITNESS: We get those in all the time.

CROSS-EXAMINING ATTORNEY: Answer my question, Mr. Doe. Did you not read Sample's Acknowledgment #108647B, previously entered as Plaintiff's Exhibit B? Yes or no, Mr. Doe?

THE WITNESS: I read the part where the blanks were filled in.

CROSS-EXAMINING ATTORNEY: It doesn't say anything about palletizing, does it?

THE WITNESS: It sure doesn't.

CROSS-EXAMINING ATTORNEY: So you read the front, but not the "terms" section on the back? Well, would you please read this part above the signature, so the jury and Her Honor can hear you? *(hands document to witness)*

THE WITNESS: *(reading)* Thank you for your order. Please immediately verify we have processed it correctly. Notify the above-listed contact of any discrepancy without delay. Your order is accepted subject to all terms on the reverse side of this order acknowledgment, which supersede all prior agreements regarding this transaction. We appreciate your business.

CROSS-EXAMINING ATTORNEY: "Please immediately verify we have processed it correctly." Did you read that?

THE WITNESS: I'm pretty sure I did.

CROSS-EXAMINING ATTORNEY: Did you make any objection to the order acknowledgment as it stated your order?

THE WITNESS: No, I didn't.

Cross-Examining Attorney: Now, Mr. Doe, please read the first two sentences of paragraph nine on the back of the form.

THE WITNESS: *(reading)* These terms encompass the entire agreement between Buyer and Seller superseding all other terms and conditions. Seller shall not be bound by any terms not written herein, unless written amendment is signed by an authorized Seller representative.

CROSS-EXAMINING ATTORNEY: You never ordered from Sample before, correct?

THE WITNESS: Correct.

CROSS-EXAMINING ATTORNEY: And the brochure sent to you said *three* dozen per skid, right?

THE WITNESS: I guess so.

CROSS-EXAMINING ATTORNEY: And you never submitted a purchase order of your own to Sample, did you?

THE WITNESS: We don't use purchase orders. It's a lot easier just to place our orders by telephone.

CROSS-EXAMINING ATTORNEY: Nor do you have any written amendment varying the terms of the order acknowledgment or specifying two dozen per pallet, right?

THE WITNESS: No, I don't.

CROSS-EXAMINING ATTORNEY: No further questions. I ask the court to now grant our motion for summary judgment against Mr. Doe's company for $62,548.74 plus costs, interest, and attorney fees."

That's the possible penalty. Between the covers of this book lies the remedy: a detailed and standardized set of forms and agreements that any businessperson can put to work as useful and effective business tools. Each form can be customized to your needs, circumstances, and desires, preferably with the help of your counsel.

BRIDGING THE GAP: LEGAL NEED V. BUSINESS EFFICIENCY

This is a book for business people. Therefore, it is not cluttered with legal references, footnotes, and citations. Much of the law applied in this volume is governed by the Uniform Commercial Code (UCC), which has been adopted in every state, except Louisiana. (Despite its loyalty to French heritage, Louisiana has codified many of the same legal principles as found in the UCC.) There is also a smattering of federal law (including tax law) references to a few other uniform laws adopted by many states, and some contributions from the common law, which is the body of court-made (as opposed to legislature-passed) law. Many of those principles are so well-known and so tested, they trace their roots back to the time of the Magna Carta under our traditions of English law.

Neither the common law nor the uniform laws (including the UCC) are necessarily identical in all states, with each legislature exercising its preroga-tive to make accommodations for pre-existing local customs and predilec-tions. Even federal law may involve different interpretations in different appeals court circuits, which remain contradictory until such time as the U.S. Supreme Court makes a final determination or Congress settles the issue by rewriting the law.

Of course, each area of the law touched on by each of the forms herein has spawned libraries of books, articles, opinions, and briefs. Virtually any of the forms could be lengthened with pages of boilerplate designed to cover all the "what-ifs," however remote. But that belies the real goals of forms develop-ment and management, which are

1. To inform the user of rights, duties, and salient data
2. To allow the user to coordinate actions and performance relative to other parties
3. To protect and preserve the rights and assets of the user
4. To promote the profitability of the user by encouraging sales, limiting costs, and projecting a true image of honesty, organization, and efficiency

Hence, the emphasis here is on good legal foundations without ignoring practical operating, marketing, and administrative needs. Too many forms books are written from the lopsided perspective of either lawyers or opera-tions-oriented nonlawyers, which make those books unattractive to the other. As a person with a foot in both camps, I believe this book bridges the gap by finding a balance between legal need and business efficiency.

FORMAT AND USE

The table of contents gives a complete rundown of the forms; this book covers all the typical (and some not-so-typical) operating transactions your business is likely to encounter. Now you can encounter them confidently prepared. Rather than chapters, the book is divided into "modules," each of which includes the forms likely to be encountered in and necessary to the particular function embodied in the module. There is some cross-referencing among (and within) modules.

To make this package even more user-friendly, an ASCII diskette is enclosed with the book, so that you can download the forms directly to your computer to make completion and customizing all the more efficient. The diskette is designed to be compatible with most word-processing programs. (Refer to your program manual for downloading and access procedures.)

Several points (both legal and operational) are worth mentioning about use of the forms:

1. Most repetitively used operational forms (e.g., purchase order, invoice, expense voucher) should be numbered for control and retrieval.

2. Businesses dealing with consumers are likely to find a more restrictive legal environment than are businesses dealing with other businesses. Consequently, forms may need to be modified from one sphere to the other. In some cases (e.g., Module VI) the distinctions are so great as to require substantially different approaches to similar transactions.

3. Where interest rates may be applied (e.g., loans, invoices, installment contracts), beware that in addition to federal statutes protecting consumers, some states have usury laws, which may apply to all kinds of transactions.

4. On many operational forms, including a contact person's name and telephone number will speed communication and save time.

5. Fax machines and modems are growing in popularity; including applicable telephone numbers (especially when inviting sales orders) makes good sense.

6. When forms are being filled out, it is recommended that all blocks, blanks, and boxes are marked, even with an X or an NA, if not applicable to the transaction. There are two advantages:

   a. It will be clear that no item was overlooked.

   b. It will be a hedge against dishonesty on such forms as employment applications, damage claims, and credit applications.

7. Eliminate extra signature lines (especially where consent is indicated) if they are not needed for a transaction, as blank lines may imply the form was not accepted by all necessary parties.

8. The form of business (corporation, partnership, limited partnership, joint venture, trust, proprietorship, charity, etc.) may require variations on some forms.

9. When obtaining signatures for an entity, be sure the person signing has the legal authority to sign on behalf of the entity. Without such authority, the document will not bind the entity.

10. Attach additional sheets if there is inadequate room on a form, but indicate on *both* the form and the attachment that they go together.

11. Notary blocks have been placed on a number of forms, but if the document is not intended for recordation or presentation to an official, the notary may not be necessary. Nevertheless, the blocks have been added where authentication may be useful to enforcement or will impress upon the signatories the gravity of the obligations and rights inherent in the document.

12. Some years ago there was a television commercial for a certain brand of

oil filters, where the mechanic, finding an engine expensively damaged by failure to replace the filter, looked into the camera and said, "You can pay me now, or you can pay me later." An attorney I know quotes that often when referring to penny-wise, pound-foolish clients who came for legal help in closing the proverbial barn door after the horse was gone. These forms refer to weighty, sometimes make-or-break matters. Each one is a guide, designed in part to warn of legal issues. Please, if you need legal help, do not be penny-wise and pound-foolish—get help.

SUMMARY

Legal problems in the field of commercial transactions are like advertising. If you knew with 100-percent accuracy which buyers would respond to which ads, you could save a lot of advertising expense by communicating only with the appropriate targets. But no one has such insight. Similarly, nobody knows which transaction will turn out to be the disputed one. That is why your business needs the safeguard of an umbrella over all your transactions. The standardized forms and agreements found in this book are designed to provide just that. With the umbrella in place, your business can proceed to maximize efficiency and profitability, without getting blindsided in the rush of transactions.

Module I

Collections

INTRODUCTION

The primary purposes of collection forms are

1. To inform the customer or client of the amount due to be paid
2. To inform the customer or client of the terms for payment
3. To prompt the customer or client to make payment according to the terms
4. To aid in control of payment accounting and tracking

A great deal of the legal material in this Module has been predetermined by the documentation establishing the transaction, especially those found in Module IX dealing with sale of goods and services. Hence, the collection forms should mirror and confirm the nature of the transaction, the duties of the customer or client, and the rights of your company as vendor.

MODULE FORMS

The 10 forms in this Module are

Invoice for Sale of Goods
Invoice for Sale of Services

Statement of Account

Demand for Payment

Final Demand for Payment

Appointment of Collection Agent

Assignment of Account for Collection

Notice of Account Assignment

Bankruptcy Court Proof of Claim

Bankruptcy Court Reaffirmation of Debt

Invoice for Sale of Goods

Definition

The invoice for sale of goods is the billing to the customer for the sale and delivery of tangibles.

Comments

a. Note the blank for listing the customer's purchase order number (Cust. P.O. No.). Not only should the purchase order number be listed to facilitate customer reference, but the body of the invoice should also tie in to the data and format of the purchase order number as confirmed by the order acknowledgment (see Module IX).

b. If sales contracts are used in place of purchase orders, use the PO blanks for identification and tie-in to the contract.

c. The boilerplate at the bottom of the invoice is the last chance to assert these rights, which presumably have been reserved (or at least not precluded) in earlier documentation for the transaction.

Distribution

Original to customer

Copy to customer for return with payment

Copy to accounting department

Copy to account salesman

Copy retained by billing department

Invoice for Sale of Services

Definition

The invoice for sale of services is the billing to the customer for the sale and delivery of services.

Comments

a. Comments regarding the goods invoice are applicable to the services invoice, as well.

b. Where the sale is mixed (goods and services), the primary thrust of the transaction should determine which form is used. If the sale is primarily for goods, but involves, say, installation services, the goods invoice is appropriate. On the other hand, if it is primarily for services, but incidentally involves goods (e.g., parts), the services invoice is preferred.

Distribution

Same as for invoice for sale of goods

Statement of Account

Definition

The statement of account alerts the customer to all invoices then outstanding, hopefully prompting payment of all of them at one time.

Comments

a. Statements usually are sent monthly, but also may be used when a certain number of invoices are open or as a prompt when a certain dollar amount is reached.

b. Note the identical reservation of rights (last line of boilerplate) as appears in the invoice forms.

Distribution

Original to customer

Copy to customer for use with payment

Copy to accounting department

Copy to collections department as a signal to dun

Demand for Payment

Definition

Essentially a letter, the demand for payment is used to promote customer payment of overdue invoices.

Comments

a. While statements are normally sent as a matter of course, demands are used when the account is in arrears.

b. Some companies will send a series of reminders, which may become increasingly strident as the customer fails to respond with payment. However, it is usually a mistake to continue carrying a customer who does not get the hint after one reminder.

Distribution

Original to customer

Copy to sales department to alert them to credit difficulty

Copy retained by collections department

Final Demand for Payment

Definition

The final demand for payment gives notice to the customer that the overdue account will be turned over for collection if payment is not forthcoming.

Comments

a. A final demand should not be used unless the threat to refer for collection will be carried out.

b. However, waiting a week or so after the deadline to actually refer for collection is usually wise; this allows reasonable time for mail delivery, especially since most poor credits will stretch the time to the limit before sending payment.

Distribution

Same as demand for payment

Appointment of Collection Agent

Definition

The appointment of a collection agent involves a contract between the vendor and the collection agent or attorney who agrees to collect on a contingency basis (i.e., taking as the collection fee only a percentage of the amount collected).

Comments

a. By appointing the collector as a legal agent, the agent is empowered to act on the vendor's behalf in obtaining payment, but does not have ownership of the account (as contrasted with assignment form).

b. The vendor-agent relationship is such that the assigning vendor is legally liable for the collection actions of the agent; hence the indemnity.

c. Special instructions may be used to define the limits within which the agent may negotiate or prescribe specific steps to be taken toward collection.

Distribution

Original to agent

Copy to collections department

Copy to accounting department

Assignment of Account for Collection

Definition

The assignment of an account for collection involves a contract between the billing party and the party who has agreed to purchase the account in anticipation of collection.

Comments

a. This form is designed to transfer an account to a party purchasing it (perhaps as a factor or discounter) with recourse, so that the billing paty (i.e., the vendor who issued the original invoice) is effectively guaranteeing payment of the account from the customer.

b. Although the form is written for an individual account, it can be used as a contract to cover a batch of accounts being assigned.

Distribution

	Assignor	Assignee
Original	collections	account management
Copy	accounting	accounting
Copy		collections

Notice of Account Assignment

Definition

The notice of account assignment is used to notify the customer or client that collection rights for the account have been assigned and that payment should therefore be made to the assignee, instead of to the vendor.

Comments

a. The notice should be sent by the assignor, as the customer's contractual relationship is with the assignor. Although many customers might respond to an assignee, receiving unanticipated notice from an unknown party is likely to prompt worry or confusion.

b. The assignee subsequently can send a confirming notice, which also helps to prompt payment.

c. A notice is not necessary when a collection agent has been appointed, unless the agent will actually be receiving the funds. In such a case, this form can be modified to indicate the agency (as opposed to assignment) relationship.

Distribution

Original to customer

Copy to assignee collections department

Copy of assignor collections department

Bankruptcy Court Proof of Claim

Definition

Once a debtor has declared or been placed in bankruptcy, anyone who is owed money must file a bankruptcy court proof of claim to have the opportunity to receive any payment on the amount owed from the debtor.

Comments

a. Bankruptcy law and procedure can be quite complicated: therefore, care in preparing the proof of claim and precision in describing the debt, relationship, and terms are essential.

b. There is a time limit within which the proof of claim must be filed; refer to the notice of bankruptcy. When in doubt, contact the clerk of the bankruptcy court or your counsel.

c. Review by counsel is recommended, especially for large debts or where the company is blessed with infrequent use of the form.

d. Filing does not guarantee a share of payment, but without filing, the opportunity for payment will be lost, unless the bankruptcy case is terminated without discharge of debts.

Distribution

Original to bankrupty court

Copy to collections department

Copy to counsel

Bankruptcy Court Reaffirmation of Debt

Definition

Bankruptcy, when properly filed and prosecuted, results in the release of the debtor from the debt. However, the bankrupt debtor can agree to repay an otherwise dischargeable debt and will be bound by such agreement, provided the proper procedures are followed. The form for reaffirmation of debt is an application to the court for approval of such an agreement.

Comments

a. Generally, a debt will not be approved for reaffirmation unless a benefit to the debtor can be shown. For example, the automobile used by the bankrupt debtor to get to work will be repossessed unless the debt is reaffirmed.

b. Penalties can be imposed by the court for the harassment or improper pressuring of a debtor to reaffirm.

c. Note the rescission ability of the debtor, which allows a debtor to pull the debt back into dischargeable bankruptcy.

d. Attempting to make a reaffirmation agreement without help of counsel can be tricky.

Distribution

Original to court

Copies to court, in accord with local rules of court

Copy to accounting department

Copy to billing (or collections) department

Copy to counsel

Copy to debtor

Copy to debtor's counsel

INVOICE FOR SALE OF GOODS

Billed to
CUSTOMER _____

Please pay
VENDOR _____

Attn _____

Attn _____

Address _____

Address _____

_____

_____

Invoice No. _____ Invoice Date _____ Terms _____

Contact Person _____ Phone _____

Cust. P.O. No. _____ P.O. Date _____ Ship Date _____

Order No. _____ Process Date _____ Salesman _____

****PLEASE make checks payable to:

_____

Serial Number	Description & Specifications	Packing Unit	Quantity Ordered	Quantity Back Ordered	Quantity Shipped	Price per Package	Total Charges

Add: Shipping charges

Taxes

Other charges

Please pay: TOTAL DUE

Number additional sheets attached: _____ pages

Interest is charged on all overdue accounts at the rate of _____% per month on the unpaid balance. Customer shall be charged with all costs of collection, including but not limited to 25% attorney fees and court costs. A $15.00 processing charge will be added for chargeback and billing of all unearned payment discounts wrongfully deducted. Your prompt payment is appreciated. No terms contained herein shall alter any terms heretofore confirmed by Vendor. All rights reserved under such terms and under the Uniform Commercial Code.

INVOICE FOR SALE OF SERVICES

Billed to
CUSTOMER _____

Please pay
VENDOR _____

Attn _____

Attn _____

Address _____

Address _____

_____

_____

Invoice No. _____ Invoice Date _____ Terms _____

Contact Person _____ Phone _____

Cust. P.O. No. _____ P.O. Date _____ Setup Date_____

Contract No._____ Process Date _____ Salesman _____

****PLEASE make checks payable to:
_____

Description of Services	Where Performed	Work Started	Work Completed	No. Time Units	Rate per Unit	Total Charges

Add: Materials charges

Taxes

Travel charges

Other charges

Please pay: TOTAL DUE

Number additional sheets attached: ____ pages

Interest is charged on all overdue accounts at the rate of ____% per month on the unpaid balance. Customer shall be charged with all costs of collection, including but not limited to 25% attorney fees and court costs. A $15.00 processing charge will be added for chargeback and billing of all unearned payment discounts wrongfully deducted. Your prompt payment is appreciated. No terms contained herein shall alter any terms heretofore confirmed by Vendor. All rights reserved under such terms and under the Uniform Commercial Code.

STATEMENT OF ACCOUNT

Billed to   Please pay
CUSTOMER _____   VENDOR _____

Attn _____   Attn _____

Address _____   Address _____

_____   _____

Contact Person _____   Phone _____

Acct. No. _____ Credit Limit $ _____ Salesman _____

***** PLEASE make checks payable to

Invoice Number	Invoice Date	Invoice Amount	Interest Amount	Other Charge	Payment Date	Payment Amount	Other Credit	Balance Due

Please pay: TOTAL DUE

Number additional sheets attached: _____ pages

Interest is charged on all overdue accounts at the rate of _____% per month on the unpaid balance. Customer shall be charged with all costs of collection, including but not limited to 25% attorney fees and court costs. A $15.00 processing charge will be added for chargeback and billing of all unearned payment discounts wrongfully deducted. Your prompt payment is appreciated. No terms contained herein shall alter any terms heretofore confirmed by Vendor. All rights reserved under such terms and under the Uniform Commercial Code.

DEMAND FOR PAYMENT

Date _____

To _____

_____

_____

Dear _____:

We currently show the following outstanding balance on your account:

Invoice No. _____ Dated _____ Amount $ _____

Invoice No. _____ Dated _____ Amount _____

Invoice No. _____ Dated _____ Amount _____

Interest through _____ @ ____% _____

Late charges _____

Less credits and payments – _____

Total balance due $ _____

This is a reminder that we have not received your payment for the above balance, which is due and payable. Your prompt attention to clear this balance would be appreciated.

Please disregard this notice if full payment has been forwarded to us.
Thank you for your cooperation.

Sincerely,

_____

cc: Sales representative

FINAL DEMAND FOR PAYMENT

Date _____

To _____

_____

_____

Dear _____:

Your account is currently in arrears as of _____, 19____, in the total amount of $_____. Despite our earlier notices to you, your account is still delinquent.

Therefore, unless payment in full in good funds is received by _____, 19____, your account will be turned over to our attorneys for collection, which may increase your total expenses and could have an adverse effect on your credit rating.

If your payment has already been sent, please ignore this letter.

We regret the necessity of this action, and urge you to cure your delinquency. We look forward to prompt payment.

Sincerely,

_____

APPOINTMENT OF COLLECTION AGENT

This Agreement is made _____, 19____, by and between the parties
_____ ("Vendor") and _____ ("Agent"),
relative to that certain Account Receivable due to Vendor from Vendor's customer known as
_____ ("Customer") whose address is _____
_____, in the amount of
_____ dollars ($_____; "Account Balance") due from
Customer, which account is hereinafter referred to as the "Receivable".

Vendor hereby appoints Agent granting full authority to Agent to collect the Receivable from
Customer on behalf of Vendor. From so much of the Receivable as is collected by Agent, Agent
shall be entitled to a fee of ____% thereof, payable upon receipt of such collected amounts, when,
as, and if received. Agent is hereby subject to the following special instructions:

_____

_____

Vendor shall furnish Agent all information Agent requests to aid collection. This Appointment
expires _____, 19____, unless extended in writing.

Vendor shall indemnify and save harmless Agent in and from any and all claims, damages,
losses, expenses, costs, attorney fees, and detriments arising from the Receivable or underlying
contract between Vendor and Customer. Agent shall indemnify and save harmless Vendor in and
from any and all claims, damages, losses, expenses, costs, attorney fees, and detriments arising from
Agent's collection efforts. Each party shall notify the other of any circumstance that may affect the
collectability of the Receivable.

Date _____, 19____

Vendor _____   Agent _____

by _____ (Seal)   by _____ (Seal)

ASSIGNMENT OF ACCOUNT FOR COLLECTION

This Assignment is made _____ 19____, by and between the parties
_____ ("Assignor") and _____ ("Assignee"),
relative to that certain Account Receivable due to Assignor from Assignor's customer known as
_____ ("Third Party") whose address is _____
_____ in the amount of
_____ dollars ($_____; "Account Balance") due from Third
Party, which account is hereinafter referred to as the "Receivable".

In consideration for the sum of _____ dollars
($_____; "Purchase Price") paid this date by Assignee to Assignor, Assignor hereby assigns unto
Assignee all right, title, and interest to collect the aforesaid Receivable, with recourse nevertheless,
as follows: If Assignee is unable to collect the same in full after _____ days, Assignee may demand
and shall receive upon such demand from Assignor that portion of the Account Balance which is
then unpaid.

Assignor shall indemnify and save harmless Assignee in and from any and all claims, damages,
losses, expenses, costs, attorney fees, and detriments arising from the Receivable or underlying
contract between Assignor and Third Party. Assignor shall furnish Assignee all information Assignee
requests to assist Assignee in collection. Assignor shall notify Third Party of this Assignment and to
promptly pay Assignee at the designated payment address. Assignor shall notify Assignee of any
circumstance that may materially affect Assignee's ability to collect.

Date _____, 19____

Assignor ————————————————   Assignee ————————————————————

by ———————————————— (Seal)   by ———————————————————— (Seal)

NOTICE OF ACCOUNT ASSIGNMENT

Date _____

To _____

_____

_____

Dear _____:

Your account with us has been assigned for collection. Until further notice, please make all payments to the following assignee:

_____

_____

_____

As of _____, 19____, we show a balance due on your account of
_____ dollars ($_____), with the next payment due
_____, 19____. Please contact us immediately by telephone at
_____ if you believe any of these items to be incorrect or in need of adjustment.

Thank you for your cooperation.

Sincerely,

_____

cc: Assignee

United States Bankruptcy Court

For the _____ **District of** _____

In re

Case No. _____

Debtor*

PROOF OF CLAIM

1. [*If claimant is an individual claiming for himself*] The undersigned, who is the claimant herein, resides at**

   [*If claimant is a partnership claiming through a member*] The undersigned, who resides at**

is a member of _____ , a partnership,
composed of the undersigned and ,
of** ,
doing business at** ,
and is authorized to make this proof of claim on behalf of the partnership.

   [*If claimant is a corporation claiming through an authorized officer*] The undersigned, who resides at**

is the _____ of _____ ,
a corporation organized under the laws of ,
and doing business at** ,
and is authorized to make this proof of claim on behalf of the corporation.

   [*If claim is made by agent*] The undersigned, who resides at**
_____ , is the agent of _____ ,
of** _____ , and is
authorized to make this proof of claim on behalf of the claimant.

2. The debtor was, at the time of the filing of the petition initiating this case, and still is indebted [*or* liable] to this claimant, in the sum of $

3. The consideration for this debt [*or* ground of liability] is as follows:

   [*If filed in a chapter 7 or 13 case*] This claim consists of $_____ in principal amount and $_____ in addition charges [*or no additional charges*]. [*Itemize all charges in addition to principal amount of debt, state basis for inclusion and computation, and set forth any other consideration relevant to the legality of the charge.*]

4. [*If the claim is founded on a writing*] The writing on which this claim is founded (or a duplicate thereof) is attached hereto [*or* cannot be attached for the reason set forth in the statement attached hereto].

5. [*If appropriate*] This claim is founded on an open account, which became [*or* will become] due on _____ , as shown by the itemized statement attached hereto. Unless it is attached hereto or its absence is explained in an attached statement, no note or other negotiable instrument has been received for the account or any part of it.

6. No judgment has been rendered on the claim except

7. The amount of all payments of this claim has been credited and deducted for the purpose of making this proof of claim.

8. This claim is not subject to any setoff or counter-claim except

9. No security interest is held for this claim except

   [*If security interest in the property of the debtor is claimed*] The undersigned claims the security interest under the writing referred to in paragraph 4 hereof [*or* under a separate writing (or a duplicate of which) is attached hereto, *or* under a separate writing which cannot be attached hereto for the reason set forth in the statement attached hereto]. Evidence of perfection of such security interest is also attached hereto.

10. This claim is a general unsecured claim, except to the extent that the security interest, if any, described in paragraph 9 is sufficient to satisfy the claim. [*If priority is claimed, state the amount and basis thereof.*]

Claim No. (office use only)	Total Amount Claimed	$

Full Name of Creditor: _____

Signature _____

Date _____

Penalty for Presenting Fraudulent Claim. Fine of not more than $5,000 or imprisonment for not more than 5 years or both — Title 18, U.S.C., ¶152.

*Include all names used by debtor within last 6 years.   ***State mailing address.*

UNITED STATES BANKRUPTCY COURT

For the _____ District of _____

SUMMARY OF REAFFIRMATION AGREEMENT

Name Of Debtor: _____

Case No.: _____

Instructions:
1. Complete Debtor's name and bankruptcy case number above.
2. PART A - Complete each item. Both the debtor and creditor must sign.
3. PART B - Must be signed by the attorney who represents the debtor(s) in bankruptcy, if any.
4. File the fully completed form by mailing or delivering it to

Clerk of Court for the above Bankruptcy Court.

PART A - AGREEMENT:

Creditor's Name & Address:

_____

_____

_____

_____

Date set for entry of Discharge:

_____

Terms of New Agreement:

a) Amount:

Principal $_____

Interest Rate (APR)_____%

Monthly Payments $_____

b) Security (collateral):

Description:_____

_____

Present Market Value $_____

The parties understand this Agreement is purely voluntary and the debtor may rescind this Agreement at any time prior to discharge or within 60 days after such Agreement is filed with the Court, whichever occurs later, by giving notice of rescission to Creditor. This Agreement was entered into before the date of discharge in the above case.

_____
Creditor Signature

Date:_____

_____
Debtor Signature

PART B - ATTORNEY'S DECLARATION
This Agreement represents a fully informed and voluntary agreement by the debtor that does not impose an undue hardship on the debtor or any dependent of debtor.

Attorney's Name & Address:

_____

_____

_____
Attorney Signature

_____
Date

23

Module II

Contract Formation and Administration

INTRODUCTION

This Module deals not only with the formation of contracts, but also with forms used to control or administer contractual relations between the parties. It is not a Module dealing with specific contract terms but, rather, is generic in scope. Hence, it is more likely to be used in conjunction with some of the contractually oriented modules, especially Modules IV, V, VI, IX, and X. The forms in Module II have three principal purposes:

1. To promote proper formalization of agreements
2. After formation, to adjust contractual terms by consent between or among the parties to the contract
3. To deal with perceived violations of the contract

MODULE FORMS

The 11 forms in this Module are

Letter of Intent (cover sheet)

Individual Acknowledgment

Attorney-in-Fact Acknowledgment
Partner's Acknowledgment
Corporate Acknowledgment
Power of Attorney
Modification Agreement
Assignment of Contract
Early Termination and Mutual Release of Contract
Notice of Breach
Agreement to Binding Arbitration

Letter of Intent (cover sheet)

Definition

Such a cover sheet is designed to be included on a letter of intent to govern its terms, as letters of intent are often subjects of disagreement as to their actual enforceability and meaning.

Comments

a. A letter of intent should be enforceable to the extent indicated in this cover sheet; if it is not at all enforceable, it is merely an "expression of interest," which lacks enforceability. Many people (including some lawyers) seem to be confused between the two. This cover sheet should eliminate the likelihood of confusion when included in any document.

b. To avoid all doubt, an "expression of interest" should include language that it is not enforceable or binding, but merely (tautologically speaking) an expression of interest.

c. Do not sign a letter of intent unless you intend it to be binding to the extent explained in this cover sheet.

Distribution

Original signature to each party

Individual Acknowledgment

Definition

Technically called a "jurat for an individual," the format for individual acknowledgment is to be followed for the notarization of one person's signature.

Comments

a. While its use is not limited to what are commonly thought of as being "contracts," the effect of the jurat is to authenticate the signature as binding the signer, so the terms of the document become enforceable against the signer in a contractual sense.

b. Although the signature line of the form indicates it is to be signed by a notary public, both state and federal law govern who may authenticate signatures.

c. Many states have adopted the "Uniform Recognition of Acknowledgments Act," which authorizes notaries, judges, clerks (including deputies), consular officers designated by the U.S. State Department, commissioned officers in the U.S. armed services (for other persons in the services and their dependents), and any person authorized within the authenticator's jurisdiction (a catchall designed primarily to give force to the laws of other countries).

Distribution

Attached to the document being notarized and distributed as a part of it

Attorney-in-Fact Acknowledgment

Definition

An attorney-in-fact is a person legally authorized, usually by a power of attorney (to be defined later) to sign for another. This type of jurat is used to authenticate such a signature as binding on the principal who appointed the attorney-in-fact.

Comments

a. Comments regarding the individual acknowledgment are applicable to the attorney-in-fact acknowledgment, as well.

b. To obtain notarization, the attorney-in-fact ordinarily must exhibit documentation proving the authority.

Distribution

Same as for individual acknowledgment

Partner's Acknowledgment

Definition

The form for partner's acknowledgment is used to authenticate the signature of a partner on behalf of the partnership.

Comments

a. Comments regarding the individual acknowledgment are applicable to the partner's acknowledgment, as well.

b. State law and the partnership agreement normally will control the ability of a partner to bind the partnership. Proof of such authority is required before the signature will be notarized.

c. When using the form for a limited partnership, the fact that the partner is a general partner should be indicated (a limited partner does not have power to bind a partnership).

Distribution

Same as for individual acknowledgment

Corporate Acknowledgment

Definition

The form for corporate acknowledgment is used to authenticate the signature of a corporate agent on behalf of the empowering corporation.

Comments

a. Comments regarding the individual acknowledgment are applicable to the corporate acknowledgment, as well.

b. A corporation's board of directors is the source for authority to bind the corporation, though such authority may be delegated to officers to redelegate. As for a partnership, proof of authority must be exhibited to the authenticating officer.

Distribution

Same as for individual acknowledgment

Power of Attorney

Definition

The form for power of attorney is a document empowering one person to act on behalf of another, usually including the power of signature.

Comments

a. There are many different formats for powers of attorney, varying almost as much as the number of tasks that may be performed. This form, therefore, is "bare bones," you may flesh it out as needed.

b. A corporate officer or partner of a partnership usually cannot grant a power of attorney to someone else without specific authority from the board of directors or the other partners.

Distribution

Original to attorney-in-fact

Copy to principal

Modification Agreement

Definition

The form used to amend the terms of an existing contract.

Comments

a. If the contract being modified has any special procedural requirements for amendment, they should be followed to be sure the modification will be legal.

b. All parties to a contract must sign to validate an amendment, unless the original contract provides otherwise.

Distribution

Original signature to each party

Assignment of Contract

Definition

The assignment of contract is used to supplant one of the parties to a contract with a substitute.

Comments

a. Assignment is really a specialized type of modification but usually does not require approval of all parties unless specifically stated.

b. Many types of contracts prohibit assignment by their terms, so that assignment in these cases is not possible unless all parties consent.

c. Certain types of contracts (e.g., personal service contracts involving special talents) are not assignable by law without consent of all parties, even if they do not so specifically designate.

d. A consent block is included in the form, as the majority of assignment parties will desire consent; however, if consent is not required, it is better to eliminate the consent block, as its existence may be misconstrued as evidence that consent is in fact required.

e. If assignment does not require consent, notice of the assignment should be given to all other parties as soon as possible.

Distribution

Original signature to each signing party

Copy to each nonsigning party

Early Termination and Mutual Release of Contract

Definition

The form for early termination and mutual release is used to end a contract and the obligations of the parties under the contract.

Comments

a. For other forms of release, see Module VII.

b. Because the effect of the form is to end absolutely the responsibilities to each other, be sure that all obligations to you have been satisfied.

c. The language of this form also eliminates any terms of the contract from being binding, even if they were originally reserved in the contract as "surviving termination." If you intend any to survive, use an addendum or insert to indicate "all EXCEPT . . .."

Distribution

Original signature to each party

Notice of Breach

Definition

The notice of breach is used to formally notify another party to a contract of a claim of a breach by such other party.

Comments

a. Certified mailing is indicated, as it is a requirement under the Uniform Commercial Code for claims on contracts relative to sales of goods, but is recommended for any type of contract claim.

b. Be sure the description of the breach is accurate, as the notice is often the first (and a key) step toward litigation. Advice of an attorney, even at this stage, is often advisable.

c. A time for cure is also a UCC requirement. If no opportunity for cure is applicable, be sure to strike the cure wording.

Distribution

Original to breaching party

Copy to all other contract parties (if any)

Copy to counsel

Copy retained by claiming party

Agreement to Binding Arbitration

Definition

The agreement to binding arbitration locks the parties into settling a dispute through binding arbitration.

Comments

a. Binding arbitration means the award made by the arbitrator has the legal effect of a court ruling and can be docketed with a court for enforcement.

b. Arbitration is usually faster than court proceedings (especially in crowded urban areas), sometimes less expensive, and offers the advantage of staying off the public record.

c. The American Arbitration Association referenced in the form is not the only organization offering arbitration services, but is among the most well known and has published relatively uncomplicated rules that generally have been recognized and accepted as valid in the courts.

d. This form is not needed if the contract itself contains a clause requiring arbitration in the event of dispute. In such a case, the procedure to be followed would be governed by the contract language.

e. Many states have adopted the Uniform Arbitration Act, which contains model procedures that may be superseded by contract.

Distribution

Original signature to each party

Original signature to the arbitrator

LETTER OF INTENT
(cover sheet)

The attached Letter of Intent (hereinafter, "Letter") bearing date of _____, 19____, and made by and between _____ and _____ regarding the described Subject is made under these letter-of-intent terms.

Subject: _____

_____

Terms: The parties further intend to form a final contract with regard to the subject of the attached Letter. Although the Letter does not form such a binding final contract, the legal force and effect of the Letter is that as to all terms described in the Letter, the terms of the final contract shall be identical to those terms, unless agreed otherwise. It shall be an actionable breach of contract if a party to the Letter shall

A. Refuse to bargain in good faith toward reaching a final contract; or

B. Fail (unless waived in writing by the other party) to meet deadlines or duties, if any, imposed toward reaching final contract by the Letter; or

C. Refuse (unless waived, in writing, by the other party) to accept any term or terms of the Letter in the final contract; or

D. To refuse to agree to reasonable proposed final contract terms not contained in and not at variance with the Letter for the purpose of avoiding a final contract containing terms of the Letter.

And, the parties to the attached letter of intent do so agree, incorporating this cover sheet into and making it a part of the attached letter of intent.

Date _____, 19__

_____ (Seal)   _____ (Seal)

INDIVIDUAL ACKNOWLEDGMENT

State of _____

_____ of _____

   On the _____ day of _____, 19____, before me personally came _____ who swore to and acknowledged the foregoing document.

_____
Notary Public

(Notary Seal)

My commission expires _____

ATTORNEY-IN-FACT ACKNOWLEDGMENT

State of _____

_____ of _____

   On the _____ day of _____, 19____, before me personally came _____ who, being by me duly sworn, did depose and declare that _____ (he/she) is the duly authorized Attorney-in-Fact for _____ ("Principal") under power of attorney from said Principal, dated _____, 19____, on whose behalf the said Attorney-in-Fact executed the foregoing document, swearing and acknowledging the same is executed with the full authority of said Principal as a true, lawful, and binding act of said Principal.

_____
Notary Public

(Notary Seal)

My commission expires _____

PARTNER'S ACKNOWLEDGMENT

State of _____

_____ of _____

    On the _____ day of _____, 19____, before me personally came _____, who, being by me duly sworn, did depose and declare that _____ (he/she) is a Partner in the Partnership named _____ (trading as _____), on which Partnership's behalf the said Partner executed the foregoing document, swearing and acknowledging the same is executed with the full authority of said Partnership as a true, lawful, and binding act of said Partnership.

                                                  _____
                                                  Notary Public

                                                      (Notary Seal)

My commission expires _____

CORPORATE ACKNOWLEDGMENT

State of _____

_____ of _____

   On the _____ day of _____, 19____, before me personally came _____ who, being by me duly sworn, did depose and declare that while being a resident of _____ the same holds the office of _____ of the Corporation bearing the legal name of _____ (trading as _____), on which Corporation's behalf the said Officer executed the foregoing document, swearing and acknowledging the same is executed with the full authority of said Corporation as a true, lawful, and binding act of said Corporation.

_____
Notary Public

(Notary Seal)

My commission expires _____

POWER OF ATTORNEY

KNOW ALL MEN BY THESE PRESENTS:

That I, _____, a legal resident of the County/City of _____, State of _____, have made, constituted, and appointed, and by these presents do hereby make, constitute, and appoint _____, a legal resident of the County/City of _____, State of _____, as my true and lawful Attorney-in-Fact for me and in my name, place, and stead, to do, execute, and perform all and every act or acts, thing or things, in law needful and necessary to be done in and about and in relation to the following Matter:

_____
_____
_____
_____

GRANTING UNTO AND AUTHORIZING my said Attorney-in-Fact full power of every kind and character, as fully, and largely, and amply to all intents and purposes whatsoever, as necessary to be exercised in relation to the said Matter as I might or could do if acting personally. This Power further includes and grants to my Attorney-in-Fact, but is not limited to, the authority to

_____
_____
_____

Further, I hereby grant unto my said attorney all of the maximum of powers as are allowed to fiduciaries by the applicable law of any jurisdiction. I specifically further include the power to substitute and delegate without limitation. Delegation may be accomplished by duly signed, dated, and notarized written instrument. All of said powers are cumulative and not exclusive, and failure to exercise forebearance in the exercise, or sporadic exercise of any such power, shall in no way constitute a waiver of such power nor a limitation of any kind on the ability of my Attorney-in-Fact (including delegatees thereof) to so exercise.

This Power of Attorney shall not terminate upon my disability, incompetency, illness, or incapacity as principal.

I hereby ratify and confirm all lawful acts and all acts undertaken in good faith by my said Attorney-in-Fact (including delegatees thereof) by virtue hereof, and no one dealing therewith shall have the duty nor the power to question the authority of my said Attorney-in-Fact (or delegatees thereof).

This Power is irrevocable and may be cancelled only by express written and notarized agreement between myself and my said Attorney.

In the event any portion hereof shall be found to be invalid or unlawful by operation of law or rule of court, then the same shall be considered severable but shall not invalidate the entire power nor any acts undertaken hereunder, and this Power of Attorney shall continue in full force and effect as if the invalid portion had never been a part hereof as to the jurisdiction or jurisdictions in which such portion is found invalid or unlawful.

WITNESS my signature and seal:

Date _____   _____ (Seal)

State of _____

_____ of _____,

The foregoing Power of Attorney was sworn to and acknowledged before me this _____ day of _____, 19____, by _____

_____
Notary Public

(Notary Seal)

My commission expires _____

MODIFICATION AGREEMENT

This Modification Agreement is made to Contract dated _____, 19____, by and between _____ and _____, modifying and amending the said Contract as follows:

_____

_____

_____

_____

_____

_____

_____

_____

_____

_____

Additional Terms:

I.   Any conflict between this Modification Agreement and the original Contract shall be construed in favor of this Modification Agreement.
II.   This Modification Agreement shall be effective upon execution by both parties unless specifically indicated otherwise.
III. This Modification Agreement is binding on neither party until executed by both parties.
IV.   In all other respects, the parties hereby ratify and confirm all the terms and conditions of the original Contract, except as modified and amended by this Modification Agreement, which becomes and is a part of such Contract, being incorporated therein and incorporating the same.

Date _____, 19____

_____ (Seal)   _____ (Seal)

ASSIGNMENT OF CONTRACT

This Assignment is made this date of _____, 19____, by and between the parties _____ ("Assignor") and _____ ("Assignee") relative to that certain contract made _____, 19____, between Assignor and the consenting third party, _____ which contract was made for the purpose of _____

_____

and which is hereinafter referred to as the "Contract".

In consideration for the mutual promises herein contained and other good and valuable consideration acknowledged as had and received, Assignor does hereby assign unto Assignee, now and forever, all right, title and interest in and to the aforesaid Contract, without recourse, including but not limited to all right to benefit from said Contract. Nevertheless, Assignor agrees to indemnify and save harmless Assignee in and from any and all claims, damages, losses, expenses, costs, attorney fees, and detriments that arise from the Contract or Assignor's duties thereunder prior to this date.

Furthermore, in like consideration, Assignee does hereby accept such assignment of the Contract and does agree to assume and undertake all unfulfilled obligations remaining on the Contract, which otherwise would be due to be fulfilled by Assignor, agreeing to indemnify and save harmless Assignor in and from any and all claims, damages, losses, expenses, costs, attorney fees, and detriments that arise from the Contract or Assignee's duties thereunder from and after this date.

The parties agree to execute such further assurances and provide such other information, data, and records as may be necessary between them to carry out the provisions of this agreement of Assignment of Contract.

Nothing herein contained shall be construed to modify the Contract, other than to substitute Assignee for Assignor in such Contract.

Date _____, 19____

Assignor _____   Assignee _____

by _____ (Seal)   by _____ (Seal)

CONSENT

_____ is the third party referred to in the foregoing Assignment of Contract and does hereby consent thereto, affirming that no modification to the Contract is made or intended hereby, except that Assignee is now and hereafter substituted for Assignor.

Date _____, 19____

_____

by _____ (Seal)

EARLY TERMINATION AND MUTUAL RELEASE
OF CONTRACT

For good and valuable consideration had and received and the mutual promises and releases herein contained, the parties known as _____ ("Vendor") and _____ ("Buyer") do hereby release each other, now and forever, in and from all further promises, liabilities, warranties, requirements, obligations, payments, and performance of the Contract dated _____, 19____, entitled _____, and made for the purpose of _____ _____ as reflected in said Contract between them.

The parties each acknowledge all matters between them regarding the said Contract have been satisfactorily adjusted between them, and the Contract has been terminated prior to its entire fulfillment and performance, as the parties have agreed such early termination is mutually desirable.

Accordingly, said Contract is hereby SUPERSEDED AND ABSOLUTELY TERMINATED.

Each party warrants each's own full power and authority to enter into this Early Termination and Mutual Release of Contract, which shall become effective only upon the signature of both parties.

Date _____

Vendor _____   Buyer _____

by _____ (Seal)   by _____ (Seal)

State of _____

_____ of _____

The foregoing Early Termination and Mutual Release of Contract was sworn to and acknowledged before me by _____ and _____ on _____, 19____.

_____
Notary Public

(Notary Seal)

My commission expires _____

NOTICE OF BREACH

To _____   From _____

_____   _____

_____   _____

    TAKE NOTICE that under Contract made _____, 19____, as evidenced by the following documents: _____ ,we are hereby holding you IN BREACH for the following reasons:

_____

_____

_____

_____

_____

    If your Breach is not cured within _____ days (i.e., cure must be completed by _____, 19____), we will take all further actions necessary to mitigate our damages and protect our rights, which may include, but are not necessarily limited to, the right to "Cover" by obtaining substitute performance and chargeback to you of all additional costs and damages incurred.

    This Notice is made under the Uniform Commercial Code *(if applicable)* and all other applicable laws. All rights are hereby reserved, none of which are waived. Any forebearance or temporary waiver from enforcement shall not constitute permanent waiver or waiver of any other right.

    You are urged to cure your Breach forthwith.

Date _____, 19____

Complaining Party _____

by _____
Authorized Signatory

AGREEMENT TO BINDING ARBITRATION

This Agreement is made this date of _____, 19____, by and between the parties _____ ("Claimant") and _____ ("Respondent") relative to that certain Contract made _____, 19____, between Claimant and Respondent regarding said Contract between them, which was made for the purpose of _____,

_____

_____

and with regard to which a dispute has arisen, which they agree may be described in general terms as follows:

_____

_____

_____

_____

Accordingly, in the interest of resolving said dispute, and without admission of liability or wrongdoing by either or both of them, they hereby agree to submit the same to binding arbitration under the auspices and Rules of the American Arbitration Association. They further agree that the final award of the Arbitrator made therein (which may include the costs and expenses of Arbitration at the discretion of the Arbitrator) may be entered as a judgment in any court of competent jurisdiction.

Upon notification of acceptance of the case, Claimant shall have the time specified in the Rules to submit a complete description of its claims, and Respondent shall then have the specified time for reply and counterclaim (if any) and the parties shall at all times abide by the Rules and the rulings of the Arbitrator in the conduct of the case.

Claimant _____   Respondent _____

by _____   by _____

Module III

Credit Extension

INTRODUCTION

The decision to extend credit is usually dependent upon the hard financial and referential data obtained about the prospective customer, client, or borrower. Forms for credit extension thus bear more heavily on decision making than do most other types of forms.

The purposes of credit extension forms are

1. To elicit adequate, verifiable information to aid the credit analyst in okaying credit and determining the size of the credit line
2. To help the collections department in chasing delinquencies
3. To use as evidence and background in court in the event the delinquency must be turned over for collection
4. To serve as a database for use in marketing and forecasting

MODULE FORMS

The seven forms in this module are

Business Credit Application
Loan Application (for consumers)
Personal Financial Statement

42

> Letter of Approval of Credit Application
> Letter of Rejection of Credit Application
> Notice of Change in Credit Terms
> Termination of Credit Line

Business Credit Application

Definition

The business credit application is to be completed by businesses applying for trade credit.

Comments

a. Be sure to obtain financial statements and references in support of the application.

b. Use credit reporting services to verify the information, not as a substitute for the application. Investigate discrepancies.

c. Require completion of every blank and block. Permitting blanks may encourage applicant to omit unfavorable information and to later claim "accidental skipping" of the question.

d. Limit distribution of the application and supporting materials, as much of it will be considered confidential by the applicant, who is, after all, a customer.

Distribution

> Original to credit department
> Copy to applicant

Loan Application (for consumers)

Definition

This loan application is to be completed by consumers who wish to receive credit.

Comments

a. Comments regarding the business credit application are applicable to the consumers' loan application, as well.

b. With the proliferation of credit cards, consumer credit extended by nonfinancial businesses has become more and more of a rarity. Most such transactions now are often cast as loans, wherein the loan proceeds are used to buy a consumer durable (e.g., furniture).

c. The approach of converting trade credit to a loan usually gives the business stronger legal rights.

   d. The application must avoid all hint of unlawful discriminatory intent (e.g., race, religion, handicap).

Distribution

Same as for business credit application

Personal Financial Statement

Definition

The personal financial statement is a detailed balance sheet showing net worth for an individual.

Comments

a. This statement is almost certain to be required from any sole proprietor, partner, or closely held business owner applying to a bank for credit. Hence, this is a good form to keep up to date for yourself.

b. It should also be required when anyone is interested in buying into the business, and may thus be used in conjunction with Module IX.

c. Check the mathematics when reviewing.

Distribution

Same as for business credit application

Letter of Approval of Credit Application

Definition

The letter of approval of credit application is notice to a credit applicant that a credit line has been established and that the applicant, by using the line, is contractually bound to the credit terms established.

Comments

a. If the applicant is a consumer, disclosure of all the terms must be made at time of application.

b. Nevertheless, reiterating the terms in the approval letter bolsters the company's claim of rights.

c. Interest and late charges rates may be limited by law for consumers.

Distribution

Original to customer

Copy to sales department

Copy retained by credit department

Letter of Rejection of Credit Application

Definition

The letter of rejection of credit application is notice to a credit applicant that no credit line can be established at the present time.

Comments

a. Not surprisingly, rejection will probably mean a lost customer. Thus credit standards should be carefully constructed and applied.

b. Consumers generally have the right to know why rejection has been issued. It may also be a good idea with both consumers and businesses to advise of such reasons (if it will not breach the lawful confidentiality of sources), as good credits, accidentally rejected, will not be lost as customers.

c. Rejections should not be widely distributed.

Distribution

Same as for letter of approval of credit application

Notice of Change in Credit Terms

Definition

The notice of change in credit terms notifies an existing credit-line customer of changes in the amount of authorized credit line.

Comments

a. This form may be used to advise of increases or decreases.

b. Increases are often used to spur additional purchases, especially if not specifically applied for.

c. Changes may come about based on the credit history of the account, as well as through updating of information from credit bureaus or other sources.

Distribution

Same as for letter of approval of credit application

Termination of Credit Line

Definition

The form for termination of credit line is used to give notice to an existing credit-line customer that the line of credit has been cancelled.

Comments

a. Most often this form will be used because of poor credit performance, in which case it ties in with Module I.

b. Other causes of termination may be customer request, death, consolidation of multiple accounts, etc.

c. Technically, a reason need not be stated; however, without such an explanation, the customer may have difficulty in correcting an error.

Distribution

Original to customer

Copy to sales department

Copy to collections department

Copy to credit department

BUSINESS CREDIT APPLICATION

Please supply ALL required information. Only FULLY COMPLETED forms will be considered.

Company Name _____

Trade Name _____

Billing Address _____

Headquarters Address _____

Telephone _____ Fax _____ Telex _____

Subsidiary of _____ Address _____

___ Corporation   ___ Partnership   ___ Proprietor   ___ Other: _____

Year Established _____ Type of Business _____

Yearly Sales $ _____ Yearly Profits $ _____ Net Worth $ _____

Resale Tax No. _____Tax Exemption No. _____ Employer ID No. _____

Please list partners (partnership), owner (proprietorship), officers (all others):

Name _____Title _____ Soc. Sec. No. _____

Address _____

Name _____Title _____ Soc. Sec. No. _____

Address _____

Name _____Title _____ Soc. Sec. No. _____

Address _____

Applicant agrees the following apply to all purchases and credit, if allowed:

1. All overdue invoices bear interest at ___% per month on unpaid balance.
2. Processing charge of $10.00 for each chargeback of unearned discounts.
3. Applicant will pay all costs of collection, including but not limited to attorney fees and court costs.
4. Credit line may be terminated, altered, suspended, or otherwise changed at any time, with or without cause by Vendor.
5. The terms of all transactions shall be as stated on Vendor's documents, which shall govern all transactions, regardless of conflicts, if any, with Applicant's documentation.
6. All transactions shall be governed by the laws of Vendor's jurisdiction.

Business Credit Application (*continued*)

Bank References

Bank Name _____   Bank Name _____

Account No. _____   Account No. _____

Address _____   Address _____

_____   _____

Telephone _____   Telephone _____

Trade Credit References

Vendor Name _____   Vendor Name _____

Account No. _____   Account No. _____

Address _____   Address _____

_____   _____

Telephone _____   Telephone _____

Other Credit References

Creditor _____   Creditor _____

Account No. _____   Account No. _____

Address _____   Address _____

_____   _____

Telephone _____   Telephone _____

Please attach most recent balance sheet and profit and loss statement or income tax return. *(Credit cannot be allowed without financial statements and references.)*

All information provided in connection with this Business Credit Application, including all financial statements, tax returns, and other materials, if any, is true, complete, and correct. Applicant agrees to update and supplement this information on demand, and further agrees to notify Vendor immediately in the event of any change in circumstances that might reasonably affect Vendor's ability to collect from Applicant, or Vendor's willingness to extend credit, or both. Applicant hereby authorizes Vendor to contact all references, whether listed herein or not, and to receive therefrom all credit information, including confidential information, as Vendor may request. Applicant understands acceptance of this Application by Vendor does not constitute an extension of credit nor a promise to extend credit. Any extension of credit by Vendor does not constitute a promise to extend additional or future credit.

_____, 19____   _____   _____
Date   Authorized Signature   Title

ACCOUNT # _____

CIS # _____

Application # _____

Loan Type _____

Date _____

Taken By _____

Approval 1 _____

Approval 2 _____

Branch # _____

LOAN APPLICATION

APPLICANT

Full Name (First, Middle, Last)	Date of Birth	Social Security No.	No. Dependents

Home Address (Street, City, State, Zip)	Years There	Home Phone

☐ Own ☐ Rent ☐ Other	Type Mortgage	If variable,	Mortgage Bal.	Mkt. Value	2nd Mtg.
Monthly Payment $ _____	Fixed ☐ Variable ☐	Maximum %	$	$	Yes ☐ No ☐

Previous Address (Street, City, State, Zip)	Years There

Employer Name and Address	Position/Occupation	Years There	Business Phone

Gross Mo. Income $	Net Mo. Income $	Previous Employer	Years There	Position/Occupation

Income from alimony, child support, or separate maintenance payments need not be revealed if you do not use it for repaying this obligation.

Other Income $	Frequency & Source	List any other names under which you have applied for or obtained credit.

Are you obligated to make monthly alimony, child support or separate maintenance payments? ☐ No ☐ Yes $

Name and Address of Nearest Relative Not Living With You	Relationship	Home Phone

Are there now, or have there been, any judgments or garnishments against you? ☐ No ☐ Yes	Have you ever been through bankruptcy or made a settlement with creditors? ☐ No ☐ Yes

Face Amount (Bank Use) $	Amount Requested $	Purpose of Loan (Describe)

Repayment Terms:

Instalment//Term: # payments _____ amount $_____ frequency _____

first payment due _____

Single Payment: Terms _____ Source of Repayment _____

Describe collateral offered, if any, and show name and social security no. of any joint owner of collateral offered.

Name: _____ SS# _____

Year _____ Body Type _____

New/Used _____ # Cylinders _____

Make _____ Model _____

ID# _____

_____

Other Collateral _____

BANK USE ONLY

Cash Price $ _____ NADA Loan Value $ _____

Trade $ _____ AT V.Top P.Seat P. Window Other Adds _____

Bal. Owed $ _____ 4 SP S/Tape A/C _____

Net $ _____ Residual Value $ _____

Value of Other Collateral $ _____ Source of Valuation _____

Will anyone else be obligated on this loan? ☐ Yes ☐ No

CO-APPLICANT - If application is for joint credit, please complete this section.

Full Name (First, Middle, Last)	Date of Birth	Social Security No.	No. Dependents

Home Address (Street, City, State, Zip)	Years There	Home Phone

Employer Name and Address	Position/Occupation	Years There	Business Phone

Gross Mo. Income $	Net Mo. Income $	Previous Employer	Years There	Position/Occupation

Income from alimony, child support, or separate maintenance payments need not be revealed if you do not use it for repaying this obligation.

Other Income $	Frequency & Source	List any other names under which you have applied for or obtained credit.

Are you obligated to make monthly alimony, child support or separate maintenance payments? ☐ No ☐ Yes $

Are there now, or have there been, any judgements or garnishments against you? ☐ No ☐ Yes	Have you ever been through bankruptcy or made a settlement with creditors? ☐ No ☐ Yes

APPLICANT AND CO-APPLICANT

CREDIT HISTORY/OBLIGATIONS - List all current obligations with banks, loan companies, finance companies, credit unions, stores, credit cards and all other creditors. Be sure to include unpaid taxes and outstanding debts to individuals. Indicate obligations of applicant with "A", of co-applicant with "C", and joint accounts with "J".

To Whom Indebted	Purpose or Account Number	A C J	Secured Yes/No	Outstanding Balance	Monthly Payment or Other Term
	Second Mortgage				
Total Debt				$	

DEPOSIT ACCOUNTS - APPLICANT AND CO-APPLICANT - Indicate accounts of applicant with "A", co-applicant with "C", and joint accounts with "J".

Name and Location of Bank and Savings Institution	A C J	Account No.	Type of Account	Amount

ASSETS OWNED - APPLICANT AND CO-APPLICANT

Description of Assets	Value	Encumbered?	Name(s) of Owner(s) of Record
Cash (Including checking and savings accounts)	$		
Time Deposits, Money Market Funds and Other (List)			
Marketable Securities (Issuer, Type, Shares)			
Automobiles (Make, Model, Year)			
Cash Value of Life Insurance (Issuer, Face Value)			
Real Estate (Location, Date Acquired)			
TOTAL ASSETS	$		

Applicant Signature _____ Date _____ Co-Applicant Signature _____ Date _____

Comments:
_____
_____
_____

LOAN REVIEW SECTION

Date: _____ Comments _____
_____
_____
_____

50

PERSONAL FINANCIAL STATEMENT
IMPORTANT: Read these directions before completing this Statement

If you are applying for individual credit in your own name and are relying on your own income or assets and not the income or assets of another person as the basis for repayment of the credit requested, complete only Sections 1 and 3.

☐ If you are applying for joint credit with another person, complete all Sections providing information in Section 2 about the joint applicant.

☐ If you are applying for individual credit, but are relying on income from alimony, child support, or separate maintenance or on the income or assets of another person as a basis for repayment of the credit requested, complete all Sections, providing information in Section 2 about the person whose alimony, support, or maintenance payments or income or assets you are relying.

☐ If this statement relates to your guaranty of the indebtedness of other person(s), firm(s) or corporation(s), complete Sections 1 and 3.

TO:

SECTION 1 - INDIVIDUAL INFORMATION (Type or Print)	SECTION 2 - OTHER PARTY INFORMATION (Type or Print)
Name	Name
Residence Address	Residence Address
City, State, Zip	City, State, Zip
Position or Occupation	Position or Occupation
Business Name	Business Name
Business Address	Business Address
City, State, Zip	City, State, Zip
Res. Phone Bus. Phone	Res. Phone Bus. Phone

SECTION 3 - STATEMENT OF FINANCIAL CONDITION AS OF _____ 19, _____

ASSETS (Do not include Assets of doubtful value)	In Dollars (Omit cents)	LIABILITIES	In Dollars (Omit cents)
Cash on hand and in banks		Notes payable to banks - secured	
U.S. Gov't. & Marketable Securities - see Sch. A		Notes payable to banks - unsecured	
Non-Marketable Securities - see Schedule B		Due to brokers	
Securities held by broker in margin accounts		Amounts payable to others - secured	
Restricted or control stocks		Amounts payable to others - unsecured	
Partial interest in Real Estate Equities - see Schedule C		Accounts and bills due	
		Unpaid income tax	
Real Estate Owned - see Schedule D		Other unpaid taxes and interest	
Loans Receivable		Real estate mortgages payable - see Schedule D	
Automobile and other personal property			
Cash value - life insurance - see Schedule E		Other debts - itemize:	
Other assets - itemize:			
		TOTAL LIABILITIES	
		NET WORTH	
TOTAL ASSETS		TOTAL LIAB. AND NET WORTH	

SOURCES OF INCOME FOR YEAR ENDED _____ , 19 _____		Do you have a will? If yes, name of executor.
Salary, bonuses & commissions	$	
Dividends		Are you a partner or officer in any other venture? If yes, decribe
Real estate income		
Other income (Alimony, child support, or separate maintenance income need not be revealed if you do not wish to have it considered as a basis for repaying this obligation)		Are any assets pledged other than as described on schedules? If yes, describe
		Income tax settled through (Date) _____
		Are you a defendant in any suits or legal actions?
		Personal Bank Accounts carried at
TOTAL	$	
CONTINGENT LIABILITIES		Have you ever declared bankruptcy? If yes, describe
Do you have any contingent liabilities? If so, describe		
		List any other names under which you applied for or obtained credit
As indorser, co-maker or guarantor?	$	
On leases or contracts?	$	Are you obligated to pay alimony, child support, or separate maintenance payments? If yes, describe
Legal claims?	$	
Other special debt?	$	Note - If separate, unsecured credit is sought, the following information need not be supplied. ☐ married ☐ unmarried ☐ separated
Amount of contested income tax liens?	$	

(COMPLETE SCHEDULES AND SIGN ON REVERSE SIDE)

51

SCHEDULE A - U.S. GOVERNMENTS & MARKETABLE SECURITIES

Number of Shares Of Face Value (Bonds)	Description	In Name Of	Are These Pledged?	Market Value

SCHEDULE B - NON-MARKETABLE SECURITIES

Number of Shares	Description	In Name Of	Are These Pledged?	Source of	Value

SCHEDULE C - PARTIAL INTERESTS IN REAL ESTATE EQUITIES

Address & Type Of Property	Title In Name Of	% Of Ownership	Date Acquired	Cost	Market Value	Mortgage Maturity	Mortgage Amount

SCHEDULE D - REAL ESTATE OWNED

Address & Type Of Property	Title In Name Of	Date Acquired	Cost	Market Value	Mortgage Maturity	Mortgage Amount

SCHEDULE E - LIFE INSURANCE CARRIED, INCLUDING N.S.L.I. AND GROUP INSURANCE

Name of Insurance Company	Owner Of Policy	Beneficiary	Face Amount	Policy Loans	Cash Surrender Value

SCHEDULE F - BANKS OR FINANCE COMPANIES WHERE CREDIT HAS BEEN OBTAINED

Name & Address of Lender	Credit In The Name Of	Secured Or Unsecured?	Original Date	High Credit	Current Balance

The information contained in this statement is provided for the purpose of obtaining, or maintaining credit with you on behalf of the undersigned, or persons, firms or corporations in whose behalf the undersigned may either severally or jointly with others, execute a guaranty in your favor. Each undersigned understands that you are relying on the information provided herein (including the designation made as to ownership of property) in deciding to grant or continue credit. Each undersigned represents and warrants that the information provided is true and complete and that you may consider this statement as continuing to be true and correct until a written notice of a change is given to you by the undersigned. You are authorized to make all inquiries you deem necessary to verify the accuracy of the statements made herein, and to determine my/our credit-worthiness. You are authorized to answer questions about your credit experience with me/us.

Signature (Individual) _____
S.S. No.: _____ Date of Birth _____

Signature (Other Party) _____
S.S. No.: _____ Date of Birth _____

Date Signed _____ 19 _____

LETTER OF APPROVAL OF CREDIT APPLICATION

Date _____

To _____

_____

_____

Dear _____:

    Thank you for your application for credit with our company. We are pleased to inform you that we have approved a line of credit for you in the amount of $_____, subject to the following terms:

    We reserve the right to change or terminate the line of credit at any time, with or without cause, and without any liability on our part for a change or termination.

    Payment terms are ___% within ___ days, net due ___ days from the invoice date.

    In the event any invoice is not paid according to its terms, a late charge of ___% will be assessed. Also, interest on the outstanding balance will also accrue monthly at ___% per month.

    If collection or enforcement action of any kind is necessary because of any failure to pay or to adhere to the terms of any agreement with us, you will be liable also for court costs, attorney fees, and all other costs of collection allowed by law.

    Your use of the line of credit constitutes acceptance of these terms.
We appreciate your patronage and look forward to a long and mutually beneficial relationship.

        Sincerely,

_____
Authorized Signatory

_____
Title

LETTER OF REJECTION OF CREDIT APPLICATION

Date _____

To _____

_____

_____

Dear _____:

    Thank you for your application for credit with our company. Unfortunately, at this time we are unable to extend credit to you. However, we do hope you will reapply at a later time. Until such time, we do welcome your purchases on a cash basis.

    Thank you again for your interest.

Sincerely,

_____

Authorized Signatory

_____

Title

NOTICE OF CHANGE IN CREDIT TERMS

Date _____

To _____

_____

_____

Dear _____:

    Please be advised that we are changing the amount of our credit line to you from $_____ to $_____, effective immediately.

    This change is made in accord with the terms under our credit approval letter, which established the account.

    Please be advised that as of this date the balance owed on your account is $_____.

    All other terms remain in full force and effect. Please contact us if you should have any questions. We appreciate your continued patronage and cooperation.

Sincerely,

_____
Authorized Signatory

_____
Title

TERMINATION OF CREDIT LINE

Date _____

To _____

_____

_____

Dear _____:

    Please be advised that, effective immediately, your credit line with this company is hereby terminated for the following reason(s):

_____

_____

_____

    This termination is made in accord with our rights under our credit approval letter, which established the account.

    Please be advised that as of this date the balance owed on your account is $_____, for which prompt payment is hereby requested.

    All terms governing payment and collection remain in full force and effect, and all rights are hereby reserved. We regret that it has become necessary to take this action.

Sincerely,

_____

Authorized Signatory

_____

Title

Module IV

Employment

INTRODUCTION

Few areas of the law have seen such dramatic change in recent years as employment law. Not only have there been great changes, but there is also substantial variation among different states, even within states. Consequently, one must proceed with great caution and often with the assistance of an experienced attorney familiar with local law.

The purposes of employment forms are

1. To aid in decision making, regarding employees
2. To provide data for managing personnel and related costs
3. To assist in compliance with laws regarding personnel and recordkeeping
4. To prevent employees from harming the company through disclosure of confidential information or by competitive activities

MODULE FORMS

The 12 forms in this module are

Employment Application
Letter Requesting Employment Verification
Authorization for Medical Examination and Testing

Physical Examination Form

Request for Medical Records

Employment Eligibility Verification (Form I-9)

Employment Contract

Employee's Covenants

Employee Confidentiality Certification

Receipt for Samples and Documents

Employee Weekly Time Sheet

Expense Voucher

Employment Application

Definition

The employment application is used to obtain and evaluate data on prospective hirees.

Comments

a. This form is targeted toward blue-collar and lower level positions, as most executive applicants will provide résumés.

b. Any implication of illegal discrimination must be avoided (e.g., race, religion, handicap). However, if a lawful need to screen on such a basis (e.g., hazards to women of childbearing age, age for restaurant employees serving liquor) can be shown, such questions may be asked.

c. Be sure to tell the appliant to read the statement of truthfulness before signing. Employees are usually favored by courts, and a failure to read may be a legitimate excuse for avoiding the terms.

Distribution

Original to screening parties during hiring process, ultimately to be returned to and retained by personnel department

Letter Requesting Employment Verification

Definition

The letter requesting employment verification is used to obtain verification and background information on employment applicants.

Comments

a. The addresses of the letter should be disclosed to the applicant to test the applicant's reaction and to be sure the applicant is giving informed consent.

b.   Verification has fallen into disfavor because of lawsuits against respondents for giving unfavorable replies. Nevertheless, inquiry remains a necessary investigative tool, which must be weighed as a factor in evaluation.

Distribution

Original to addressee

Copy retained by personnel department

Authorization for Medical Examination and Testing

Definition

The authorization for medical examination and testing allows an employer to arrange for medical tests of the person giving consent.

Comments

a.   Such tests must be reasonably related to employment requirements to be made a condition of employment.

b.   This form is the one to use if drug testing of employees is desired. But proceed with caution, as the employer's right to require drug testing is subject to many restrictions, may be challenged, and can result in liability if handled improperly.

c.   No arrangements for testing should be undertaken until the existence of adequate liability insurance coverage has been confirmed.

Distribution

Original to personnel department

Copy to medical examiner

Copy to consenting employee or applicant

Physical Examination Form

Definition

The physical examination form is a document on which the results of a physical exam of an employee or applicant are reported.

Comments

a.   This form was developed by the American Trucking Association to meet U.S. Department of Transportation (DOT) requirements. It is, however, an excellent model for any type of employee medical reporting.

b.   The accompanying instructions are not needed when not used in connection with a DOT-covered position.

    c. Like most employee data, this form should be maintained in strict confidence.

Distribution

Original to personnel department

Copy to employee or applicant

Copy retained by physician

Request for Medical Records

Definition

The request for medical records is used to obtain existing medical records of an employee from third parties (e.g., physicians, former employers)

Comments

a. The employee's/applicant's signed consent is mandatory.

b. While it may be possible to substitute existing medical records for a new exam, it is risky as health changes. Usually, the old records are desired as additional background.

Distribution

Original to records custodian

Copy to employee or applicant

Copy retained by personnel department

Employment Eligibility Verification (Form I-9)

Definition

Form I-9 is used to verify an applicant's eligibility for employment.

Comments

a. Federal law now requires all new hirees to complete the I-9 to prevent employment of illegal aliens. Employers who fail to obtain and retain I-9's are subject to fines and other penalties.

b. Conversely, I-9's on file offer a safe harbor to the employer, showing intent to comply with the law to not hire illegal aliens.

c. In obtaining an I-9, the employer must walk a fine line to avoid appearing to practice discrimination. The safe way to do so is to offer the position to the applicant *before* presenting the I-9, with the caveat to the applicant that the I-9 information must be acceptable as required by law.

d. Follow the instructions and be sure the new employee understands and follows them as well.

Distribution

Original to personnel department

Copy to employee (if requested)

Employment Contract

Definition

The employment contract is a written agreement covering the terms of employment.

Comments

a. Employment contracts are very much individualized creations of local law. This form is designed to reflect the more common points but should not be used without advice of counsel.

b. Ambiguities will generally be construed against the employer, so precision in language is especially important.

Distribution

Original to personnel department

Original to employee

Employee's Covenants

Definition

The employee's covenants are promises of the employee required as conditions of employment.

Comments

a. Comments regarding the employment contract are applicable to the employee's covenants, as well.

b. Some companies prefer these to full-blown contracts, as they do not place explicit responsibility on the company.

c. However, to be valid, they generally must be signed right at the point of hiring or when a new benefit (e.g., raise, promotion) is offered to the employee, as most jurisdictions require a showing of consideration.

d. This form is used primarily for white-collar employees, especially those having access to sensitive data.

Distribution

Same as for employment contract

Employee Confidentiality Certification

Definition

The employee confidentiality certification is a promise of nondisclosure made by an employee as a condition of employment.

Comments

a. Comments regarding the employee's covenants are applicable to the employee confidentiality certification, as well.

b. This form is applicable to all employees, as nearly all have information that can be useful intelligence to competitors.

Distribution

Same as for employment contract

Receipt for Samples and Documents

Definition

The receipt for samples and documents is a promise of faithful custodianship by an employee entrusted with valuable samples and/or sensitive documents.

Comments

a. This form is used most often for field personnel, such as salespersons and customer-site repairpersons.

b. Failure to safeguard will not subject the employee to liability for payment for damage (in the absence of willful destruction) in most jurisdictions; rather it is cause for dismissal.

c. The greater value of the form is for recovery of the samples and documents upon termination of employment.

Distribution

Original to personnel department

Copy to employee's immediate superior

Copy to employee

Employee Weekly Time Sheet

Definition

The employee weekly time sheet is used to keep track of an employee's work hours.

Comments

a. Time sheets are mandatory records for hourly employees.
b. Where a time clock or similar device is used, the results should still be verified by the employee.
c. Note the policies enumerated at the bottom of the form, which may vary from employer to employer.

Distribution

Original to payroll department

Copy to employee's immediate superior

Expense Voucher

Definition

The expense voucher is to be used by an employee to obtain reimbursement for expenditures made on behalf of the employer.

Comments

a. Proof of expenditures is required by tax authorities.
b. Payment on the voucher alone, without verifying receipts, is a dangerous practice. At minimum, an explanation of why receipts are not provided should be required.
c. If the advance amount exceeds the total expense, the employee should be required to return the difference.

Distribution

Original to accounting department

Copy to employee's immediate superior

Copy to employee

EMPLOYMENT APPLICATION

Company _____ Location _____

Applicant Name _____ Social Security No. _____

Address _____ Telephone _____

_____ Years at present address _____

Name, relation, and address of nearest relative _____

_____

I am/am not (circle one) at least 18 years old.   Driver's License No. _____ State _____

Position applied for _____ Salary Desired $_____/_____

Referred by _____ Applied to our company previously? _____

If so, when? _____

EMPLOYMENT HISTORY *(Please list current or most recent employment first.)*

From	To	Employer	Address	Position	Salary	Reason for leaving

EDUCATION *(Please list current or most recent schooling first.)*

From	To	School Name	Address	Program	Degree	Reason for leaving

SKILLS *(Please list skills in order of usefulness to the position applied for.)*

Skill	How acquired	When acquired	Rate your ability

Page 1 of 2. Please initial. _____

Employment Application (*continued*)

If you have ever been convicted of any crime (including traffic violations), please describe.

Date	Nature of crime	Court	Disposition	On parole now?

Are you legally able to be employed in the U.S.? _____

When would you like to begin work? _____

How will you get to work? _____

What work schedule do you prefer? _____

Please list any reason(s) you believe may require you to cease work if employed. _____

_____

Please list any health problem(s) that could affect your employment. _____

_____

Please provide any other information you think may assist evaluation. _____

_____

STATEMENT OF TRUTHFULNESS

By signing below, I agree that acceptance of the application is no guarantee employment will be offered. All employment is strictly "at will," meaning it may be terminated any time by the company with or without cause and for any reason. In submitting this application, I authorize the Company to contact all persons and organizations listed. I agree to submit to various tests, if so requested, such as for skills or substance abuse, and refusal to submit to tests constitutes withdrawal of this application and my rejection of any employment offer. If offered employment, I agree a condition for acceptance is my agreement to covenants to not compete and for confidentiality, and my refusal to agree thereto in writing constitutes withdrawal of this application and rejection of any employment offer. I have had the opportunity to confidentially disclose any special status (e.g., handicap, veteran, minority) that I believe applicable for equal opportunity purposes. I agree any part of the foregoing found to be invalid under law shall stand as severed from this application and statement of truthfulness. I certify all the foregoing and all information provided by me is true, correct, and complete to the best of my knowledge and belief, and any false or incorrect statement is cause for termination of the "at will" employment at the option of the company. I HAVE READ ALL THE ABOVE, ASKED ALL QUESTIONS I DESIRED, AND UNDERSTAND AND AGREE.

Date _____, 19____   _____
                                        Applicant's signature

LETTER REQUESTING EMPLOYMENT VERIFICATION

Date _____

To _____

_____

_____

Dear _____ :

_____ (Social Security No. ____ - ____ - ____) has applied to this company for employment in the position of _____. With the permission of your former employee, as shown below, we request that the following information be provided to us:

Employment History

From	To	Position	Initial salary	Ending salary

Please list any commendations or awards. _____

_____

Please state the reason(s) for separation. _____

_____

We welcome any additional comments or information. Many thanks for your assistance.

Cordially,

_____

- -

I hereby irrevocably authorize release of all requested employment information to the above-listed requesting company.

Date _____   _____
                                      Applicant's signature

AUTHORIZATION FOR MEDICAL EXAMINATION AND TESTING

I, the undersigned person, declaring that I am a competent adult of at least eighteen (18) years of age do hereby irrevocably grant permission and authorization for the following medical examination and test procedures to be performed on me:

_____

_____

_____

I further agree and recognize that such testing may involve the temporary invasion or penetration of my body by medical instruments, light, sound, x-rays, or other imaging and diagnostic media, and may further involve the obtainment of bodily fluids, tissue, products or waste, all of which I relinquish any claim to.

I further certify that all such contemplated procedures have been explained to me and that I have provided complete and honest responses to all questions posed to me regarding my health and medical condition and status, including pregnancy, disabilities, allergies, and susceptibilities, if any.

I further acknowledge that these medical procedures are not being performed for my benefit, but are instead performed for the benefit of _____, which I hereby release from any and all responsibility for treatment, advice, referral, or diagnosis.

I grant this authorization in consideration for the opportunity to be considered for employment, or for immediate or future advancement in employment, or because examination and tests are required by applicable law, and I understand and agree such medical examination and tests are necessary and relevant to my employment.

I make this grant voluntarily and without reservation.

Date _____

_____
Applicant's signature

Witness _____

PHYSICAL EXAMINATION FORM

(MEETS DEPARTMENT OF TRANSPORTATION REQUIREMENTS)

FORM C0730, Reorder from:
American Trucking Associations
2200 Mill Road
Alexandria, VA 22314
1 800 ATA-LINE   2/88

Date of Examination _____   New Certification ☐
                                    Recertification ☐

To Be Filled In By Examining Physician *(Please Print):*

Driver's Name _____

Address _____

Soc. Sec. No. _____ Date of Birth _____ Age _____

Health History:

Yes	No		Yes	No		Yes	No	
☐	☐	Asthma	☐	☐	Nervous stomach	☐	☐	Head or spinal injuries
☐	☐	Kidney	☐	☐	Rheumatic fever	☐	☐	Seizures, fits, convulsions, or fainting
☐	☐	Tuberculosis	☐	☐	Muscular disease	☐	☐	Extensive confinement by illness or injury
☐	☐	Syphilis	☐	☐	Psychiatric disorder	☐	☐	Any other nervous disorder
☐	☐	Gonorrhea	☐	☐	Cardiovascular disease	☐	☐	Suffering from any other disease
☐	☐	Diabetes	☐	☐	Gastrointestinal ulcer	☐	☐	Permanent defect from illness, disease or injury

If answer to any of the above is yes, explain: _____

General appearance and development: Good _____ Fair _____ Poor _____

Vision: For Distance: Right 20/_____ Left 20/_____ Both 20/_____ ☐ Without corrective lenses ☐ With corrective lenses, if worn

Evidence of disease or injury: Right _____ Left _____

Color Test _____ Horizontal field of vision: Right _____ Left _____

Hearing: Right ear _____ Left ear _____

Disease or injury _____

Audiometric test: *(if audiometer is used to test hearing)* Decibel loss at 500 Hz _____ 1,000 Hz _____ 2,000 Hz _____ 4,000 Hz _____ 6,000 Hz _____

Throat: _____

Thorax: Heart _____

If organic disease is present, is it fully compensated? _____

Blood pressure: Systolic _____ Diastolic _____

Pulse: Before exercise _____ Immediately after exercise _____

Lungs _____

Abdomen: Scars _____ Abnormal masses _____ Tenderness _____

Hernia: Yes _____ No _____ If so, where? _____ Is truss worn? _____

Gastrointestinal: Ulceration or other diseases: Yes _____ No _____

Genito-Urinary: Scars _____ Urethral discharge _____

Reflexes: Rhomberg _____

Pupillary _____ Light: R _____ L _____

Accommodation: Right _____ Left _____

Knee jerks: Right: Normal _____ Increased _____ Absent _____

Left: Normal _____ Increased _____ Absent _____

Remarks: _____

Extremities: Upper _____ Lower _____ Spine _____

Laboratory and Other Special Findings: Urine: Spec. Gr. _____ Alb. _____ Sugar _____

Other Laboratory Data (Serology, etc) _____

Radiological Data _____ Electrocardiograph _____

☐ CHECK HERE IF NOT QUALIFIED

General Comments: _____

_____

Name of Examining Doctor (Print) _____ Signature _____

Address of Examining Doctor _____

MEDICAL EXAMINER'S CERTIFICATE TO BE COMPLETED ONLY IF DRIVER IS FOUND QUALIFIED

MEDICAL EXAMINER'S CERTIFICATE
(I certify that I have examined)

_____
(Driver's name (Print))

in accordance with the Federal Motor Carrier Safety Regulations (49 CFR 391.41-3 91.49) and with the knowledge of his duties, I find him qualified under the regulations.
☐ Qualified only when wearing corrective lenses
☐ Qualified only when wearing a hearing aid
A complete examination form for this person is on file in my office at:

_____
Address

_____
(Date of examination)   (Name of examining doctor (Print))

_____
(Signature of examining doctor)

_____
(Signature of driver)

_____
(Address of driver)

The following will be completed only when the visual test is conducted by a licensed ophthalmologist or optometrist.

_____
(Date of Examination)

_____
(Name of Ophthalmologist or Optometrist (Print))

_____
(Address of Ophthalmologist or Optometrist)

_____
(Signature of Ophthalmologist or Optometrist)

INSTRUCTIONS ON REVERSE SIDE

68

Physical Examination Form (*continued*)

DEPT. OF TRANSPORTATION PHYSICAL QUALIFICATIONS & EXAMINATIONS OF DRIVERS

A person is physically qualified to drive a motor vehicle if he—

(1) Has no loss of a foot, a leg, a hand, or an arm, or has been granted a waiver pursuant to §391.49;

(2) Has no impairment of the use of a foot, a leg, a hand, fingers, or an arm, and no other structural defect or limitation, which is likely to interfere with his ability to control and safely drive a motor vehicle, or has been granted a waiver pursuant to §391.49 upon a determination that the impairment will not interfere with his ability to control and safely drive a motor vehicle;

(3) Has no established medical history or clinical diagnosis of diabetes mellitus currently requiring insulin for control;

(4) Has no current clinical diagnosis of myocardial infarction, angina pectoris, coronary insufficiency, thrombosis, or any other cardiovascular disease of a variety known to be accompanied by syncope, dyspnea, collapse, or congestive cardiac failure;

(5) Has no established medical history or clinical diagnosis of a respiratory dysfunction likely to interfere with his ability to control and drive a motor vehicle safely;

(6) Has no current clinical diagnosis of high blood pressure likely to interfere with his ability to operate a motor vehicle safely;

(7) Has no established medical history or clinical diagnosis of rheumatic, arthritic, orthopedic, muscular, neuromuscular, or vascular disease which interferes with his ability to control and operate a motor vehicle safely;

(8) Has no established medical history or clinical diagnosis of epilepsy or any other condition which is likely to cause loss of consciousness or any loss of ability to control a motor vehicle;

(9) Has no mental, nervous, organic or functional disease or psychiatric disorder likely to interfere with his ability to drive a motor vehicle safely;

(10) Has distant visual acuity of at least 20/40 (Snellen) in each eye without corrective lenses or visual acuity separately corrected to 20/40 (Snellen) or better with corrective lenses, distant binocular acuity of at least 20/40 (Snellen) in both eyes with or without corrective lenses, field of vision of at least 70° in the horizontal meridian in each eye, and the ability to recognize the colors of traffic signals and devices showing standard red, green, and amber;

(11) First perceives a forced whispered voice in the better ear at not less than 5 feet with or without the use of a hearing aid or, if tested by use of an audiometric device, does not have an average hearing loss in the better ear greater than 40 decibels at 500 Hz, 1,000 Hz, and 2,000 Hz with or without a hearing aid when the audiometric device is calibrated to American National Standard (formerly ASA Standard) Z24.5 — 1951.

(12) Does not use a drug or other substance identified in the Drug Enforcement Administration's Schedule I - Controlled Substances, an amphetamine, narcotic, or any other habit - forming drug; and

(13) Has no current clinical diagnosis of alcoholism.

INSTRUCTIONS FOR PERFORMING AND RECORDING PHYSICAL EXAMINATIONS

The examining physician should review these instructions before performing the physical examination. Answer each question yes or no where appropriate.

The examining physician should be aware of the rigorous physical demands and mental and emotional responsibilities placed on the driver of a commercial motor vehicle. In the interest of public safety the examining physician is required to certify that the driver does not have any physical, mental, or organic defect of such a nature as to affect the driver's ability to operate safely a commercial motor vehicle.

General information. The purpose of this history and physical examination is to detect the presence of physical, mental or organic defects of such a character and extent as to affect the applicant's ability to operate a motor vehicle safely. The examination should be made carefully and at least as complete as indicated by the attached form. History of certain defects may be cause for rejection or indicate the need for making certain laboratory tests or a further, and more stringent, examination. Defects may be recorded which do not, because of their character or degree, indicate that certification of physical fitness should be denied. However, these defects should be discussed with the applicant and he should be advised to take the necessary steps to ensure correction, particularly of those which, if neglected, might lead to a condition likely to affect his ability to drive safely.

General appearance and development. Note marked overweight. Note any posture defect, perceptible limp, tremor, or other defects that might be caused by alcoholism, thyroid intoxication, or other illnesses. The Federal Motor Carrier Safety Regulations provide that no driver shall use a narcotic or other habit-forming drug.

Head-eyes. When other than the Snellen chart is used, the results of such test must be expressed in values comparable to the standard Snellen test. If the applicant wears corrective lenses, these should be worn while applicant's visual acuity is being tested. If appropriate, indicate on the Medical Examiner's Certificate by checking the box, "Qualified only when wearing corrective lenses." In recording distance vision use 20 feet as normal. Report all vision as a fraction with 20 as numerator and the smallest type read at 20 feet as denominator. Note ptosis, discharge, visual fields, ocular muscle imbalance, color blindness, corneal scar, exophthalmos, or strabismus, uncorrected by corrective lenses. Monocular drivers are not qualified to operate commercial motor vehicles under existing Federal Motor Carrier Safety Regulations.

If the driver habitually wears contact lenses, or intends to do so while driving, there should be sufficient evidence to indicate that he has good tolerance and is well adapted to their use. The use of contact lenses should be noted on the record.

Ears. Note evidence of mastoid or middle ear disease, discharge, symptoms of aura vertigo, or Meniere's Syndrome. When recording hearing, record distance from patient at which a forced whispered voice can first be heard. If audiometer is used to test hearing, record decibel loss at 500 Hz, 1,000 Hz, and 2,000 Hz.

Throat. Note evidence of disease, irremediable deformities of the throat likely to interfere with eating or breathing, or any laryngeal condition which could interfere with the safe operation or a motor vehicle.

Thorax-heart. Stethoscopic examination is required. Note murmurs and arrhythmias, and any past or present history of cardio-vascular disease, of a variety known to be accompanied by syncope, dyspnea, collapse, enlarged heart, or congestive heart failures. Electrocardiogram is required when findings so indicate.

Blood pressure. Record with either spring or mercury column type of sphygomomanometer. If the blood pressure is consistently above 160/90 mm. Hg., further tests may be necessary to determine whether the driver is qualified to operate a motor vehicle.

Lungs. If any lung disease is detected, state whether active or arrested; if arrested, your opinion as to how long it has been quiescent.

Gastrointestinal system. Note any diseases of the gastrointestinal system.

Abdomen. Note wounds, injuries, scars, or weakness of muscles of abdominal walls sufficient to interfere with normal function. Any hernia should be noted if present. State how long and if adequately contained by truss.

Abnormal masses. If present, not location, if tender, and whether or not applicant knows how long they have been present. If the diagnosis suggests that the condition might interfere with the control and safe operation of a motor vehicle, more stringent tests must be made before the applicant can be certified.

Tenderness. When noted, state where most pronounced, and suspected cause. If the diagnosis suggests that the condition might interfere with the control and safe operation of a motor vehicle, more stringent tests must be made before the applicant can be certified.

Genito-urinary. Urinalysis is required. Acute infections of the genito-urinary tract, as defined by local and State public health laws, indications from urinalysis of uncontrolled diabetes, symptomatic albumin-urea in the urine, or other findings indicative of health conditions likely to interfere with the control and safe operation of a motor vehicle, will disqualify an applicant from operating a motor vehicle.

Neurological. If positive Rhomberg is reported, indicate degrees of impairment. Pupillary reflexes should be reported for both light and accommodation. Knee jerks are to be reported absent only when not obtainable upon reinforcement and as increased when foot is actually lifted from the floor following a light blow on the patella, sensory vibratory and positional abnormalities should be noted.

Extremities. Carefully examine upper and lower extremities. Record the loss or impairment of a leg, foot, toe, arm, hand, or fingers. Note any and all deformities, the presence of atrophy, semiparalysis or paralysis, or varicose veins. If a hand or finger deformity exists, determine whether sufficient grasp is present to enable the driver to secure and maintain a grip on the steering wheel. If a leg deformity exists, determine whether sufficient mobility and strength exist to enable the driver to operate pedals properly. Particular attention should be given to and a record should be made of, any impairment or structural defect which may interfere with the driver's ability to operate a motor vehicle safely.

Spine. Note deformities, limitation of motion, or any history of pain, injuries, or disease, past or presently experienced in the cervical or lumbar spine region. If findings so dictate, radiologic and other examinations should be used to diagnose congenital or acquired defects; or spondylolisthesis and scoliosis.

Recto-genital studies. Diseases or conditions causing discomfort should be evaluated carefully to determine the extent to which the condition might be handicapping while lifting, pulling, or during periods of prolonged driving that might be necessary as part of the driver's duties.

Laboratory and other special findings. Urinalysis is required, as well as such other tests as the medical history or findings upon physical examination may indicate are necessary. A serological test is required if the applicant has a history of luetic infection or present physical findings indicate the possibility of latent syphilis. Other studies deemed advisable may be ordered by the examining physician.

Diabetes. If insulin is necessary to control a diabetic condition, the driver is not qualified to operate a motor vehicle. If mild diabetes is noted at the time of examination and it is stabilized by use of a hypoglycemic drug and a diet that can be obtained while the driver is on duty, it should not be considered disqualifying. However, the driver must remain under adequate medical supervision.

The physician must date and sign his findings upon completion of the examination.

The medical examination shall be performed by a licensed doctor of medicine or osteopathy. A licensed ophthalmologist or optometrist may perform examinations pertaining to visual acuity, field of vision and ability to recognize colors.

If the medical examiner finds that the person he examined is physically qualified to drive a motor vehicle he shall complete the Medical Examiner's Certificate and furnish one copy to the person examined and one copy to the motor carrier employer.

REQUEST FOR MEDICAL RECORDS

Date _____

To _____

_____

_____

Dear _____:

_____ (Social Security No. ___ – ___ – _____) has applied to this company for employment in the position of _____. Because of the physical requirements this position entails, we request the following medical records:

_____

_____

_____

Please note the signature of the applicant granting permission below. Thank you for your cooperation.

Sincerely,

_____

— —

I irrevocably authorize release of all requested medical information to the above-listed requesting company.

Date _____   _____
                                 Applicant's signature

EMPLOYMENT ELIGIBILITY VERIFICATION (Form I-9)

1 EMPLOYEE INFORMATION AND VERIFICATION: (To be completed and signed by employee.)

Name: (Print or Type) Last	First	Middle	Birth Name

Address: Street Name and Number	City	State	ZIP Code

Date of Birth (Month/Day Year)	Social Security Number

I attest, under penalty of perjury, that I am (check a box):

☐ 1. A citizen or national of the United States.

☐ 2. An alien lawfully admitted for permanent residence (Alien Number A _____).

☐ 3. An alien authorized by the Immigration and Naturalization Service to work in the United States (Alien Number A _____ .
or Admission Number _____ , expiration of employment authorization, if any _____).

I attest, under penalty of perjury, the documents that I have presented as evidence of identity and employment eligibility are genuine and relate to me. I am aware that federal law provides for imprisonment and/or fine for any false statements or use of false documents in connection with this certificate.

Signature	Date (Month/Day/Year)

PREPARER TRANSLATOR CERTIFICATION (To be completed if prepared by person other than the employee). I attest, under penalty of perjury, that the above was prepared by me at the request of the named individual and is based on all information of which I have any knowledge.

Signature	Name (Print or Type)		
Address (Street Name and Number)	City	State	Zip Code

2 EMPLOYER REVIEW AND VERIFICATION: (To be completed and signed by employer.)

Instructions:

Examine one document from List A and check the appropriate box. *OR* examine one document from List B *and* one from List C and check the appropriate boxes. Provide the *Document Identification Number* and *Expiration Date* for the document checked.

List A Documents that Establish Identity and Employment Eligibility	List B Documents that Establish Identity	**and**	List C Documents that Establish Employment Eligibility
☐ 1. United States Passport	☐ 1. A State-issued driver's license or a State-issued I.D. card with a photograph, or information, including name, sex, date of birth, height, weight, and color of eyes. (Specify State)_____)		☐ 1. Original Social Security Number Card (other than a card stating it is not valid for employment)
☐ 2. Certificate of United States Citizenship	☐ 2. U.S. Military Card		☐ 2. A birth certificate issued by State, county, or municipal authority bearing a seal or other certification
☐ 3. Certificate of Naturalization	☐ 3. Other (Specify document and issuing authority)		☐ 3. Unexpired INS Employment Authorization Specify form
☐ 4. Unexpired foreign passport with attached Employment Authorization	_____		# _____
☐ 5. Alien Registration Card with photograph			
Document Identification	*Document Identification*		*Document Identification*
# _____	# _____		# _____
Expiration Date (if any)	*Expiration Date (if any)*		*Expiration Date (if any)*
_____	_____		_____

CERTIFICATION: I attest, under penalty of perjury, that I have examined the documents presented by the above individual, that they appear to be genuine and to relate to the individual named, and that the individual, to the best of my knowledge, is eligible to work in the United States.

Signature	Name (Print or Type)	Title
Employer Name	Address	Date

Form I-9 (05/07/87)
OMB No. 1115-0136

U.S. Department of Justice
Immigration and Naturalization Service

71

Employment Eligibility Verification

> **NOTICE:** Authority for collecting the information on this form is in Title 8, United States Code, Section 1324A, which requires employers to verify employment eligibility of individuals on a form approved by the Attorney General. This form will be used to verify the individual's eligibility for employment in the United States. Failure to present this form for inspection to officers of the Immigration and Naturalization Service or Department of Labor within the time period specified by regulation, or improper completion or retention of this form, may be a violation of the above law and may result in a civil money penalty.

Section 1. Instructions to Employee/Preparer for completing this form

Instructions for the employee.

All employees, upon being hired, must complete Section 1 of this form. Any person hired after November 6, 1986 must complete this form. (For the purpose of completion of this form the term "hired" applies to those employed, recruited or referred for a fee.)

All employees must print or type their complete name, address, date of birth, and Social Security Number. The block which correctly indicates the employee's immigration status must be checked. If the second block is checked, the employee's Alien Registration Number must be provided. If the third block is checked, the employee's Alien Registration Number *or* Admission Number must be provided, as well as the date of expiration of that status, if it expires.

All employees whose present names differ from birth names, because of marriage or other reasons, must print or type their birth names in the appropriate space of Section 1. Also, employees whose names change after employment verification should report these changes to their employer.

All employees must sign and date the form.

Instructions for the preparer of the form, if not the employee.

If a person assists the employee with completing this form, the preparer must certify the form by signing it and printing or typing his or her complete name and address.

Section 2. Instructions to Employer for completing this form

(For the purpose of completion of this form, the term "employer" applies to employers and those who recruit or refer for a fee.)

Employers must complete this section by examining evidence of identity and employment eligibility, and:
- checking the appropriate box in List A *or* boxes in both Lists B and C;
- recording the document identification number and expiration date (if any);
- recording the type of form if not specifically identified in the list;
- signing the certification section.

NOTE: Employers are responsible for reverifying employment eligibility of employees whose employment eligibility documents carry an expiration date.

Copies of documentation presented by an individual for the purpose of establishing identity and employment eligibility may be copied and retained for the purpose of complying with the requirements of this form and no other purpose. Any copies of documentation made for this purpose should be maintained with this form.

Name changes of employees which occur after preparation of this form should be recorded on the form by lining through the old name, printing the new name and the reason (such as marriage), and dating and initialing the changes. Employers should not attempt to delete or erase the old name in any fashion.

RETENTION OF RECORDS.

The completed form must be retained by the employer for:
- three years after the date of hiring; or
- one year after the date the employment is terminated, whichever is later.

> Employers may photocopy or reprint this form as necessary.

U.S. Department of Justice
Immigration and Naturalization Service

OMB #1115-0136
Form I-9 (05 07 87)

EMPLOYMENT CONTRACT

THIS CONTRACT is made between _____ ("Employee"), who is a resident of _____ and _____ ("Company") as follows:

1. EMPLOYMENT Company hereby employs Employee, who accepts employment with Company in the position of _____ on a strictly "at will" basis, all per the terms of this Contract. Employee agrees to devote all work time and attention to fulfill the duties listed in the job description, diligently and to the best of Employee's ability. Employee agrees to make every effort to promote the Company's interest, subject to the direction and control of the Company, and shall adhere to all lawful Company rules and regulations and directions of superiors.

2. COMPENSATION Employee's compensation during the term of employment shall be earned by Employee as follows:

    a. Base salary of _____ dollars ($_____) per _____.
    b. Other compensation (including contingency compensation): _____

    _____

    c. Employee shall be entitled to receive the same fringe benefits as other employees of similar stature and seniority.
    d. Compensation to be paid in accord with Company's normal payroll procedures. Company and Employee may mutually agree to changes in compensation.

3. TRADE SECRETS Employee agrees there are certain trade, business, and financial secrets in connection with the business of Company and its affiliates. Employee covenants to not, at any time, directly or indirectly, during the term of this Agreement or afterwards, divulge to any party of any character, unless directed by the Board of Directors, any of the information hereafter or previously acquired by Employee about Company or its affiliates, including, but not limited to, trade secrets, customer lists, financial statements, documents, correspondence, quotes, processes, patents, formulas, intellectual property, research, costs, expenses, or other trade secrets or confidential information of any kind, or any other data which could be used by third parties to the disadvantage of Company. This Paragraph shall survive the term and termination of the Contract.

4. TERM and TERMINATION Unless terminated sooner as provided below, employment shall commence on _____ and continue until terminated by either party, or until the death or disability of Employee or dissolution of Company. Employee must give Company at least two (2) weeks notice of voluntary termination.

5. RESTRICTIVE COVENANT During this Contract's term and every extension and renewal hereof and for a period of one (1) year after termination, Employee hereby covenants and agrees to refrain from all the following:

    a. Soliciting Company's customers, employees, staff, vendors, subcontractors, or prospects with respect to any services or products of the nature of those being sold by Company or affiliates of Company;
    b. Engaging in or promoting, directly or indirectly, as a principal, employee, contractor, partner, associate, manager, agent, or otherwise, or by means of any entity, any business in the same or a similar business as Company or its affiliates within the geographic area defined as

    _____

Employment Contract (*continued*)

If Employee breaches this Covenant, Company shall have the right, in addition to all other rights available hereunder and by law, to enjoin Employee from continuing such breach. Employee acknowledges having had the opportunity to fully discuss and negotiate this Restrictive Covenant and affirms understanding and acceptance. If any part of this Restrictive Covenant is declared invalid, then Employee agrees to be bound by a Restrictive Covenant as near to the original as lawfully possible. This Paragraph shall survive the term and termination of this Contract. Employee shall further be liable for all costs of enforcement including but not limited to attorney fees.

6. EXPENSES Employee shall be reimbursed for all vouchered, preauthorized expenses expended by Employee in the course of the performance of job duties.

7. TIME OFF Employee shall be entitled to _____ of paid time off after _____ of continuous employment. Additionally, Employee shall be entitled to paid holidays as designated by Company. Unless agreed by Company, Employee may not work and receive additional compensation in lieu of time off or holiday time in cash. Termination of employment at any time for any reason voids Employee's entitlements to vacation and holiday pay.

8. WAIVER No waiver of a right by Company constitutes a waiver of any other right of Company, and temporary waiver or forebearance by Company shall not constitute a permanent waiver or any additional temporary waiver.

9. ASSIGNMENT This Agreement is personal as to Employee and may not be assigned by Employee, but is and shall be binding on all heirs, executors, and successors-in-interest of Employee. Company may assign this Agreement, and upon assignment, this Agreement shall inure to the benefit of and be binding on all successors-in-interest of every kind and character of Company.

10. MODIFICATION This Contract contains the entire agreement between the parties and may not be modified except in writing signed by both parties.

11. SEVERABILITY If any portion hereof is declared invalid by rule of court or operation of law, the same shall not invalidate the entire Contract which shall continue in effect as if the invalid portion had never been part hereof.

12. GOVERNING LAW This Contract shall be governed under the laws of _____.

Dated _____, 19____

Employee _____

_____ (Seal)

Company _____

by _____
Authorized Signatory

EMPLOYEE'S COVENANTS

_____ ("Employee"), a resident of _____ and employed by or about to be employed by _____ ("Company"), hereby makes these Covenants to Company in consideration for

___ hiring by Company of Employee in the position of _____

OR

___ continued employment by Company of Employee, with the following change in the nature of employment agreed to by Company for the benefit of Employee:

_____

Covenant No. 1: TRADE SECRETS

Employee agrees there are certain trade, business, and financial secrets in connection with the business of Company and its affiliates. Employee covenants to not, at any time, directly or indirectly, during the term of this Agreement or afterwards, divulge to any party of any character, unless directed by the Board of Directors, any of the information hereafter or previously acquired by Employee about Company or its affiliates, including, but not limited to, trade secrets, customer lists, financial statements, documents, correspondence, quotes, processes, patents, formulas, intellectual property, research, costs, expenses, or other trade secrets or confidential information of any kind, or any other data that could be used by third parties to the disadvantage of Company. This Paragraph shall survive the term of employment.

Covenant No. 2: RESTRICTIVE COVENANT

During the term of employment and every extension and renewal and for a period of one (1) year after termination, Employee hereby covenants and agrees to refrain from all the following:

a. Soliciting Company's customers, employees, staff, vendors, subcontractors, or prospects with respect to any services or products of the nature of those being sold by Company or affiliates of Company;

b. Engaging in or promoting, directly or indirectly, as a principal, employee, contractor, partner, associate, manager, agent, or otherwise, or by means of any entity, any business in the same or a similar business as Company or its affiliates within the geographic area defined as

_____

Covenant No. 3: COMPANY RIGHTS on BREACH

If Employee breaches this covenant, Company shall have the right, in addition to all other rights available hereunder and by law, to enjoin Employee from continuing such breach. Employee acknowledges having had the opportunity to fully discuss and negotiate this Restrictive Covenant and affirms understanding and acceptance. If any part of this Restrictive Covenant is declared invalid, then Employee agrees to be bound by a Restrictive Covenant as near to the original as lawfully possible. This Paragraph shall survive the term and termination of employment. Employee shall further be liable for all costs of enforcement, including but not limited to attorney fees.

Covenant No. 4: ADDITIONAL GOVERNING TERMS

No waiver of a right by Company constitutes a waiver of any other right of Company, and temporary waiver or forebearance by Company shall not constitute a permanent waiver or any additional temporary waiver. These Covenants may not be modified except in writing signed by Employee and Company. If any portion hereof is declared invalid by rule of court or operation of law, the same shall not invalidate the entire Instrument which shall continue in effect as if the invalid portion had never been part hereof. These Covenants shall be governed under the laws of

_____.

Dated _____, 19____

Employee _____ (Seal)

Accepted by Company _____
Authorized Signatory

EMPLOYEE CONFIDENTIALITY CERTIFICATION

As an Employee of _____ ("Company") I hereby certify that I understand I am likely to become privy to and/or gain access to certain confidential trade secrets and information, including, but not limited to, client lists, financial statements, tax returns, bid methods, bid prices, cost allocations, proposal techniques, business development procedures, contractual arrangements, organizational methods, operational processes, minutes, bylaws, accounting methods, prices, charges, allocation procedures, vendor lists, contact lists, prospect lists, job listings, bid solicitations, work solicitations, proprietary formulas, personnel data, salary structures, employment policies, and the like, which I covenant, agree, and promise to keep confidential and not to disclose to any person nor to use in any manner outside of my employment with the Company and for the sole benefit of the Company, unless authorized to do so in advance in writing by an Officer of the Company for so long as I am employed and for not less than five (5) years after my employment with the Company terminates for any reason.

Date _____

_____ (Seal)
Employee

RECEIPT FOR SAMPLES AND DOCUMENTS

I, _____, employed in the position of _____, confirm that I have received from my employer the following samples:

No. Rec'd.	Serial No.	Description	Value Each	Total Value

I further confirm that I have received the following documents:

_____

_____

_____

_____

_____

_____

I accept responsibility for safeguarding all these materials, for preventing the disclosure of confidential material and for returning these (except those authorized for and delivered to customers) to my employer upon demand and, in any event, upon termination of employment.

Date _____   _____
                                Employee

EMPLOYEE WEEKLY TIME SHEET

For the week ending date of _____ (Day _____)

Employee Name _____ Employee ID No. _____

Department _____ Social Security No. _____

Day	:	Time In	:	Time Out	:	Hours Regular	:	Hours Overtime	:	Comments
	:		:		:		:		:	
	:		:		:		:		:	
	:		:		:		:		:	
	:		:		:		:		:	
	:		:		:		:		:	
	:		:		:		:		:	
	:		:		:		:		:	

_____ Total Hours

I certify this time sheet to be accurate, honest, and complete.

Employee signature _____   Approval _____

1. Every employee is required to take the lunch period allowed, unless approval to work through lunch has been granted by the employee's supervisor.
2. All overtime (nonemergency) must be approved *prior* to working.
3. Include time for *holiday, sick, vacation,* or other leave under "Comments."
4. Falsification of a time sheet is a cause for discharge from employment.

EXPENSE VOUCHER

Employee _____ Position Title _____

Social Security No. _____ Department _____

I hereby certify the following expenses were incurred and paid by me on behalf of my employer, and I request reimbursement in accord with the expense reimbursement policy of my employer.

Exp. No. *	Date	Paid to	Purpose/Reason	Charge to	Amount
1					
2					
3					
4					
5					
6					
7					
8					
9					
10					
11					
12					

Total Expense

Less Advance   −

Net Reimbursement Due

*Please attach receipts, in order, numbered to key to Expense No.

Voucher Date _____, 19____   _____
                                            Employee Signature

Approval _____

Approval Date _____, 19____

Module V

Leases

INTRODUCTION

Leasing has come into its own as a financing mechanism in the second half of the 20th century. Changes in tax laws, major shifts in the marketplace cost of capital, and modernization of accounting conventions make leasing an important option in asset financing. Because of the hoary, but still vibrant legal distinctions between real property and personalty, the forms for leases in the two spheres vary substantially, even though the purposes are more or less identical.

These purposes are

1. Protection of the owner's property value while allowing beneficial use to the lessee
2. Clear division of responsibilities for the maintenance and upkeep of the leased assets
3. Proper documentation for tax and accounting

It is worth mentioning that part of the distinction between realty and personalty stems from the fact that realty law is largely local in character, while the pervasive Uniform Commercial Code has a major impact on transactions involving personalty.

MODULE FORMS

The eight forms in this Module are

Equipment Lease
Lease (for real estate)
Guaranty of Realty Lease
Memorandum of Lease
Assignment of Equipment Lease by Lessor
Assignment of Equipment Lease by Lessee
Assignment of Realty Lease by Lessor
Assignment of Realty Lease by Lessee

Equipment Lease

Definition

An equipment lease is a rental agreement for personalty.

Comments

a. Although called an "equipment lease," the form can be used for any type of personalty, including vehicles.
b. This form is a third-party lease; that is, the supplier of the equipment is not the lessor. The supplier, however, may be a manufacturer and the lessor may be a distributor. Some manufacturers find it advantageous (for tax, accounting, and/or liability reasons) to use a captive leasing subsidiary.
c. Financing statements should be recorded to perfect security in the leased equipment so that the lessor's ownership is protected. (See Module VI for financing statement.)

Distribution

Original to lessor
Copy to lessee
Copy to supplier

Lease (for real estate)

Definition

The real estate lease is a rental agreement for real property.

Comments

a. Few transactions have as great an effect on business operations as entering into a realty lease. Such leases should always be reviewed in advance by counsel for both sides.

b. This lease form is a fairly evenhanded document, which would not be out of place in most cities. However, local laws and customs vary widely, and this form is designed to raise the principal commercial real estate issues between the parties.

Distribution

Original signature to lessor

Original signature to lessee

Copy to lease broker

Copy to counsel for each party

Guaranty of Realty Lease

Definition

The guaranty of realty lease is a personal commitment to make good on the lessee's obligation in the event of lessee default.

Comments

a. Guarantees are usually required on commercial property from owners of closely held businesses.

b. The guaranty is a companion document to the lease itself and should be executed at the same time as the lease.

c. Local laws create major variations in guaranty terms.

Distribution

Same as for lease being guaranteed

Memorandum of Lease

Definition

The memorandum of lease is an abstract of the lease terms, used to put others on notice of the existence of lessee rights in the property under lease.

Comments

a. The main purpose of a memorandum is to prevent the property from being transferred to someone else who is not bound by the lease.

b. Language in the lease itself making it binding on successors and the like will provide protection to those who acquire through the lessor, but will not necessarily protect against foreclosing lienholders or some other kinds of successors, depending upon local law.

Distribution

Original to land records

Copy to lessor

Copy to lessee

Assignment of Equipment Lease by Lessor

Definition

The lessor's assignment of equipment lease is an agreement transferring lessor's rights in the lease to a third-party buyer of the equipment.

Comments

a. Most assignments by lessor do not require lessee consent.

b. However, notice should be given to lessee by the former lessor so that lessee will make payments to the new lessor.

c. The form must be used when the equipment is sold, in order to convey all of lessor's right, title, and interest to the buyer.

d. Rents should be allocated as of the date of transfer between the old and new lessors.

Distribution

Original signature to new lessor

Original signature to former lessor

Copy to lessee

Assignment of Equipment Lease by Lessee

Definition

The lessee's assignment of equipment lease is an agreement transferring lessee's rights in the lease to a third party.

Comments

a. In contrast to a lessor's assignment, an assignment by a lessee usually requires the lessor's approval to be valid.

b. If consent is not required, the consent block should be eliminated to avoid a false impression; further the lessor should be given notice by the former lessee.

Distribution

Original signature to each party

Assignment of Realty Lease by Lessor

Definition

The lessor's assignment of realty lease is an agreement transferring lessor's rights in the realty lease to a third-party buyer of the real estate.

Comments

a. Lessor assignments almost never require lessee agreement.

b. However, notice should be given to lessee by the former lessor so that lessee will make payments to the new lessor.

c. Security deposits should be transferred and rents prorated between the old and new lessors.

Distribution

An original to each lessor

Copy to lessee

Assignment of Realty Lease by Lessee

Definition

The lessee's assignment of realty lease is an agreement transferring lessee's rights in the realty lease to a third party.

Comments

a. Comments regarding the assignment of equipment lease by lessee are applicable to the assignment of realty lease by lessee, as well.

b. Because approval of the landlord is often needed, most business sales (which naturally involve transfer of the lease) are contingent on lessor approval.

Distribution

Original signature to each party

EQUIPMENT LEASE

LEASE
NUMBER _____

NAME AND ADDRESS OF LESSEE	SUPPLIER OF EQUIPMENT (Complete Address)
_____	_____
_____	_____
_____	_____
_____	_____

NAME PERSON TO CONTACT: _____ SALESMAN: _____

QUANTITY	ITEM	MODEL NO.	SERIES NO.	PRICE
E Q U I P M E N T L E A S E D				$
			TOTAL LIST	_____
			FEDERAL EXCISE TAX (If any)	_____
			TRANSPORTATION (If any)	_____
			OTHER	_____
			SALES TAX	_____
	THIS LEASE _____ DOES _____ DOES NOT INCLUDE MAINTENANCE SERVICES.		LESS TRADE-IN (If any)	_____

LOCATION OF EQUIPMENT: STREET ADDRESS _____

CITY _____ STATE _____	TOTAL COST	$

TERMS OF PAYMENT	PRE-PAID RENTAL	TERMS OF PAYMENT	
MONTHLY RENTAL $_____ TAX _____ TOTAL MONTHLY PAYMENTS $_____	PAYMENTS WILL BE MADE: **MONTHLY** MONTHS IN ADVANCE	INITIAL TERMS OF LEASE (NO. OF MONTHS)	NO. OF RENT PAYMENTS

Terms and Conditions of Lease

1.   LEASE.   Lessee hereby leases from lessor, and lessor leases to lessee, the personal property described above and in any schedule made a part hereof by the parties hereto (herein called "equipment").

2.   SELECTION OF EQUIPMENT.   Lessee has requested equipment of the type and quantity specified above and has selected the supplier named above. Lessor agrees to order such equipment from said supplier, but shall not be liable for specific performance of this lease or for damages if for any reason the supplier delays or fails to fill the order. Lessee shall accept such equipment of delivered in good repair, and hereby authorizes lessor to add to this lease the serial number of each item of equipment so delivered. Any delay in such delivery shall not affect the validity of this lease.

3.   ERRORS IN ESTIMATED COST.   As used herein, "actual cost" means the cost to lessor of purchasing and delivering the equipment to lessee, including taxes, transportation charges and other charges. The amount of each rent payment, the pre-paid rent, and the renewal rental initially set forth above are based on the total cost initially set forth above, which is an estimate, and shall each of the adjusted proportionally if the actual cost of the equipment differs from said estimate. Lessee hereby authorizes lessor to correct the figures set forth above when the actual cost is known, and to add to the amount of each rent payment any sales tax that may be imposed on or measured by the rent payments.

4.   WARRANTIES.   LESSOR WILL REQUEST THE SUPPLIER TO AUTHORIZE LESSEE TO ENFORCE IN ITS OWN NAME ALL WARRANTIES, AGREEMENTS OR REPRESENTATIONS, IF ANY, WHICH MAY BE MADE BY THE SUPPLIER TO LESSEE OR LESSOR, BUT LESSOR ITSELF MAKES NO EXPRESS OR IMPLIED WARRANTIES AS TO ANY MATTER WHATSOEVER, INCLUDING, WITHOUT LIMITATION, THE CONDITION OF EQUIPMENT, ITS MERCHANTABILITY OR ITS FITNESS FOR ANY PARTICULAR PURPOSE. NO DEFECT OR UNFITNESS OF THE EQUIPMENT SHALL RELIEVE LESSEE OF THE OBLIGATION TO PAY RENT OR OF ANY OTHER OBLIGATION UNDER THIS LEASE.

5.   INITIAL TERM.   The initial term of this lease commences upon the execution hereof by lessor and ends upon the expiration of the number of months specified above.

SEE REVERSE SIDE FOR ADDITIONAL TERMS AND CONDITIONS WHICH ARE PART OF THIS LEASE

The undersigned agree to all terms and conditions set forth above and on reverse side hereof, and in witness thereof hereby execute this lease.

DATE _____

DATE _____

LESSOR:

NAME OF LESSEE _____ (SEAL)
(FULL LEGAL NAME)

BY _____

BY _____
LESSEE'S SIGNATURE IN INK   TITLE

ATTEST OR WITNESS _____

PERSONAL GUARANTOR: _____

WITNESS: _____

6. RENT. Lessee agrees to pay during the initial term of this lease to rent equal to the amount of each rental payment as specified above multiplied by the number of such payments as specified above. The prepayment of rent as specified above is due and payable upon signing of this lease. The first regular rental payment is due and payable thirty (30) days from date of the signing of the lease. All rent shall be paid to lessor at its address set forth above, or as otherwise directed by lessor or his assignees in writing.

7. PRE PAID RENT. Shall not apply to cure any default of lessee in the monthly rental payments.

8. RENEWAL. After its initial term, this lease may be renewed upon agreement of the parties.

9. LOCATION. The equipment shall be delivered and thereafter kept at the location specified above or, if none is specified, at lessee's address as set forth above, and shall not be removed therefrom without lessor's prior written consent. Lessor shall have the right to inspect the equipment without notice during lessee's business hours.

10. NOTICE OF DEFECTS. Unless lessee gives lessor written notice of each defect or other proper objection to an item of equipment within five (5) business days after receipt thereof, it shall be conclusively presumed, as between lessee and lessor, that the item was delivered in good repair and that lessee accepts it as an item of equipment described in this lease.

11. USE. Lessee shall use the equipment in a careful manner and shall comply with all laws relating to its possession, use or maintenance. Lessee is responsible for purchase of all supplies and shall use only supplies approved by lessor in order to assure the safe operation of the equipment.

12. LABELS. If lessor supplies lessee with labels stating that the equipment is owned by lessor, lessee shall affix and keep the same upon a prominent place on each item of equipment.

13. REPAIRS. Lessee, at its expense, shall keep the equipment in good repair and furnish all parts, mechanisms and devices required therefor, unless maintenance services are included in the price and noted as such herein. If included, lessee shall be responsible only for cleaning.

14. ALTERATIONS. Lessee shall not make any alterations, additions or improvements to the equipment without lessor's prior written consent. All conditions and improvements made to the equipment shall belong to lessor.

15. SURRENDER. Upon the expiration or earlier termination of this lease, lessee, at its expense, shall return the equipment in good repair, ordinary wear and tear resulting from proper use thereof alone excepted, by delivering it, packed and ready for shipment, to such place or carrier as lessor may specify.

16. LOSS AND DAMAGE. Lessee shall bear the entire risk of loss, theft, damage or destruction of the equipment from any cause whatsoever; and no loss, theft, damage or destruction of the equipment shall relieve lessee of the obligation to pay rent or of any other obligation under this lease:

In the event of damage to any item of equipment, lessee shall immediately notify lessor. If lessor determines that any item of equipment is lost, stolen, destroyed or damaged beyond repair, lessee at the option of lessor shall:

(a) replace the same with the like equipment in good repair, or

(b) pay lessor in cash all of the following: (i) all amounts then owed by lessee to lessor under this lease, (ii) an amount equal to ten percent (10%) of the actual cost of said item, and (iii) the unpaid balance of the total rent for the initial term of this lease attributable to said item. Upon lessor's receipt of such payment, lessee shall be entitled to whatever interest lessor may have in said item, in its then condition and location, without warranty express or implied. The parties hereto agree that the sum of the amounts numbered (ii) and (iii) will equal the fair value of said item on the date of such loss, theft, damage or destruction.

17. INSURANCE; LIENS; TAXES. Lessee shall provide and maintain insurance against loss, theft, damage or destruction of the equipment in an amount not less than the total rent payable hereunder, with loss payable to lessor. Each policy shall expressly provide that said insurance as to lessor and its assigns shall not be invalidated by any act, omission or neglect of lessee. Lessor may apply the proceeds of said insurance to replace or repair the equipment and/or to satisfy lessee's obligations hereunder. At lessor's request, lessee shall furnish proof of said insurance.

Lessee shall keep the equipment free and clear of all levies, liens and encumbrances. Lessee shall pay all charges and taxes (local, state and federal) which may now or hereafter be imposed upon the ownership, leasing, rental, sale, purchase, possession or use of the equipment, excluding however, all taxes on or measured by lessor's income.

If lessee fails to procure or maintain said insurance or to pay said charges and taxes, lessor shall have the right, but shall not be obligated, to effect such insurance, or pay said charges and taxes. In that event, lessee shall repay to lessor the cost thereof with the next payment of rent.

18. INDEMNITY. Lessee shall indemnify lessor against, and hold lessor harmless from, any and all claims, actions, proceedings, expenses, damages and liabilities, including attorneys' fees, arising in connection with the equipment, including, without limitation, its manufacture, selection, purchase, delivery, possession, use, operation or return and the recovery of claims under insurance policies thereon.

19. ASSIGNMENT. Without lessor's prior written consent, lessee shall not (a) assign, transfer, pledge, hypothecate or otherwise dispose of this lease or any interest therein, or (b) sublet or lend the equipment or permit it to be used by anyone other than lessee or lessee's employees.

Lessor may assign this lease and/or mortgagee the equipment, in whole or in part, without notice to lessee; and its assignee or mortgage may reassign this lease and/or such mortgage, without notice to lessee. Each such assignee and/or mortgagee shall have all of the rights but none of the obligations of lessor under this lease. Lessee shall recognize each such assignment and/or mortgage and shall not assert against the assignee and/or mortgagee any defense, counterclaim, or set-off that lessee may have against lessor. Subject to the foregoing, this lease insures to the benefit of and is binding upon the heirs, legatees, personal representatives, survivors and assigns of the parties hereto.

20. LATE CHARGES. Should lessee fail to pay any part of the rent herein reserved within five days (5) after due date thereof, lessee shall pay unto lessor a late charge equal to five (5) percent of the payment due with a minimum amount of two dollars ($2.00) for each month the delinquency continues. It is expressly understood that the charge herein is not an interest charge, but a charge to cover the additional expenses involved in such delinquency.

21. DEFAULT. If lessee fails to pay any rent or other amount herein provided within five (5) days after the same is due and payable, or if lessee fails to perform any other provision hereof within five (5) days after lessor shall have demanded in writing performance thereof, or if any proceeding in bankruptcy, receivership or insolvency shall be commenced by or against lessee or its property, or if lessee makes any assignment for the benefit of its creditors, lessor shall have the right but shall not be obligated, to exercise any one or more of the following remedies: (a) to sue for and recover all rents and other amounts then due or thereafter accruing under this lease; (b) to take possession of any or all of the equipment, wherever it may be located, without demand or notice, without any court order or other process of law, and without incurring any liability to lessee for any damages occasioned by such taking of possession; (c) to sell any or all of the equipment at public or private sale for cash or on credit and to recover from lessee all costs of taking possession, storing, repairing and selling the equipment, an amount equal to ten percent (10%) of the actual cost to lessor of the equipment sold, and the unpaid balance of the total rent for the initial term of this lease attributable to the equipment sold, less the net proceeds of such sale; (d) to terminate this lease as to any or all items of equipment; (e) in the event lessor elects to terminate this lease as to any or all items of equipment, to recover from lessee as to each item subject to said termination the worth at the time of such termination, of the excess, if any, of the amount of rent reserved herein for said item for the balance of the term hereof over the then reasonable rental value of said item for the same period of time; (f) to pursue any other remedy now or hereafter existing at law or in equity.

Notwithstanding any such action that lessor may take, including taking possession of any or all of the equipment, lessee shall remain liable for the full performance of all its obligations hereunder, provided, however, that if lessor in writing terminates this lease, as to any item of equipment, lessee shall not be liable for rent in respect of such item accruing after the date of such termination.

In addition to the foregoing, lessee shall pay lessor all costs and expenses, including reasonable attorneys' fees incurred by lessor in exercising any of its rights or remedies hereunder.

22. NOTICES. Any written notice or demand under this agreement may be given to a party by mailing it to the party at its address set forth above, or at such address as the party may provide in writing from time to time. Notice or demand so mailed shall be effective when deposited in the United States mail, duly addressed and with postage prepaid.

23. MULTIPLE LESSEE. If more than one lessee is named in this lease, the liability of each shall be joint and several.

24. CHOICE OF LAW. This lease shall be governed by and construed in accordance with the law of the Commonwealth of Virginia.

25. OWNERSHIP. The equipment is, and shall at all times remain, the property of lessor; and lessee shall have no right, title or interest herein or thereto except as expressly set forth in this lease. Lessee shall promptly comply with Lessor requests for financial statements and further assurances of lessor's ownership and security interest on said equipment.

26. ENTIRE AGREEMENT: WAIVER. This instrument constitutes the entire agreement between lessor and lessee. No agent or employee of the supplier is authorized to bind lessor to this lease, to waive or alter any term or condition printed herein or add any provision hereto. Except as provided in paragraph 3 hereof, a provision may be added hereto or a provision hereof may be altered or varied only by a writing signed and made a part hereof by an authorized officer of lessor. Waiver by lessor of any provision hereof in one instance shall not constitute a waiver as to any other instance.

LEASE

THIS LEASE ("Lease") is made as of the _____ day of _____, 19____, by and between _____ ("Lessor") and _____ ("Lessee"), whereby Lessor does hereby demise and lease to Lessee, for the term and lease payments hereinafter set forth, the premises consisting of _____ square feet, designated as _____ ("Premises"), at _____ ("Building"), on the following terms and conditions:

1. *Term* The initial term of this Lease ("Initial Term") shall be for _____ (___) years commencing on _____, 19____, and ending on _____, 19____. Lessee shall have the option, exercisable by written notice to Lessor at least ninety (90) days prior to the end of the Initial Term, to extend the terms of this Lease for an additional _____ (___) years period ("Renewal Term").

2. *Rent* The rent to be paid by Lessee shall be as follows:

   a. *Initial Term* During the Initial Term, Lessee shall pay as base rent _____ dollars ($_____) per month on or before the first day of each and every month, commencing _____, 19____, with appropriate proration made for any period less than one month, subject to the adjustment described in Paragraph 3 below.

   b. *Renewal Term* If Lessee exercises the renewal option, as in Paragraph 1 above, the Lessee shall pay an annual rent in monthly installments, to be determined by negotiation between Lessor and Lessee, within six (6) months prior to the termination date of the initial term.

   c. *Location* All payments of rent shall be made in good funds payable to and delivered to Lessor at Lessor's offices having the address of _____ or to such other person and place as may be reasonably designated by notice in writing from Lessor to Lessee from time to time.

   d. *Allocation of Rent* No payment by Lessee or receipt by Lessor of a lesser amount than the monthly installments of rent herein stipulated shall be deemed to be other than on account of the earliest stipulated rent, nor shall any endorsement or statements on any check or any letter accompanying any check or payment as rent be deemed an accord and satisfaction, and Lessor may accept such check for payment without prejudice to Lessor's right to recover the balance of such rent or pursue any other remedy provided in this Lease.

3. *Rent Escalation* Each year that this Lease remains in effect after the first full lease year, Lessee shall pay to Lessor an increased monthly base rent to be determined as follows:

   The monthly base rent shall be increased by a ratio, the numerator of which shall be the value of the Consumer Price Index as published by the U.S. Bureau of Labor Statistics for the last month of the prior lease year, and the denominator of which shall be the value of the same index for the month immediately preceding the prior lease year.

4. *Delinquent Payments* If Lessee shall fail to pay any installment of rent within five (5) days of the due date, Lessee shall pay to Lessor as additional rent a late charge of five percent (5%) of each delinquent rent installment. This provision for payment by Lessee of a late fee is not a waiver by Lessor of Lessee's obligation to pay rent on the first day of each and every month.

5. *Condition of Premises* Lessee covenants and agrees that (i) Lessee will take good care of the Premises and the fixtures and equipment therein; (ii) Lessee will not suffer or commit any waste of or about the Premises; and (iii) upon expiration of the Initial Term or Renewal Term, or upon surrender or abandonment of the Premises, Lessee will leave the premises in as good a condition as when first occupied by Lessee, ordinary wear and tear and casualty loss expected.

6. *Utilities* Lessee shall pay the costs of all utilities serving the Premises and shall be responsible for payment and maintenance of gas and electric equipment used in connection with the Premises.

7. *Use of Premises* Lessee shall use the Premises as and for _____ only, and shall not use or permit the Premises to be used for any other purpose without the prior written consent of Lessor.

8. *Subletting and Assignment* Lessee will not sublet the Premises or any part thereof or transfer possession or occupancy thereof to any person, firm, or corporation, or transfer or assign this Lease without the prior written consent of Lessor, not to be unreasonably withheld, nor shall any sublet or assignment hereof be affected by operation of law or otherwise other than with the prior written consent of Lessor.

9. *Casualty Insurance* Lessee will not do or permit anything to be done in the Premises, or bring or keep anything therein, which shall in any way increase the rate of fire or other insurance in the Building, or on the property kept therein, or obstruct or interfere with the rights of other tenants, or conflict with the fire laws or regulations, or with any insurance policy upon the Building or any part thereof, or with any statutes, rules, or regulations enacted or established by the appropriate governmental authority regarding the Building.

10. *Services* Lessor shall use best efforts to furnish all services to the Premises to which Lessee is entitled, including, without limitation, plumbing, air conditioning, heat, electricity, and elevator. Lessor shall make all necessary structural and capital repairs to the Premises and Building as necessary. Lessor shall not be liable to Lessee for personal injury or damage or loss of property arising from this Lease or Lessee's occupancy hereunder, except for Lessor's negligence or willful misconduct.

11. *Lessee's Property* Lessor and Lessee acknowledge and confirm that Lessee may install and place in and about the Premises furniture, equipment, supplies, and fixtures that are and shall remain the property of Lessee. Lessee shall have the right during the term of this Lease and any subsequent renewals thereof, and upon the termination of this Lease, to remove said furniture, equipment, supplies, and fixtures; provided, however, that Lessee shall be responsible for and shall bear the cost and expense solely for such removal, and shall reimburse Lessor for any and all costs and damages incurred by Lessor regarding the condition of the Premises as a result of said removal.

12. *Alterations and Additions* Lessor will provide, at its own expense, the baseboard, partitions doors, painting and electrical outlets for the Premises as per Lessee's drawings. Lessor will also provide for the relocation of ceiling light fixtures and air ducts for the Premises. Lessee may make, in its discretion and at its expense, additional improvements or alterations to the Premises with the prior consent of the Lessor which shall not be unreasonably withheld.

13. *Destruction* The payments of rent under this Lease shall cease if the Premises are rendered untenantable by the absence for thirty (30) consecutive days or more of the basic services described in Paragraph 10 above, or by fire or other casualty loss, and Lessee may terminate this Lease upon proper written notice thereof to Lessor.

14. *Access* Lessee agrees that it will allow Lessor, its agents or employees, to enter the Premises at all reasonable times to examine, inspect, or to protect the same, or prevent damage or injury to the Premises or to make such repairs to the Premises as are necessary and reasonable; or to exhibit the Premises to prospective tenants during the last ninety (90) days of either the Initial Term or the Renewal Term.

15. *Defaults* It is agreed that if Lessee shall fail to pay the rent, or any installments thereof as aforesaid, at the time the same shall become due and payable although no demand shall have been made for the same, and such default continues for a period of fifteen (15) days after written notice of such failure from Lessor, or if Lessee shall violate or fail or neglect to keep and perform any of the covenants, conditions, and agreements herein contained on the part of the Lessee to be kept and performed, or if the Premises shall become vacant or deserted, and such default continues to a period of fifteen (15) days after written notice of such default from Lessor, then, at the option of Lessor, Lessee's right of possession shall thereupon cease and terminate, and Lessor shall be entitled to the possession of the Premises and to re-enter the same without demand of rent or demand of possession of the Premises by process of law, any notice to quit or of intention to re-enter the same, being hereby expressly waived by Lessee. In the event of such re-entry by process of law or otherwise, Lessee nevertheless agrees to remain answerable for any and all damages, including attorney's fees, deficiency or loss of rent that Lessor may sustain by such re-entry; and in such case, Lessor reserves full power, which is hereby acceded to by Lessee, to relet the Premises for the benefit of Lessee in liquidation and discharge, in whole or in part, as the case may be, of the liability of Lessee under the terms and provisions of this Lease. No provisions of this Lease shall be deemed to have been waived unless such waiver shall be in writing signed by the party seeking to enforce said provision.

16. *Quiet Enjoyment* Lessor covenants that if Lessee pays the rent and all other charges provided for herein, performs all of its obligations provided for hereunder and observes all of the other provisions hereof,

Lease (*continued*)

Lessee shall at all times during the term hereof peaceably and quietly have, hold, and enjoy the Premises, without any interruption or disturbance from Lessor, or anyone claiming through or under Lessor, subject to the terms hereof.

17. *Successors* All rights, remedies, and liabilities herein given to or imposed upon either of the parties hereto, shall extend to such party's respective successors and assigns, except as specifically prohibited herein.

18. *Attorney's Fees* In the event either party requires the services of an attorney in connection with enforcing the terms of this Lease or in the event suit is brought for the recovery of any rent due under this Lease or for the breach of any covenant or condition of this Lease, or for the restitution of the Premises to Lessor and/or eviction of Lessee during said term of after the expiration thereof, the prevailing party shall be entitled to a reasonable sum of attorney's fees and court costs.

19. *Notice* Unless agreed otherwise, any notice hereunder shall be in writing, sent by registered mail, to the addresses listed below.

Lessor: Lessee:

_____   _____

_____   _____

_____   _____

_____   _____

20. *Governing Law* The terms and provisions of this Lease shall be governed under the laws of the State of _____.

21. *Security Deposit* Lessee shall place with Lessor the sum of _____ dollars ($_____) and said deposit shall be considered a security for the payment and performance by Lessee of Lessee's obligations, covenants, conditions and agreements under this Lease, and shall be held by Lessor. Said security deposit represents _____ (__) months rent, and should Lessee make all rent payments as due and perform all Lease obligations required of Lessee throughout the term of the Lease and all extensions, modifications and renewals thereof, then at the end of the final term Lessor shall return said security deposit to Lessee. Lessor shall have the right, in the event of any default by Lessee hereunder, but shall not be obligated, to apply all or any portion of the deposit to cure such default, in which event Lessee shall be obligated to promptly deposit with Lessor the amount necessary to restore the deposit to its full amount.

22. *Insurance and Liability.* Lessor shall have no liability or responsibility whatsoever with respect to the conduct and operation of the business to be conducted in the demised premises. Lessor shall not be liable for any accident to or injury to any person or persons or property in or about the demised premises that is caused by the conduct or operation of said business or by virtue of equipment or property of Lessee in said premises. Lessee agrees to hold Lessor harmless against all such claims.

    a. Without limiting the above, Lessee agrees to purchase liability insurance with a recognized insurance company in the amount of $300,000 to $1,000,000 combined single limits, which insurance shall protect the Lessor, and to deposit evidence of same with said Lessor. The evidence of insurance deposited with Lessor shall name the Lessor as a co-insured party. Said insurance shall not be cancellable without notice to Lessor.

    b. Lessee shall indemnify and save harmless Lessor from and against any and all loss, cost (including attorney's fees), damages, expenses, liability (including statutory liability), and claims for damages as a result of injury or death of any person or damage to any property that arise from or in any manner grow out of any act or neglect on or about the leased premises by Lessee, Lessee's partners, agents, employees, customers, invitees, contractors, or subcontractors.

23. *Subordination to Mortgage* This Lease shall be subject to the lien of any mortgage or deed of trust now on the demised premises, and subject to the lien of any mortgage or deed of trust which may at any time hereafter be made a lien upon the premises. The Lessee shall execute and deliver such further instruments subordinating this Lease to the lien of any mortgagee or secured party or proposed mortgagee or proposed secured party. All costs and expense in connection with such transaction shall be borne and paid for by Lessor.

24. *Lessee's Waiver* Lessee hereby waives and releases any and all lien and claim or right to lien, or other security interest or right of any nature provided under any statute upon any apparatus, fixtures, or other

merchandise placed upon the premises by the Lessee or by any person for or on Lessee's behalf and which is or may become subject to the security interest of the Lessee or any of its partners, officers, directors, and/or stockholders, and AGREES THAT SUCH PROPERTY SHALL REMAIN FOR ALL PURPOSES SUBJECT TO THE LESSOR'S STATUTORY LIEN FOR RENT, which lien shall be superior to all other lien rights in favor of Lessee, its partners, officers, directors, and/or stockholders whether evidenced by filed financing statements and/or other security documents. Lessee agrees not to remove and repossess such apparatus, fixtures, or other merchandise from the leased premises without the prior written consent of the Lessor.

25. *Bankruptcy* If Lessee shall make an assignment for the benefit of creditors, or if Lessee shall file a voluntary petition in bankruptcy or receivership, or a bankruptcy petition be filed against Lessee and the same not be dismissed within thirty (30) days of the filing thereof, or if Lessee be adjudged bankrupt, then and in any of said events this Lease shall immediately cease and terminate at the option of the Lessor with the same force and effect as though the date of said event was the day herein fixed for expiration of the term of this Lease.

26. *Licenses* Lessee will obtain all necessary permits and licenses, and Lessee shall save Lessor harmless from any failure to obtain proper licenses and permits.

27. *Estoppels* The Lessee shall from time to time at the Lessor's request execute and deliver letters or certificates of estoppel addressed as the Lessor may direct, evidencing that this Lease is in effect and remains umodified, or if modified, the nature of the modifications, and the Lessor is not in breach or violation of any term or provision thereof, or, alternatively, the nature of such breach. The failure of Lessee to so execute and deliver shall constitute a material breach of this Lease.

28. *Surrender of Possession* If Lessee shall not immediately surrender possession of the premises at the expiration or other termination of this Lease, Lessee shall become a month-to-month Tenant, at twice the monthly rental as that in effect just prior to termination of this Lease, said rental to be paid in advance; Lessor may accept such rental from Lessee, and notwithstanding the same, Lessor shall continue to be entitled to retake possession of the premises without any prior notice to Lessee. If Lessee shall fail to surrender possession of the premises immediately upon expiration of the term hereof, Lessee hereby agrees that all of obligations of Lessee shall be equally applicable during such period of subsequent occupancy, whether or not a month-to-month tenancy shall have been created as aforesaid. Lessee shall be liable for any damages suffered by Lessor by reason of Lessee's failure to immediately surrender the premises.

29. *Recordation* Either party may at any time record either this Lease or a memorandum of this Lease. Any such recordation shall be at the sole cost and expense of the parties seeking the same.

30. *Entire Agreement* This Lease contains all the agreements and conditions made between the parties hereto and may not be modified orally or in any other manner than by agreement in writing signed by all parties or their respective successors in interest.

Witness _____   Lessor _____
Witness _____   Lessor _____

Witness _____   Lessee _____
Witness _____   Lessee _____

GUARANTY OF REALTY LEASE

IN CONSIDERATION OF, and as a material inducement and incentive to, _____ ("Land-lord"), executing and delivering simultaneously herewith, in reliance upon this Guaranty, a Lease dated _____, 19____, between Landlord and

_____ ("Tenant"), for leasing of the

Premises located at and known as

_____

_____

the undersigned do(es) hereby unconditionally and absolutely guarantee unto Landlord, it successors and assigns, the full, prompt, and complete payment by Tenant of the rent and additional rents provided in the Lease and the prompt, faithful, and complete performance and observance by Tenant of all of the terms, covenants, and conditions of the Lease on the Tenant's part to be performed and/or observed.

Guarantor hereby waives notice of any and all defaults on the part of the Tenant, waives acceptance and notice of acceptance of this Guaranty, and waives all demands for payment and/or performance. Guarantor agrees that no delay on the part of the Landlord in enforcing any of its rights and remedies or insisting there-upon, nor any extension of time nor any change or modifications in or to, or in connection with the Lease, shall in any way limit, affect, or impair the liability of Guarantor hereunder. Guarantor hereby expressly consents to and approves hereof with the same force and effect as though its written consent had been given to each such delay, extension, change, and modification.

This Guaranty is independent of and in addition to any security or other remedies that Landlord has or may have for the performance of any of the obligations on the part of Tenant. Guarantor agrees Landlord shall not be required to resort to any other security or other remedies before proceeding upon this Guaranty. Landlord may proceed hereunder against Guarantor at any time it sees fit, independently or concurrently with any other remedies it may have.

It is understood Guarantor's liability shall continue for and during the entire term of the Lease and all renewals and extensions, notwithstanding any assignment of the Lease or subletting of all or any portion of the demised Premises under the Lease. This Guaranty is not limited as to time, and at all time shall include the full indebtedness and all other liability and obligation of Tenant (and/or any assignee or subtenant of Tenant) to Landlord under the Lease.

If this Guaranty is executed by two or more parties, their liability is and shall be joint and several.

This Guaranty shall be binding upon the undersigned, its successors and assigns, and shall inure to the benefit of Landlord, its successors and assigns.

IN WITNESS WHEREOF, the undersigned has (have) duly executed this Guaranty under seal on _____, ____.

Guarantor: Guarantor:

_____ (Seal)   _____ (Seal)

State of _____

_____ of _____

The foregoing Guaranty was sworn to and acknowledged before me on _____, 19____, by _____ and _____.

_____
Notary Public

(Notary Seal)

My commission expires _____

MEMORANDUM OF LEASE

THIS IS A MEMORANDUM OF A CERTAIN LEASE, which Lease bears date of _____, 19____, and which Lease was then made by and between _____ ("Landlord") and _____ ("Tenant"), concerning the following described real estate ("Property"):

_____

_____

_____

Said Lease was made for good and valuable consideration, wherein the Landlord leases to Tenant the above-described Propety, together with all rights, improvements, and appurtenances thereto, and Tenant hires the same from Landlord for the term and for the rents and under the conditions contained in the said Lease, which Lease is hereby incorporated verbatim herein by reference, as if the entirety thereof were repeated herein.

The Lease term begins _____, 19____, and ends _____,____, unless terminated sooner in accord with the terms of the Lease. The Lease may be renewed up to _____ (____) times for additional terms of _____, at the option of _____, and if all renewals are in fact exercised and performed, the Lease will then finally terminate on _____, ____.

The addresses of the Landlord and Tenant are

Landlord: Tenant:

_____   _____

_____   _____

_____   _____

_____   _____

This Memorandum is NOT a complete summary of the Lease. Provisions herein shall not be used in interpreting the Lease provisions. In the event of a conflict between this Memorandum and the Lease, the Lease shall control.

This Memorandum of Lease may be recorded.

WITNESS the following signatures and seals:

Dated _____, 19____.

Landlord: Tenant:

_____ (Seal)   _____ (Seal)

Memorandum of Lease (*continued*)

State of _____

_____ of _____

The foregoing Memorandum of Lease was sworn to and acknowledged by

_____ ("Landlord") and by

_____ ("Tenant") on _____, 19____.

_____
Notary Public

(Notary Seal)

My commission expires _____

ASSIGNMENT OF EQUIPMENT LEASE BY LESSOR

_____, heretofore the Owner of the
Equipment described as
_____

Quantity	Item	Model No.	Series No.	Price

having sold, bargained, and conveyed all of the said Equipment to Purchaser,
_____, hereby assigns, effective _____, to Purchaser without
recourse all right, title, and interest in and to the Lease to which the Equipment is subject, dated
_____, and made to the Lessee, _____, and
which Purchaser agrees to honor according to all its terms and conditions.

The parties to this Agreement confirm that all responsibilities and duties incident to this Assignment are current and have been satisfactorily adjusted. Each party warrants full power and authority
to consummate this Assignment.

(A copy of said Lease is ___/is not____ attached.)

Date _____

Former Lessor: New Lessor:

_____   _____

State of _____

_____ of _____

Personally appeared before me _____
_____, who each and all swore to and acknowledged the foregoing.

_____
Notary Public

(Notary Seal)

My commission expires _____

ASSIGNMENT OF EQUIPMENT LEASE BY LESSEE

_____, heretofore Lessee of Equipment described as

Quantity	Item	Model No.	Series No.	Price

hereby assigns without recourse, effective _____, unto Assignee, _____, all right, title, and interest in and to said Equipment and to the Lease dated _____, made with the Lessor, _____, which Assignee agrees to honor according to all its terms and conditions.

The parties confirm that all responsibilities and duties incident to this Assignment are current and have been satisfactorily adjusted. Assignee accepts the Equipment in its physical condition "as is," and shall be responsible for all matters regarding physical condition to the extent required by and in accord with the said Lease.

(A copy of said Lease is___/is not____ attached.)

Date _____

Former Lessee: Accepted—New Lessee:

_____   _____

Approved—Lessor:

_____

State of _____

_____ of _____

Personally appeared before me _____

_____, who each and all swore to and acknowledged the foregoing.

_____
Notary Public

(Notary Seal)

My commission expires _____

ASSIGNMENT OF REALTY LEASE BY LESSOR

_____, heretofore Owner of Real Property at
_____ having
sold, bargained, and conveyed the said Real Property unto Purchaser,
_____, hereby assigns, effective _____, to Purchaser
without recourse all right, title, and interest in and to the Lease, dated _____, to which the
property is subject, made to the Lessee, _____, and which Purchaser
agrees to honor according to all its terms and conditions.

   The parties hereto confirm that all responsibilities and duties incident to this Assignment are
current and have been satisfactorily adjusted. Each party warrants full power and authority to
consummate this Assignment.

   (A copy of said Lease is___/is not___ attached.)

Date _____

                                        Former Owner/Lessor:

                                        _____

Accepted—New Owner/Lessor:

_____

State of _____

_____ of _____

Personally appeared before me _____

_____, who each and all swore to and acknowledged the foregoing.

                                        _____
                                        Notary Public

                                                (Notary Seal)

My commission expires _____

ASSIGNMENT OF REALTY LEASE BY LESSEE

_____, heretofore Tenant at Real Property at
_____ having
moved from the said Real property, hereby transfers all right, title, and interest in and to the Leasehold (including Security Deposit of $_____) at said Real Property to
_____, Assignee, subject to the Lease dated _____, made
with the Landlord, _____, and which Assignee agrees to honor
according to all its terms and conditions.

The parties confirm that all responsibilities and duties incident to this Assignment are current and
have been satisfactorily adjusted. Assignee accepts the property in its physical condition "as is," and
shall be responsible for all matters regarding physical condition to the extent required by and in
accord with the said Lease.

(A copy of said Lease is___/is not___ attached.)

Date _____

Former Tenant/Lessee: Accepted—New Tenant/Assignee:

_____   _____

Approved—Landlord:

_____

State of _____

_____ of _____

Personally appeared before me _____

_____, who each and all swore to and acknowledged the foregoing.

_____
Notary Public
(Notary Seal)

My commission expires _____

Module VI

Loans and Security

INTRODUCTION

This Module deals with transactions in which most every business will find itself on both sides of the document from time to time. Many of the documents presented are of the type likely to be encountered when borrowing from a financial institution. The business person should be familiar with these, especially as personal liability is often a loan condition. However, most businesses sometimes also find themselves in the position of lender, even if inadvertently through extension of trade credit or advances to employees, so the business person must be ready to undertake the lender's role in a responsible fashion.

The purposes of loan and security documents are

1. To evidence the borrowing, terms of repayment, and security
2. To provide protection to the lender, through collateral and third-party promises, in the event repayment is not made
3. To protect the borrower (especially a consumer) against overreaching by the lender

One special comment: Distribution is not shown for any forms in Module VI because internal distribution varies so greatly by transaction. However, in every case, each party should receive a copy.

99

MODULE FORMS

The law makes significant distinctions between business borrowers and consumers. Hence, there are often two kinds of forms for each task. As a result, this is the largest of the Modules, with 17 forms:

Truth in Lending Disclosure
Promissory Note (simple)
Commercial Loan Note
Consumer Loan Note (Instalment)
Promissory Note of Employee
Confess Judgment Promissory Note
Borrower's Waiver of Right of Rescission
Notice to Cosigner
Consumer Security Agreement
Guaranty (commercial)
Loan and Security Agreement
Deed of Trust
Financing Statement (UCC)
Receipt for Collateral
Collateral Substitution Agreement
Warehousing Agreement
Non-Negotiable Warehouse Receipt

Truth in Lending Disclosure

Definition

The truth in lending disclosure is required by federal law to be given to consumer borrowers in advance of the loan to inform the borrower of loan terms.

Comments

a. The disclosure form requirement is applicable to most consumer instalment purchase transactions, as well as straight loans.

b. Signature by the borrower is necessary to validate compliance by the lender, but the terms expressed in the disclosure cannot be held against the borrower, and if they vary from the terms of the loan documents, will place the lender's rights in jeopardy, including the possibility the loan can be avoided.

c. Proper completion of the form requires some training. It is advisable to get help from your counsel and/or your banker.

Promissory Note (simple)

Definition

The promissory note is used for evidencing the promise of the borrower to repay the loan amount to the lender.

Comments

a. Assumability prevents the borrower from passing along the obligation to someone else who may not be creditworthy.

b. On the other hand, the note can be assigned by the noteholder, as there is no prohibition stated.

c. As the note is payable to order, it is governed by the Uniform Commercial Code as adopted in the state where it is signed.

d. Notes should not be duplicated without being labeled as copies, and borrowers should never sign more than one for the same transaction, as each appears on its face to constitute a separate debt.

Commercial Loan Note

Definition

The commercial loan note is used as evidence of business indebtedness, stating terms.

Comments

a. Little protection is granted by law to business borrowers, who are presumed (rightly or wrongly) to negotiate from equal strength.

b. This form may be used for either secured or unsecured transactions, at either fixed or variable rates, and offers options on other terms as well as those negotiated between the parties.

c. For significant amounts, whether lending or borrowing, have the assistance of counsel.

Consumer Loan Note (Instalment)

Definition

The consumer loan note is used for the typical consumer loan transaction.

Comments

a. This particular note form has several other forms built into it: truth in lending (minus the itemization), notice to cosigner (which is also described below), and a consumer guaranty.

b. It is most commonly used in conjunction with a security agreement, but may be used for unsecured loans as well.

c. It is the type of form for use by sellers of goods (usually durables and vehicles) to consumers on credit.

d. It should be reviewed by counsel to be sure it matches to local requirements.

Promissory Note of Employee

Definition

The promissory note of employee is used as evidence of an employee's debt including advances.

Comments

a. Special note terms relate to the termination of employment, so the employer is hopefully able to recover the funds out of wages due.

b. Be sure that local law, which often favors employees, does not contradict the terms of the note.

c. Also be sure that there are no contractual limitations (e.g., union contracts) on the terms of the note.

Confess Judgment Promissory Note

Definition

A confess judgment (CJ) promissory note is a document that can be immediately entered as a court-enforceable judgment upon default of the borrower.

Comments

a. State laws heavily govern CJ notes, and they are not recognized in all jurisdictions.

b. The actual format of the note should be reviewed by counsel, as failure to comply with precisely all the technical requirements will invalidate the judgment.

c. The CJ promissory notes are most often used in settling a claim against a poor credit, giving the credit time to pay but retaining the hammer of rapid judgment if default occurs again.

Borrower's Waiver of Right of Rescission

Definition

The borrower's waiver of right of rescission allows a consumer to waive the three-day rescission period on a regulated loan.

Comments

a. Federal consumer protection statutes give a borrower three days to repudiate most consumer loan transactions.

b. A waiver is allowable in certain cases, provided the borrower will face a hardship if the waiver is not allowed, as the lender is under no obligation to advance the funds until the rescission period has run.

c. It is usually unlawful to charge interest to the consumer until the funds have been delivered after the three-day rescission time.

d. This is a very highly technical area of the law and requires assistance of counsel to evaluate applicability.

Notice to Cosigner

Definition

The notice to cosigner is a statutorily required notice to consumers, guaranteeing the debt of another.

Comments

a. The language for this form is more or less mandated and should not be changed without assistance of counsel.

b. The notice must be provided to the guarantor at or before the time the guarantee is signed.

Consumer Security Agreement

Definition

The consumer security agreement is a pledge of collateral on a consumer loan.

Comments

a. The most common kind of collateral is a motor vehicle. To perfect the security interest, the law in most states requires evidence of the lien on the title through the state's motor vehicle office.

b. This form is not a note, but must be used with one.

c. It may also be used by a guarantor of the note, who pledges security as part of the guarantee.

Guaranty (commercial)

Definition

The commercial guaranty is a personal promise to pay a business's debt if the business defaults.

Comments

a. This kind of guaranty is usually required on loans by financial institutions to closely held companies.

b. Where one business is lending to another, even on trade credit, obtainment of a guaranty is a great asset if it can be obtained without destroying a customer relationship.

c. This particular form is very stringent, and its principal thrust (i.e., the promise to make good on the business's debt) can be accomplished with a shorter document (albeit, with lesser lender rights).

Loan and Security Agreement

Definition

The loan and security agreement is used commercially as a pledge of collateral and grant of a security interest as part of the loan transaction.

Comments

a. The form shown uses receivables as the example for collateral, as this is a very common kind of transaction subject, but other kinds of collateral can be used instead of or with receivables.

b. This form also provides for a line of credit that can be drawn on by the borrower subject to adequate collateral being verified.

c. Each advance will be separately documented.

d. See the forms in Module I regarding collections, especially assignments, which relate to this type of receivables transaction.

Deed of Trust

Definition

The deed of trust is used to encumber real estate as security for the loan.

Comments

a. Some jurisdictions use mortgages in place of deeds of trust; others allow both. Check state law to be sure of applicability and format requirements and limitations.

b. The deed of trust creates the security interest, not the debt, so it must be used in conjunction with a note.

c. The deed of trust will not be effective until recorded in the land records against the real estate, so no security interest is perfected until recording has occurred.

d. Errors in completing the deed of trust can invalidate it. Assistance of counsel is urged.

Financing Statement (UCC)

Definition

The UCC financing statement is prescribed by the Uniform Commercial Code to record and perfect the security interest of the lender in the asset of the borrower.

Comments

a. Financing statements do not by themselves create the debt, and, if the instrument contains all the necessary features, the debt instrument itself may be recorded in lieu of the financing statement.

b. Financing statements may be used for transactions besides straight loans, such as leases of personalty (see Module V) and instalment sales contracts.

c. Financing statements technically do not bind realty, only personalty, although the personalty may be attached to realty, and thus real estate may be "affected."

d. Surprisingly, there is no UCC requirement the lender sign, although some lenders do so.

e. Like a deed of trust, no security interest is perfected until recording of the financing statement has occurred.

Receipt for Collateral

Definition

The receipt for collateral is used to evidence delivery of collateral to the lender, stating the terms of the lender's custodianship.

Comments

a. This form should be used whenever the property of another is accepted as collateral, even if the lender is merely holding it until the loan is paid, without security interest filing or perfection.

b. Do not use in an instalment sale where title does not pass to the buyer until final payment.

c. When holding motor vehicles or other assets involving registered title, be sure also to get the registration document, as enforcement of the security is otherwise difficult, if not impossible.

d. Require return of the receipt to lender when the collateral is redelivered to the borrower, so the receipt can be cancelled.

Collateral Substitution Agreement

Definition

The collateral substitution agreement is used to reflect replacement of one asset of collateral with another for the convenience of the borrower, with the permission of the lender.

Comments

a. This form is often used in "floor plan" arrangements, where inventory secures the debt, but substitution becomes necessary as inventory is sold and replenished. However, it can be used for any kind of substitution circumstance.

b. If title documents are involved, the lien must be released from the old collateral and listed on the title of the new.

Warehousing Agreement

Definition

The warehousing agreement is used for establishing a warehouse financing arrangement, where the inventory in the warehouse is secured to the lender and in the custody of a third-party "warehouseman" who has responsibilities to both lender and borrower.

Comments

a. This form is promulgated by the American Warehousemen's Association.

b. Warehousing agreements are governed by UCC Article 7.

c. Warehousing arrangements are common in some industries and un-heard of in others. If you contemplate such an arrangement but have not used one before, obtain the assistance of counsel.

Non-Negotiable Warehouse Receipt

Definition

The non-negotiable warehouse receipt is issued by the warehouseman under a warehousing arrangement, showing receipt of the collateral goods being warehoused.

Comments

a. Comments regarding the warehousing agreement are applicable to the non-negotiable warehouse receipt, as well.

b. The warehouseman does not guarantee the goods, only adherence to the terms of custody.

TRUTH IN LENDING DISCLOSURE
(Federal Reserve Regulation Z)

ANNUAL PERCENTAGE RATE The cost of my credit as a yearly rate: ___%

FINANCE CHARGE The dollar amount the credit will cost me: $_____

AMOUNT FINANCED The amount of credit provided to me or on my behalf: $_____

TOTAL of PAYMENTS The amount I will have paid after I have made all scheduled payments:
$_____

PAYMENT SCHEDULE   ("e" means an estimate)
My payment schedule will be as follows:

Number of Payments   Amount of Payments   When Payments Are Due

INTEREST RATE The interest rate on my loan is
    ___fixed at ___%
    ___variable, as follows: _____

SECURITY I am giving a security interest in
    ___the goods or property being purchased
    ___other (brief description of other property) _____

INSURANCE As a condition of the loan, I must keep the security insured for at least the amount of the loan, with a loss payable clause to the lender, through any insurance company acceptable to the lender.

Filing fees: $_____   Non-filing insurance: $_____

LATE CHARGE If a payment is late, I will be charged _____.

TERM The term of my loan is _____ years.
    There _____ (is/is not) a demand feature.
    I _____ (do/do not) have the right to prepay the loan.

PREPAYMENT If I pay off early,
    I _____ (will/will not) have to pay a prepayment penalty of _____.
    I _____ (may/may not) be entitled to a refund of part of the finance charge.

OTHER INFORMATION My contract documents have additional information about nonpayment, default, any required repayment before the scheduled date, and prepayment refunds and penalties. I acknowledge receiving a copy hereof after it was explained to me. (See Itemization of Amount Financed.)

_____   Date _____, 19____
Borrower

_____   Date _____, 19____
Co-Borrower

Truth in Lending Disclosure (*continued*)

ITEMIZATION OF AMOUNT FINANCED

Face amount of Loan $_____

Less includible prepaid finance charges:

    Prepaid interest charges $_____

    Origination fee $_____

    Discount fee $_____

    Other _____ $_____

Amount Financed $_____

Amounts paid to others on my behalf, excludible from finance charges:

To public officials for filing fees $_____

To insurors $_____

To _____ $_____

To _____ $_____

To _____ $_____

I acknowledge receiving a copy hereof after it was explained to me.

_____   Date _____, 19____
Borrower

_____   Date _____, 19____
Co-Borrower

PROMISSORY NOTE

U.S. $_____   Signed at: _____

    FOR VALUE RECEIVED, the undersigned _____ ("Borrower")
hereby promise(s) to pay unto _____ ("Noteholder"), or order,
the principal sum of _____ dollars ($_____), with interest on
the unpaid principal balance from the date of this Note, until paid, at the rate of _____ percent
(_____%) per annum, or the applicable federal funds rate at the date hereof, whichever is higher.
Principal and interest shall be payable at _____ or such other
place as Noteholder may designate, in consecutive _____ instalments of _____
dollars ($_____), including interest, beginning _____, 19____, and continuing on the
_____ day of each _____ thereafter until paid, except that if not sooner paid, this
Note shall be due and payable in full on _____, _____.

    This Note may be prepaid in whole or in part at any time without penalty. This Note is not
assumable without written express consent of the Noteholder, which consent is not to be unreasonably withheld.

    In the event of default, Borrower shall be responsible for all costs of collection, including but not
limited to a 15% attorney fee. If more than one Borrower, all shall be jointly and severally liable,
and notice to one shall constitute notice to all.

Date _____   _____ (Seal)
                                              Borrower

Date _____   _____ (Seal)
                                              Borrower

_____ , 19 _____

Acct. No. _____ **COMMERCIAL LOAN NOTE** _____

Note No. _____ ☐ Unsecured ☐ Secured $ _____

FOR VALUE RECEIVED, the undersigned (the Maker, whether one or more) jointly and severally promise to pay to the order of

_____ (the Holder), at any of the offices of the Holder, the sum of _____

_____ Dollars ($ _____)

plus interest as shown in the following Schedule of Payments and Interest:

SCHEDULE OF PAYMENTS AND INTEREST

☐ On Demand (principal and interest);

☐ One principal payment in full on or before _____ , 19 _____ ;

☐ In consecutive [ ] monthly [ ] quarterly principal instalments of $ _____ each on the _____ day of

each _____ hereafter beginning _____ , 19 _____ , and if applicable, one final

payment of $ _____ on _____ , 19 _____ ;

☐ As follows: _____

_____

☐ This Note shall be payable in _____ consecutive monthly instalments of principal and interest of $ _____ each, on

the _____ day of each month hereafter beginning _____ , 19 _____ , and continuing on the same day of each

month thereafter until this Note is paid in full.

Interest hereon shall accrue on the unpaid balance at a per annum rate of

☐ _____ %,

☐ _____ % plus the announced prime rate of the Holder in effect from time to time, adjusted when and as such announced prime rate is changed. For purposes hereof, the announced prime rate of the Holder means the rate of interest announced by the Holder as its then applicable prime rate of interest to be used as an index in determining actual interest rates to be charged to certain of the Holder's borrowers. The Holder may price loans at, above or below its announced prime rate.

Interest hereon shall be computed for actual days elapsed on the basis of [ ] a 360-day [ ] 365 (or 366, as the case may be) day year.

Interest hereon shall be payable [ ] monthly [ ] quarterly beginning _____ , 19 _____ , and continuing on

the _____ day of each _____ thereafter; [ ] as follows: _____

_____

☐ A fee of $ _____ will be payable as follows: _____ .

Collateral. If this Note is marked above as "Unsecured", the references on the reverse hereof to "Collateral" and "security" do not apply, but all other provisions hereof are applicable. If this Note is marked above as "Secured", the Maker has either (i) executed a security agreement giving to the Holder a security interest in the property described below, or (ii) deposited with, and does hereby assign and pledge to the Holder as collateral the property described below. In either event such property and the proceeds thereof constitute collateral for the payment of this and any other liability, contingent or otherwise (including overdrafts and future advances), of the Maker to the Holder, now due or to become due or which may hereafter be contracted. Further, as security for the full and timely payment of the indebtedness evidenced by this Note, the Maker hereby grants to the Holder a security interest in all monies, bank deposits or credits held by the Holder for or owed by the Holder to the Maker. The property constituting the collateral

security for this Note (the Collateral) is described as follows: _____

_____

_____

Prepayment. The unpaid balance of this Note may be prepaid at any time in whole or in part. A prepayment penalty of _____ % of the amount prepaid will be imposed. Partial prepayments shall be applied to instalments in the inverse order of their maturities. The Maker shall pay accrued interest through the date of prepayment. No portion of any fee or service charge will be refunded upon a prepayment.

Change of Rate. The Maker agrees that, with respect to any loan (other than loans where the rate fluctuates according to the Holder's announced prime rate), the Holder at its option may change the interest rate shown above at any time. Upon making any such change, the Holder will send notice thereof to the Maker at the address on the Holder's records.

Default Charges. The Maker agrees to pay a late charge of 5% of the amount of any payment which is 10 days or more past due. After maturity or in event of default, the Maker agrees to pay interest on all outstanding amounts at the interest rate then being charged on this Note and all collection costs and expenses, including attorney's fees.

REFERENCE IS MADE SPECIFICALLY TO THE PROVISIONS APPEARING ON THE REVERSE SIDE HEREOF, ALL OF WHICH ARE EXPRESSLY MADE PARTS, TERMS AND CONDITIONS OF THIS NOTE.

Witness the following signatures and seals as of the date first above written.

_____ (SEAL)

_____ (SEAL)

_____ (SEAL)

ADDITIONAL PROVISIONS

All payments hereunder shall be made in immediately available funds and shall at the Holder's option be applied first to late charges and costs of collection, if any, then to interest , then to principal.

If the Collateral described on the face of this Note is in the nature of securities, it includes all stock dividends, dividends representing distribution of capital assets and rights to subscribe to additional capital stock to which the owner of the securities herein deposited as Collateral is now or may hereafter become entitled or possessed by virtue of owning such securities, with authority to collect, sell, transfer and rehypothecate such Collateral, it being understood that on payment or tender of the amount so due, the Holder may return to the Maker the securities deposited or an equal quantity of the same. In the event the securities pledged as Collateral should at any time and for any reason become inadequate as collateral security in the sole judgment of the Holder, the Maker agrees to deposit with the Holder such additional securities as the Holder may require to render the Collateral adequate.

In case of (i) failure to make any payment of principal or interest of the Note when due, or (ii) failure to deposit additional collateral security upon request, or (iii) upon assignment for the benefit of creditors by any Maker, guarantor, surety, endorser or other party hereto (collectively called a Party), or (iv) upon the failure of a Party to observe or perform any obligation, or warranty to or agreement with the Holder or furnished in connection herewith, or (v) in the event any representation or warranty at any time made by a Party to the Holder in connection herewith or in any other agreement between a Party and the Holder, or in any document or instrument delivered to the holder in connection herewith or pursuant to such other agreement, shall have been materially false at the time it was made, or (vi) upon application for the appointment of a receiver for a Party or for property of a Party or (vii) upon the filing of a petition in bankruptcy by or against a Party, or (viii) upon the issuance of an attachment or the entry of a judgment against a Party, or (ix) upon the making or sending of a notice of an intended bulk sale by a Party, or (x) upon a default by a Party with respect to any other indebtedness due to the Holder, or (xi) upon the death, dissolution or insolvency of any Party, or (xii) upon the good faith determination by the Holder that it deems itself insecure or that a material adverse change in the financial condition of a Party has occurred since the date hereof or that the Holder's prospect of payment hereunder has been impaired, the entire unpaid amount hereof shall become due and payable forthwith at the election of the Holder and without notice. Upon the occurence of any of the foregoing events, or in the event of non-payment of this Note in full at maturity, whether by acceleration or otherwise, the Holder is hereby authorized to collect or compromise or to sell at any exchange or at public or private sale, at the option of the Holder, at any time or times thereafter, without demand, advertisement or notice, the Collateral or any part thereof, or any substitute therefor or any additions thereto or any other collateral that may in any way come into the possession and custody of the Holder either as a deposit with the Holder or as collateral security for this or any other liability of a Party to the Holder, due or to become due, or that may be hereafter contracted. It is also agreed that upon any sales of any of the Collateral or any other collateral, the Holder may become the purchaser thereof absolutely free from any claim of a Party hereto.

Upon default and at any time thereafter the Holder shall have, where applicable and in addition to the foregoing, all rights and remedies of a secured party under the Uniform Commerical Code and all rights provided herein or in any applicable security or loan agreement, all of which rights and remedies shall, to the full extent permitted by law, be cumulative. After deducting from the proceeds all legal (including attorney's fees) and other costs and expenses of collection, compromise, sale and delivery of the Collateral, the Holder is authorized to apply the residue of the proceeds to the payment of any of the liabilities to the Holder of a Party hereto as the Holder may deem proper, returning the remainder, if any, to the appropriate Party, as determined by the Holder, and the Maker and each other Party agree to be and remain liable to the Holder for any deficiency.

Each Party to this Note hereby waives presentment, demand, protest and notice of dishonor and protest, and also waives the benefit of the Homestead Exemption and all other exemptions, and agrees that extension or extensions of the time of payment of this Note or any instalment or part thereof may be made before, at or after maturity by agreement by the Holder with any one or more of the Parties hereto without notice to and without releasing the liability of any other Party. Each Party consents that payment of any of the securities held as Collateral for this Note may be extended by the Holder in whole or in part at any time without notice to any Party hereto, and that any or all of the Collateral may be exchanged, surrendered, released, compromised or its terms extended or compromised by the Holder at any time without notice to any Party hereto. Upon default hereunder the Holder shall have the right to offset the amount owed by a Party hereunder or under any other obligation to the Holder against any account, checking, savings or otherwise, which a Party may have with the Holder, or against any amounts owed by the Holder in any capacity to any Party, whether or not due, and the Holder shall be deemed to have exercised such right of offset and to have made a charge against any such account or amounts immediately upon the occurence of a default hereunder even though such charge is made or entered on the books of the Holder subsequent thereto.

Any failure by the Holder to exercise any right hereunder shall not be constituted as a waiver of the right to exercise the same or any other right at any time. No agreement with respect to this Note or any Collateral shall be binding upon the Holder unless in writing and signed by it.

This Note shall apply to and bind the successors, heirs and personal representatives of the Maker and all Parties hereto and shall inure to the benefit of the Holder, its successors and assigns. This Note shall be governed by and interpreted in accordance with the laws of

_____ .

(FOR BANK USE ONLY)

RENEWAL

1. Charge DDA# _____ Interest $ _____

    Principal $ _____ Late Charges $ _____

2. Check Attached $ _____ Interest $ _____

    Principal $ _____ Late Charge $ _____

Interest Rate _____ %

Life Insurance $ _____ Age _____ Fee $ _____

3. Collateral Code _____

4. Loan Purpose Code _____

The undersigned endorser(s) hereby expressly acknowledge and agree to all terms, provisions and stipulations set forth in the Note.

_____

_____

Loan # _____   Date _____
CIS # _____   Approval _____
Application # _____   _____

CONSUMER LOAN NOTE
INSTALMENT

BORROWER (Name and Address)	BORROWER (Name and Address)
Social Security # _____	Social Security # _____

Promise to Pay. I, the Borrower, promise to pay to the order of you, SIGNET BANK/Virginia (the Bank), at any of your branches, the principal sum of _____ Dollars ($ _____)
plus interest and other charges as scheduled below until everything I owe under this note has been paid.

Interest.   I will pay interest beginning on the date of this note or _____ , whichever is later until all amounts due and remaining unpaid have been paid, whether at maturity, upon acceleration or otherwise.

☐ **Fixed.**   I will pay simple interest which will accrue daily on my unpaid balance at a fixed annual rate of _____%.

☐ **Variable.**   I will pay simple interest which will accrue daily on my unpaid balance. My annual simple interest rate is the Bank's Consumer Base Rate (which today is _____%) plus _____%. The Bank's Consumer Base Rate may change monthly effective on the second Friday of each month. For purposes hereof, the Bank's Consumer Base Rate means the rate of interest from time to time established and publicly or privately announced by the Bank as its then applicable Consumer Base Rate to be used as an index in determining actual interest rates to be charged to certain of the Bank's borrowers. Your interest rate will be determined on the date of this note and will be adjusted effective on the second Friday of each month. Any rate adjustments will remain in effect until a subsequent change. In no event will the interest rate exceed the maximum rate permitted by law.

Payments.   If this is a variable rate note, I know the number of monthly payments I must make may increase or decrease if my interest rate changes. My payments will be applied first to interest, then to insurance premiums, then to the other amounts financed, and finally to other fees and charges. I know that the day I actually make my payment compared to the payment due date will affect the interest I pay and the number of payments I make.

Filing Fees. $ _____ .

Service Charge.   I will pay a service charge of $ _____ on the date of this note.

ANNUAL PERCENTAGE RATE The cost of my credit as a yearly rate.	FINANCE CHARGE The dollar amount the credit will cost me.	Amount Financed The amount of credit provided to me or on my behalf.	Total of Payments The amount I will have paid after I have made all payments as scheduled.
_____%	$ _____	$ _____	$ _____

	NUMBER OF PAYMENTS	AMOUNT OF PAYMENTS	WHEN PAYMENTS ARE DUE
MY PAYMENT		$	Monthly beginning
SCHEDULE		$	
WILL BE		$	
		$	
		$	

Late Payment: I will pay a late charge of 5% of any payment that is more than 7 days late.

Prepayment: If I pay off early, I will not pay a prepayment penalty and I will not be entitled to a refund of the finance charge.

Variable Rate: If I have a variable rate note, my Annual Percentage Rate may increase if the Bank's Consumer Base Rate increases. Changes in the Consumer Base Rate are at your discretion. The following other conditions apply: _____
If my rate increases, I will pay more payments of the same amount.
For example, my loan is for $10,000 at 12% for 48 months, with monthly payments of $263.34. If my rate increased to 14% beginning with my 13th payment, I would make 37 additional payments of $263.34 plus a final payment of $80.73.

Security: This note is secured by a ☐ Security Agreement ☐ Pledge Agreement ☐ Assignment ☐ Other _____
covering the following property _____ (the Collateral).
In addition, this note will also be secured by my checking and savings accounts with you and by any collateral (other than my principal dwelling or my household goods) that secures any other present or future obligations I may have with you.

Assumption If this note is to finance the purchase of my principal dwelling, someone buying my dwelling may not be allowed to assume the remaining obligation on the original terms of this note.

Additional Information: I will refer to my contract documents for additional information about nonpayment, default, prepayment refunds, any required prepayment in full before the scheduled date, security interests and other matters relating to this loan.

Acknowledgment. I have read and agree to the provisions on both sides of this note and acknowledge receipt of a completely filled in copy of this note. I certify that my social security number shown above is correct.

_____ (SEAL)
Borrower's Signature

_____ (SEAL)
Borrower's Signature

_____ (SEAL)
Borrower's Signature

Additional Charges. I will pay you interest on all amounts remaining unpaid at maturity or upon acceleration at the interest rate in effect at that time.

Return Check Charge. If a check or electronic fund transfer I used for payment on this note is returned or not honored, I will pay you a return check charge of $18.00. This charge is in addition to any other return check charge that I may pay, and I will pay it on demand.

Collection Costs. I will pay you on demand all collection costs that you incur, including reasonable attorney's fees and costs, in connection with the enforcement or collection of this note.

Prepayment. No part of the service charge will be refunded. If I make a partial prepayment, there will be no delays in the due dates of the monthly payments. If I have credit insurance and I pay off early, I may be entitled to a refund.

Default. I will be in default if:
  (a) I do not make a payment, together with my late charges, within 10 days of the due date;
  (b) I am in bankruptcy, receivership, or insolvency proceedings;
  (c) I die or any Guarantor or Co-owner dies;
  (d) I have made a false or misleading statement to you;
  (e) a judgment, tax lien, attachment or garnishment is entered or filed against me or against any Guarantor or Co-Owner or against any property, assets or income of mine or theirs;
  (f) I fail to perform any promise I have made to you in this note or any other agreement I may have with you now or in the future; or
  (g) anything else happens that you think endangers the collateral or my ability to repay.

I agree that if you remedy a default in order to protect your interests (for example, by paying taxes or insurance premiums), then such remedy will not cure the default and you may enforce all of your rights available upon default.

Acceleration. If a default occurs, you have the right, at your option and without giving me prior notice or demand, to require me to pay immediately the full amount I owe under this note together with any finance charge that has accrued up to the date of payment and any other amount due and payable under this note. If you accept payment of an overdue instalment or the late charge on the overdue instalment, or both, you may still require me to pay immediately the entire unpaid balance, together with any finance charge or other amounts payable under this note.

Offset. If I am in default, you may take any money I have in any accounts with you and apply it to the payment of my obligations under this note or any other agreement I may have with you. If you obtain a refund on optional insurance or service contracts, you will use it to reduce my debt. The refund will be applied in inverse order of my scheduled payments and will not delay the due date of my next payment.

Delay in Enforcement. You may delay enforcing any of your rights under this note without losing them.

Governing Law. I know that this note is governed by   law.

Modification. Any change in, or waiver of the terms of this note must first be approved by you in writing.

Severability. If any part of this note is found to be invalid, it will be unenforceable only to the extent of its invalidity. I know it will not affect the enforceability of any other part.

Borrower's Responsibility. The words I and me mean each Borrower who signs this note. Although more than one Borrower may sign this note, I know that each of us is totally (jointly and severally) responsible for complying with all promises and agreements made in this note. You do not have to notify me that this note has not been paid. You may change the terms of repayment or release any of the Collateral without notifying me and without releasing me from responsibility for this note.

NOTICE: ANY HOLDER OF THIS CONSUMER CREDIT CONTRACT IS SUBJECT TO ALL CLAIMS AND DEFENSES WHICH THE DEBTOR COULD ASSERT AGAINST THE SELLER OF GOODS OR SERVICES OBTAINED PURSUANT HERETO OR WITH THE PROCEEDS HEREOF. RECOVERY HEREUNDER BY THE DEBTOR SHALL NOT EXCEED AMOUNTS PAID BY THE DEBTOR HEREUNDER.

This notice applies only if (a) I bought the goods primarily for personal, family or household use and the Amount Financed does not exceed $25,000 or (b) the goods are being used as a principal dwelling. In all other cases, I will not assert against any subsequent holder or assignee of this note any claims or defenses that I may have against you or against the manufacturer of the goods obtained with the proceeds hereof.

NOTICE TO CO-SIGNER

I am being asked to guarantee this debt. I have thought about it. I know that if the Borrower doesn't pay the debt, I will have to pay up to the full amount of the debt, including late fees and collection costs, which may increase this amount. I can afford it and want to accept this responsibility.

You can collect this debt from me without first trying to collect from the Borrower and can use the same collection methods against me that can be used against the Borrower, such as suing me, garnishing my wages, etc. If this debt is ever in default, that fact may become part of **my** credit record.

This notice is not the contract that makes me liable for the debt.

GUARANTY OF PAYMENT

In order to get the Bank to enter into this note, each Guarantor, jointly and severally, guarantees the prompt performance of all of the Borrower's promises under this note. Each Guarantor agrees to pay the entire amount owed, including collection costs and attorney's fees, promptly on demand. Each Guarantor agrees to be liable even if the Bank gives the Borrower more time to make a payment, gives a full or partial release to the Borrower or to any other Guarantor, releases any security, or modifies or renews this note. Each Guarantor certifies that the social security number below such Guarantor's signature is correct and acknowledges receipt of a completed copy of this note.

Guarantor's Signature _____

Address _____

_____

Social Security # _____

Witness _____

Guarantor's Signature _____

Address _____

_____

Social Security # _____

Witness _____

Guarantor's Signature _____

Address _____

_____

Social Security # _____

Witness _____

PROMISSORY NOTE OF EMPLOYEE

I, _____ ("Employee"), an employee of _____ ("Lender"), am indebted to Lender in the principal amount borrowed of _____ ($_____) dollars loaned or advanced to me by Lender, on the date written below.

I agree to repay the same with interest at _____ percent (___%) per annum on the unpaid balance until paid, and to make payments thereon of _____ dollars ($_____) per pay period, which I specifically authorize Lender to deduct from each of my paychecks as earned and issued to me hereafter until all amounts owing hereunder are paid in full.

This Note may be prepaid in whole or in part at any time without penalty, but partial prepayment shall not interrupt the aforesaid deductions from my paychecks, which shall instead cease sooner because of such partial prepayment.

If my employment terminates at any time for any reason, with or without cause, then, immediately upon such termination and without notice, the entire unpaid balance, including interest, shall be then due and payable in full, and I authorize and direct Lender to offset such balance to the fullest extent allowable by law from all money, if any, then owed to me by Lender or afterwards due to my estate from Lender for any reason. If any balance remains after such offset, I agree to pay the same upon demand and bind my estate and personal representatives to do the same. I agree to pay all collection costs, including but not limited to court costs and twenty-five percent (25%) attorney fees.

The loan evidenced hereby was made at my request, and I voluntarily agree to all terms listed herein after having read and understood them.

Date _____

_____
Employee

Employee ID No. _____

Social Security No. _____

CONFESS JUDGMENT PROMISSORY NOTE

$_____   _____, 19____

    FOR VALUE RECEIVED, _____ (individually and collectively referred to herein as "Makers"), promise to pay to _____ ("Noteholder") the total sum of _____ dollars ($_____), with interest thereon at the rate of _____ percent (___%) per annum, payable according to the following payment schedule:

               Due Date   *Payment Amount*

    If not sooner paid, all outstanding indebtedness, including accrued interest and other charges, if any, shall be due and payable in full on _____, 19____.

    All payments shall be made in good funds payable to the order of _____ and delivered to

_____

_____

or such other place as Noteholder may designate in writing.

    Any payment not received by Noteholder within five (5) calendar days of the due date shall incur a late charge of five percent (5%) of the full amount of such payment. Notwithstanding the above, nonpayment of any payment on the date it is due under this Note shall constitute a default hereunder.

    This Note may be prepaid in whole or in part without penalty at any time, with any prepayments to be first credited to other charges, then to interest, and lastly to principal.

    Default hereunder shall include any breach of the terms of this Note, including, but not limited to, nonpayment, filing of a petition in bankruptcy by any of the Makers hereof, or any other act, omission, or breach reasonably causing the Noteholder to believe Noteholder to be insecure.

    In the event of default, Noteholder may accelerate and declare the entire unpaid balance, plus all accrued unpaid interest and all late charges, to be immediately due and payable. Further, upon default, Makers shall further be jointly and severally liable for all costs of collection, including, but not limited to, court costs and twenty-five percent (25%) attorney fees.

    Makers individually and collectively waive all notice not specifically required herein and as subject to the terms herein. Makers do further individually and collectively waive all rights in the event of default for themselves and for any sureties, guarantors, endorsers, or successors hereof, including, but not limited to, waiver of demand, presentment, notice, dishonor, protest, offset, and the benefit of the homestead exemption. Any forebearance or temporary waiver in enforcement by Noteholder shall not constitute a permanent waiver or waiver of any other right. All of Noteholder's rights are cumulative and not exclusive. Each and all of Makers are jointly and severally liable hereunder.

    Further, in the event of default, each and all of Makers jointly and severally, collectively and individually, appoint _____ as the Attorney-in-Fact for each and all of them to CONFESS JUDGMENT against each and all of them, or any number or any combination of them, in any court of competent jurisdiction at the sole discretion and direction of the Noteholder for the balance

Confess Judgment Promissory Note (*continued*)

of this Note then unpaid, together with all accrued unpaid interest and all other charges that are then unpaid, plus all costs and twenty-five percent (25%) attorney fees.

Our said Attorney-in-Fact is further empowered to accede to enforcement of the judgment so obtained in any other court, or before any other tribunal, or in any other forum having jurisdiction over any one or more of Makers. Failure to confess judgment or accede to the enforcement of judgment against less than all of the Makers at any time or times, shall not constitute any kind of waiver or release, nor prevent our Attorney-in-Fact from confessing at a later time or times or acceding at a later time or times. If required by law, notice shall be given to each of the Makers of each such confession and accession at the address listed below the signature of each Maker.

Witness the following seals and signatures:

Makers:

_____ (Seal)   _____ (Seal)
Signature   Signature

_____   _____
Social Security Number   Social Security Number

Address: Address:

_____   _____

_____   _____

_____   _____

State of _____

City/County of _____ , to wit

On _____, 19___, _____ and _____, Makers on the foregoing Confess Judgment Promissory Note appeared in person before me and did sign, swear to, and acknowledge the same as their voluntary act and deed.

                                        _____
                                        Notary Public

                                                (Notary Seal)

My commission expires _____

116

BORROWER'S WAIVER OF RIGHT OF RESCISSION

I, _____, hereby waive the Right of Rescission applicable to the loan to be secured by my home in favor of the Lender, _____ , as the requirement of delaying disbursement will cause a hardship for me in that

Now, therefore, I do hereby WAIVE irrevocably the three-day Right of Rescission, accepting the aforesaid loan and being bound thereby according to its terms:

Date _____   _____
                                                 Borrower

State of _____
City/County of _____ , to wit

Sworn to and acknowledged before me this _____ day of _____, 19____, by
_____.

                                                 _____
                                                 Notary Public

                                                      (Notary Seal)

My commission expires _____

NOTICE TO COSIGNER

You are being asked to guarantee this debt. Think carefully before you do. If the borrower does not pay the debt, you will have to. Be sure you can afford to pay if you have to, and that you want to accept this responsibility.

You may have to pay up to the full amount of the debt if the borrower does not pay. You may also have to pay late fees or collection costs, which increase this amount.

The lender can collect this debt from you without first trying to collect from the borrower. The lender can use the same collection methods against you that can be used against the borrower, such as suing you or garnishing your wages. If this debt is ever in default, that fact may become a part of your credit record.

This notice is not the contract that makes you liable for the debt.

Acknowledgment _____, 19____

When you sign below, you acknowledge that on this date you received a copy of this notice.

_____
Cosigner

This notice is furnished by

_____

Address _____

CONSUMER SECURITY AGREEMENT
(Consumer Goods, Stocks, Vehicles, Boats)

In this agreement the following definitions are used:
- "I", "me", "my" and "mine" refer to each and all those signing this agreement as an owner.
- "You", "your" and "yours" refer to _____ , and its successors and assigns.
- "Secured Debt" means the Obligations which my property secures under this agreement.
- "Collateral" means the property in which I have given you a security interest.

1. **Security Interest.** I give you a security interest in the following property:

NEW/USED	YEAR	MAKE/BRAND	MODEL/BODY STYLE	NO. CYL.	IDENTIFICATION NO.	MILEAGE
☐ New						
☐ Used						

OTHER COLLATERAL

together with the proceeds thereof and any other property installed in or attached to it, any substitutions for it, including licenses, tires, tools, equipment, accessories and accessions, and any money or property received as a result of it being damaged, sold, leased or otherwise disposed of. (This is not an authorization for me to sell, lease or dispose of the Collateral.) I also give you a security interest in any other property of mine securing other debts with you now or in the future, except for my principal dwelling or my household goods, and in any funds I have on deposit with you in any checking, savings or time deposit or account. All of the foregoing is referred to as the "Collateral".

I also give you a security interest in all rights to which I am now or may in the future become entitled because I own the Collateral including, but not limited to, income, interest, dividends of any type, additional securities as proceeds from a stock split (which I will promptly deliver to you) and rights to acquire stock or other property.

2. **Obligations Secured.** I give you a security interest in the Collateral to secure the payment of:

   (a) **All of My Obligations —** All the money any I owe you for any reason both now and at any time in the future, regardless of amount or how the debt was created or incurred and whether it is matured or unmatured, direct or indirect, absolute or contingent, including extensions, modifications, amendments, and renewals thereof. This includes, but is not limited to, money owed you in connection with future loans or advances (even if not currently planned and even if made after all current loans have been repaid), loans arranged through someone else (such as a car dealer) which are assigned to you, this agreement and any other obligations owed to you at any time even if not a loan. All of the foregoing is referred to as the "Obligations".

   (b) Obligations of _____ ("Borrower") —
   (Check one. If no box is checked, the first box will be deemed checked and applicable.)

   ☐ In addition to my Obligations, all the money Borrower, or any one of them if more than one, owes you for any reason both now and at any time in the future, regardless of amount. This includes, but is not limited to, money owed you in connection with future loans or advances (even if not currently planned and even if made after all current loans have been repaid), loans arranged through some else (such as a car dealer) which are assigned to us, this agreement and any other Obligations owed to you at any time even if not a loan.

   ☐ In addition to my Obligations, all the money Borrower owes you in connection with a $ _____ loan or line of credit evidenced by _____
   _____ and any extensions, renewals or modifications of it.
   If this is a line of credit, you may increase the credit limit or loan more money at any time, but my Collateral may not be used to repay more of the Borrower's obligations with respect to the line of credit than an amount equal to the amount shown here, plus interest, plus costs.

3. **Nature of the Collateral.** The Collateral is (check all that apply):
   ☐ Stock or other investment securities.
   ☐ Principal and income of an irrevocable trust of which you are beneficiary.
   ☐ Goods used primarily for personal, family or household purposes.
   If the Collateral is being purchased with proceeds of your loan, I promise that the proceeds will not be used for any other purpose and I agree that you may pay the proceeds directly to the seller.

4. **Location of Collateral.** Until all Secured Debt is repaid and this agreement terminated, the Collateral will be:
   ☐ Kept at my residence as shown below.
   ☐ Kept at _____
   ☐ Delivered to you to hold.
   I promise not to change the permanent location of the Collateral without your prior written permission. You have the right to inspect the Collateral at any time.

   I promise to promptly transfer to you any documents representing any of the Collateral (such as stock certificates, including any additional stock later received as a result of a stock split, exchange or dividend) and to promptly deliver to you any certificates of title for any titled Collateral (such as a motor vehicle) with your security interest properly recorded on the certificates. If you require, I will also deliver to you any dividends, interest, payments, or other proceeds I receive in connection with Collateral.

5. **My Residence.** I reside at: _____ .
   which is in the ☐ City ☐ County of _____
   I promise to notify you of any change of my address. (Note: If the Collateral is located at my residence, I know I must get your prior written permission to change its permanent location.)

6. **Other Side.** See the other side of this page for additional terms of this agreement.

   If more than one of us signed this agreement, I know that each of us is totally (jointly and severally) responsible for complying with all promises and agreements made in it. By signing this agreement, I agree to its terms and I acknowledge that:

   (a) it was appropriately filled out (to the best of my knowledge) when I signed it; and
   (b) I have read it and any questions I had about it were answered.

Consumer Security Agreement (*continued*)

7. **Ownership.** I promise that I now own the Collateral and that no one else (except you) has an interest in it, or lien or claim against it and that no financing statement is on file in any public office with respect to the Collateral except as I have disclosed to you in writing. I promise to defend the Collateral against anyone else's claim. I promise not to sell, lease, give away, abandon, give a security interest in or otherwise dispose of the Collateral without first getting your written permission. The proceeds of any such disposition shall be given to you immediately; however, doing so will not preclude you from exercising any other default rights you deem appropriate. I agree to obtain and deliver to you certificates of title covering the Collateral showing a security interest in your favor.

8. **Use and Maintenance.** I promise:

    (a) to keep the Collateral repaired and in good condition, to use it for its intended use in a normal fashion, and not to use it for any illegal or commercial purpose or for hire;
    (b) not to make any major changes, substitutions or additions to it;
    (c) not to take it outside Virginia (except temporarily in its normal use) and not to change its permanent location, without your prior written permission;
    (d) to notify you immediately if the Collateral is stolen, lost or damaged in any way; and
    (e) to allow you to inspect it at any reasonable time.

    I know I will still have to pay everything I owe you even if the Collateral is lost, stolen or damaged. You may maintain or repair the Collateral if I do not. You may do anything else necessary to protect the Collateral. I agree to reimburse you for any such expense with interest at the interest rate in effect on the Secured Debt at that time.

9. **Insurance and Taxes.** If the Collateral includes a motor vehicle, boat, real property, consumer goods or equipment, I promise to keep it fully insured against loss and damage (collision and comprehensive for motor vehicles) in such amounts and with an insurer satisfactory to you. I will make sure the policy has a loss payable endorsement to you, that the policy cannot be cancelled unless you receive 10 days' prior written notice from the insurer, and that the policy is delivered to you promptly.

    I give you a security interest in the insurance proceeds and any unearned premiums, which I will have made payable to you. I appoint you my attorney-in-fact with power to act in my name in all respects concerning my insurance, and you may settle any claim on your own and endorse my name on any proceeds check. You may use the insurance proceeds at your option to repair the Collateral or to reduce the Secured Debt.

    I agree to pay promptly when due all insurance premiums, taxes, fees and liens on the Collateral. If I do not pay them on time, you may pay them for me. If you cannot assure yourselves upon reasonable inquiry that the required insurance coverage exists, you may obtain insurance protecting just your interest. I agree to reimburse you for any insurance premium, tax or other expense you incur with interest at the interest rate in effect on the Secured Debt at that time.

10. **Stocks and Trusts.** I am responsible for doing everything necessary to maintain all my rights against other parties liable on any property (such as investment securities) given as Collateral under this agreement. You are not responsible for this even if you are holding the Collateral. You are also not responsible for finding out or telling me about any changes in value, maturities, calls, conversions, exchanges, tenders or similar matters relating to any of this property. If the value of this property goes down for any reason, I promise to make up the difference by furnishing additional Collateral acceptable to you. Until this agreement is in default, I may vote any investment securities you are holding under this agreement.

    You may, at any time, whether before or after an event of default occurs, without notice and at my expense: (a) notify the obligors on any Collateral of the security interest and assignment created by this agreement and (b) notify the obligors on any Collateral to make payment directly to you of any or all dividends, interest, principal or other sums now or later payable on account of the Collateral and (c) collect those sums, endorse in our name any checks or other documents which are the Collateral or which are received in connection with the Collateral and apply any amounts collected to reduce the outstanding balance of the Secured Debt.

11. **Default.** An event of default occurs whenever any portion of the Secured Debt is not paid when due or is otherwise in default according to its agreement. An event of default also occurs if I made any false or misleading statement to you or fail to do anything I have promised to do in either this agreement (such as keeping the Collateral insured) or any other agreement I may have with you at any time.

12. **Default Rights.** When an event of default occurs, you may take any one or more of the following actions WITHOUT GIVING ANY NOTICE OR ANY RIGHT TO A HEARING TO ME (OR TO THE BORROWER):
    (a) repossess any of the Collateral or render it unusable without prior notice, hearing or court action;
    (b) have any investment security (and related right or option) of mine which is Collateral under this agreement registered in your name or anyone else's name;
    (c) take advantage of and enforce your rights in the Collateral and any other security for the Secured Debt, including the Collateral.
    (d) offset the amount of the Secured Debt against any account, checking, savings or otherwise, which I may have with you.

    In addition, you may take advantage of other rights and remedies you have under law, such as the Uniform Commercial Code, or by any agreement I may have with you, including this agreement. You may take any of these actions at the same time or at different times and in any order and as many times as you want.

13. **Repossession.** I agree that your right to repossess the Collateral will be a right of possession superior to that of any other person in possession of the Collateral. You (or your agent) may peacefully enter on or into my property or the property where the Collateral is stored without giving notice and without resort to judicial process to repossess the Collateral. Upon notice from you I authorize any obligor/payor of any Collateral to make payment directly to you of any dividends, interest or other amount payable in connection with the Collateral. I authorize you to collect such amounts by legal process or otherwise and to endorse in your name any checks or other documents received in connection with the Collateral. If you ask, I agree to assemble the Collateral and make it available to you at a place we choose which is reasonably convenient to you. I UNDERSTAND THAT I MAY HAVE A RIGHT UNDER LAW TO NOTICE AND A HEARING PRIOR TO REPOSSESSION OF THE COLLATERAL. AS AN INDUCEMENT TO YOU TO ENTER INTO THIS TRANSACTION, I EXPRESSLY WAIVE ALL RIGHT CONFERRED BY EXISTING OR FUTURE LAW TO NOTICE AND A HEARING PRIOR TO SUCH REPOSSESSION BY YOU OR ANY OFFICER AUTHORIZED BY LAW TO EFFECT REPOSSESSION, AND I RELEASE YOU FROM ANY LIABILITY FOR MAKING SUCH REPOSSESSION.

14. **Disposition of Collateral.** If an event of default occurs, at your option you may sell, lease or otherwise dispose of any of the Collateral and apply the proceeds to partially or fully repay any portion of the Secured Debt you may see fit. You may be the purchaser at any such sale. If notice is required by law, I agree that reasonable notice is given if mailed to my last address on your records, or given in any other reasonable manner, 10 days in advance of such disposition. I know I may redeem the Collateral before the disposition if I pay you the entire amount of the Secured Debt, including the costs of taking and storing the Collateral and other costs you have. If I do not redeem the Collateral before the date on the notice, you may sell it. After paying any late charges, any charges for taking and storing the Collateral, cleaning, advertising, attorneys' fees, court costs, and other costs you have, you will apply the net proceeds of sale to the Secured Debt. If I owe you less than the net proceeds of the sale, you will pay me the difference, unless you are required to pay it to someone else such as someone who may also have taken a security interest in the Collateral. If I owe you more than the net proceeds of the sale, I will pay you the difference whenever you ask for it. If I don't, I will pay interest at the interest rate in effect on the Secured Debt at that time. Any collection costs, attorneys' fees actually incurred, and costs for repossessing, storing, preparing and disposing of any Collateral, will become part of the Secured Debt. Your failure at any time to honor any demand to sell any Collateral will not of itself be considered a failure to exercise ordinary care in the custody or preservation of any Collateral in your possession.

15. **Other Property Taken.** I agree that you may take possession of any other property which is in the repossessed Collateral and that you may hold it for me at my sole risk and liability. Your only duty will be to make a reasonable inspection of the Collateral. If you discover any such other property you may dispose of it in any way you see fit and apply any proceeds to the Secured Debt, if I don't claim it within 30 days of the date of repossession and apply any proceeds to the Secured Debt. If you do not discover any such other property and I do not notify you in writing that you have it 48 hours after you repossess the Collateral, I give up any right of action or claim I might have against you in the future as a result of your disposing of such other property with the Collateral or as a result of any loss of or damage to such other property.

16. **Your Right to Take Action.** If I fail to do anything I have agreed to do in this agreement (such as repair or insure the Collateral or defend claims against it), or if you believe the Collateral or your interest in the Collateral may be in jeopardy, you may do anything you think appropriate to remedy my failure or to protect the Collateral and your interest in it. However, you do not have to take any action. I agree to help in any way necessary to protect the Collateral or your security interest in it, including signing any titles, financing statements or additional documents. I agree to pay all filing costs to record, preserve or release your interest. I agree to reimburse you for any money you spend or expenses you incur in connection with this agreement or the Collateral, including reasonable attorneys' fees. Also, you may add the amount of such expense to the outstanding balance of any loan I may have with you and I will pay you interest on the amount at the rate in effect on the Secured Debt.

17. **Miscellaneous.** Unless you say so in writing, you will not waive, release or otherwise affect your rights by anything you do or do not do under this agreement or in connection with the Collateral or any Secured Debt. For example, without affecting your rights you may agree to change the terms on which the Secured Debt is to be repaid (such as by extending the time for repayment or revising the payment schedule) or change any other aspect or condition of the Secured Debt; or you may release or fail to perfect your security interest in other property which also secures the Secured Debt; or, you may release any surety (such as a guarantor) for the Secured Debt; or, you may accept any late or partial payment. You may make additional loans or increase the credit limit on any line of credit to anyone of us or to the Borrower at any time, in any amount, without notice to me, without my consent and without releasing or otherwise affecting the security interest I have given you in the Collateral. The security interest and rights given you in this agreement are in addition to any other security interest or right I have given or may in the future give you by any other agreement. No part of this agreement will be affected because any other part is unenforceable. The headings used in this agreement are for convenience only and may not be used to interpret the agreement. Virginia law governs this agreement.

Owner _____
                    (Signature)

            _____
                    (Print Name Here)

            _____
                    (Date)

Owner _____
                    (Signature)

            _____
                    (Print Name Here)

            _____
                    (Date)

Owner _____
                    (Signature)

            _____
                    (Print Name Here)

            _____
                    (Date)

Owner _____
                    (Signature)

            _____
                    (Print Name Here)

            _____
                    (Date)

GUARANTY

In consideration of loans, advances, or other credit heretofore or hereafter granted by _____ ("Lender") to _____, a _____ corporation ("Borrower"), and to enable such loans, advances, or other credit to be maintained or obtained by Borrower, and to induce Lender to extend credit to Borrower, Guarantor (if more than one, each of them, jointly and severally; ("Guarantor") hereby guarantees to Lender the full and prompt payment when due, whether by acceleration or otherwise, of all obligations of Borrower to Lender, as contained in all instruments and documents evidencing the Loan, dated _____, 19__, between Lender and Borrower set forth above ("Loan Agreement"), including interest that may accrue thereon either before or after maturity. The undersigned recognizes that future loans and advances may be required by Borrower, but the exact amounts of such loans and advances cannot presently be determined, and acknowledges and agrees that while Lender is not obligated to make such loans and advances, such loans and advances, if and when made, will be deemed to have been induced, in part, by the continuity of this Guaranty, and will be covered by and subject to this Guaranty. The undersigned further acknowledges and agrees that this Guaranty is made upon and subject to the following terms and conditions.

1. This Guaranty is a guaranty of payment and not of collection. If any obligation is not satisfied when due, Guarantor shall forthwith satisfy such obligation or, at the option of Lender, all obligations of Borrower upon demand, and no such satisfaction shall discharge the obligations of Guarantor hereunder until all obligations guaranteed hereby have been satisfied in full. Lender may collect such obligations, or any part thereof, from Guarantor (or any one or more of them) without first exercising rights against Borrower or any collateral, and Guarantor waives any right to require Lender to pursue Borrower or any part of the collateral before enforcing the obligations of Gurantor hereunder. Until all the obligations guaranteed hereby have been paid in full, Guarantor shall not be subrogated to any of Lender's rights against Borrower or any collateral, and any funds or other property at any time received by Guarantor from Borrower shall be held in trust for and shall be paid or transferred to Lender upon demand therefor.

2. Guarantor hereby

    a. Waives notice of presentment, demand, notice of nonpayment, protest and notice of protest as to the obligations and any other demands and notices required by law and

    b. Consents to the provisions of all agreements heretofore or hereafter made with Lender by Borrower and

    c. Consents and agrees that Lender may

        i.   exchange, release, or surrender to Borrower any collateral or waive, release or subordinate any security interest, in whole or in part, now or hereafter held as security for any obligations, or any other indebtedness of Borrower to Lender

        ii. waive or delay the exercise of any rights or remedies against Borrower or any surety or guarantor, or any collateral for any obligations

        iii. release or enter into compromises with Borrower, or any surety or guarantor of the obligations

        iv. renew, extend, waive, or modify the terms of any obligation guaranteed hereby or any instrument or agreement evidencing the same

        v.   apply payments by Borrower or Guarantor to any obligation guaranteed hereunder and

    d. Waives all notices whatsoever with respect to this Guaranty or with respect to the obligations, including without limitation, notice of

        i.   Lender's acceptance hereof and its intention to act or its action in reliance hereon

        ii. the present existence or future incurrence of any obligation or any terms or amounts thereof or of any change therein

        iii. any default by the Borrower or by any surety or guarantor with respect to any of the obligations

        iv. the obtaining of any guarantee or surety agreement (in addition to this guaranty), pledge, assignment, or other security for any obligation and

        v.   the release of any guarantor or surety or any obligation or of any pledgor or assignor whose pledge or assignment has been given as security for any obligation and

    e. Waives any and all defenses of Borrower to the obligations guaranteed hereby and any claim or offset or counterclaim by the Borrower or loss of contribution from any co-guarantor with respect thereto.

3. The obligations of Guarantor hereunder are primary and unconditional, without regard to the obligations of any other party or person, and shall be effective regardless of the solvency or insolvency of Borrower at any time or the extension or modification of the obligations of Borrower by operation of law or otherwise, and shall not in any manner be affected by reason of any action taken or not taken by Lender, which action or inaction is hereby consented and agreed to, or of any lack of prior enforcement or retention of any rights against Borrower, Guarantor, or any other person or any property, or of the partial or complete unenforceability or invalidity of any other guaranty or surety agreement, pledge, assignment, or other security for any obligation or of the value, genuineness, validity, regularity, or enforceability of any of the obligations. Lender may release all or any part of the obligations of any other surety or guarantor of any obligation, and any such release shall not affect or release any obligation hereunder of Guarantor. No delay in making demand on Guarantor for satisfaction of the obligations of Guarantor hereunder shall prejudice Lender's right to enforce such satisfaction. All of Lender's rights and remedies shall be cumulative, and any failure of Lender to exercise any right hereunder shall not be construed as a waiver of the right to exercise the same or any other right at any time thereafter.

4. Guarantor hereby subordinates to the obligations guaranteed hereby, whether now existing or hereafter arising, all indebtedness of the Borrower owing to Guarantor (or to any one or more of them), whether now existing or hereafter arising. Guarantor assumes the responsibility for being and keeping informed of the financial condition of Borrower and of all other circumstances bearing upon the risk of nonpayment and nonperformance of the obligations; and absent written request for such information by Guarantor, Lender shall have no duty to advise Guarantor of information known to Lender regarding such condition or any such circumstances. The liability of Guarantor hereunder shall be reinstated and revived, and the rights of Lender shall continue if and to the extent that for any reason any payment by or on behalf of Borrower or any of Guarantor is rescinded or must be otherwise restored by Lender, whether as a result of any proceedings in bankruptcy or reorganization or otherwise, provided, however, that if Lender chooses to contest any such matter at the request of Guarantor, Guarantor agrees to indemnify and hold Lender harmless with respect to all costs (including, without limitation, attorney's fees) of such litigation.

5. This Guaranty shall be a continuing guarantee and shall be binding upon Guarantor regardless of how long before or after the date hereof any obligation was or is incurred, provided, however, that any of Guarantor may terminate this Guaranty by written notice sent to Lender by certified or registered mail stating an effective day of termination not less than 30 days after receipt of such notice by Lender, and the party giving such notice shall not be obligated to Lender with respect to any obligation incurred after the permitted effective date of termination stated in such notice. Notwithstanding the foregoing, this Guaranty shall continue as to each of Guarantor who has not given such notice and shall also continue as to each of Guarantor who has given such notice with respect to (a) any obligation that was incurred prior to such date of termination or that is thereafter incurred in renewal, extension, or modification of any such obligation, and (b) any obligation incurred after such date of termination pursuant to an agreement theretofore entered into which bound Lender to permit such obligation to be incurred. In the event this Guaranty is preceded or followed by any other agreement of guaranty or suretyship by Guarantor or others, all such agreements shall be deemed to be cumulative and the obligations of Guarantor hereunder shall be in addition to those stated in any other guaranty or suretyship agreement.

6. All obligations of Guarantor under this Guaranty shall mature, at the option of Lender, immediately upon the insolvency of Borrower, the commission of an act of bankruptcy by Borrower, the appointment of a receiver for Borrower or any Borrower properties, the filing of voluntary or involuntary petition in bankruptcy, reorganization or arrangement, the making of an assignment for the benefit of creditors of the calling of a meeting of creditors by Borrower or the occurence of any default in any agreement between Borrower and Lender.

7. Guarantor agrees to pay all costs and expenses incurred in enforcing the obligations of Borrower and of Guarantor under this Guaranty, including reasonable attorney's fees in the event this Guaranty is placed in the hands of an attorney for collection, or Lender finds it necessary or desirable to secure the services of advice of an attorney with regard to the collection of the obligations or the obligations of this Guaranty. Guarantor waives to the maximum extent permitted by law the benefit of any homestead exemption and all other exemption or insolvency laws to this Guaranty. The books and records of Lender showing the accounts between Lender and Borrower shall be admissible in evidence in any action or proceeding thereon as prima facie proof of the items set forth therein. The undersigned agrees that payment or per-

Guaranty (*continued*)

formance of any of the obligations or other acts that shall toll any statute of limitations applicable to the obligations shall also toll the statute of limitations applicable to the liability of Guarantor under this Guaranty.

8. All notices to or demands on Guarantor shall be deemed effective when given, and shall be in writing and sent by telex or telegram, confirmed by registered or certified mail, or sent by registered or certified mail, addressed to Guarantor at the address specified on the signature page hereof, and addressed to Lender at the address specified in the Loan Agreement. Lender and Guarantor may give notice in the manner specified herein of any change in address for such notices. Rejection or other refusal to accept, or inability to deliver because of a changed address of which no notice was given, shall not affect the date of such notice, election, or demand sent as aforesaid.

9. This Guaranty is made, executed, and delivered in the State of _____ and shall be construed and enforced in accordance with its laws. No provisions of this Guaranty may be modified, deleted, or amended in any manner except by an agreement in writing executed by the parties, and this Guaranty shall be binding upon Guarantor and the heirs, assigns, and personal representatives thereof, and shall inure to the benefit of and be enforceable by Lender and its successors and assigns.

WITNESS the following signatures and seals as of the _____ day of _____, 19____

Signature(s) of Guarantor(s):

_____ (Seal)

_____
(Street Address)

_____
(City and State)

_____ (Seal)

_____
(Street Address)

_____
(City and State)

_____ (Seal)

_____
(Street Address)

_____
(City and State)

_____ (Seal)

_____
(Street Address)

_____
(City and State)

LOAN AND SECURITY AGREEMENT

THIS AGREEMENT, dated as of _____, 19___, between _____, a _____ corporation ("Borrower"), whose mailing address is _____, and _____, a _____ corporation ("Lender"), whose mailing address is _____.

1. *Definitions* As used herein, the following terms, when initial capital letters are used, shall have the respective meanings set forth below. Further, all terms defined in Articles 1 and 9 of the Uniform Commercial Code (UCC) as enacted in this jurisdiction shall have the meanings given therein unless otherwise defined herein.

   1.1. *Receivables* means all accounts, contract rights, instruments, documents, chattel paper, and general intangibles (as those terms are defined in Articles 1 and 9 of the UCC as enacted in this jurisdiction), whether secured or unsecured, now owned or hereafter acquired by Borrower.

   1.2 *Eligible Receivables* means such Receivables which are and at all times shall continue to be acceptable to Lender in all respects. Criteria for eligibility shall be fixed and revised from time to time solely by Lender in its exclusive judgement. In general, a Receivable shall in no event be deemed eligible unless (a) delivery of the goods or rendition of services has been completed; (b) no return, rejection, or repossession has occurred; (c) such goods or services have been finally accepted by the customer without dispute, offset, defense, or counterclaim; (d) such Receivable continues to be in full conformity with the representations and warranties made by Borrower to Lender with respect thereto; (e) no more than ____ days have elapsed from invoice date; and (f) Lender is and continues to be satisfied with the credit standing of the Debtor (as defined in 1.4) in relation to the amount of credit extended.

   1.3 *Collateral* means (a) all Receivables and all other items of personalty (including inventory, equipment, and machinery) now owned or hereafter acquired by Borrower or in which Borrower has granted or may in the future grant a security interest to Lender hereunder or in any amendment or supplement hereto or otherwise; (b) all Borrower's right, title, and interest in and to all goods and other property represented by or securing any of the Receivables, including all goods that may be reclaimed or repossessed from or returned by Debtors; (c) all of Borrower's rights as an unpaid seller, including stoppage in transit, detinue, and reclamation; (d) all additional amounts due to Borrower from any Debtor (as defined in 1.4), irrespective of whether such additional amounts have been specifically assigned to Lender; (e) all guaranties and other agreements and property securing or relating to any of the items in (a) above, or acquired for the purpose of securing and enforcing any of such items; and (f) all proceeds of any of the foregoing in whatever form, including cash, negotiable instruments and other evidences of indebtedness, chattel paper, security agreements, and other documents.

   1.4 *Debtor* means the account debtor with respect to any of Borrower's Receivables and/or the prospective purchaser with respect to any contract right, and/or any party who enters into or proposes to enter into any contract or other arrangement with Borrower pursuant to which Borrower is to deliver any goods or perform any service.

   1.5 *Obligations* means, without limitation, all Loans (as defined in 2 hereof) and all other indebtedness and liabilities of Borrower to Lender of every kind, nature and description, now existing or hereafter arising, regardless of how they arise or by what agreement or instrument evidenced or whether evidenced by any agreement or instrument, and whether liquidated or unliquidated, secured or unsecured, direct or indirect (i.e., whether the same are due directly from Borrower to Lender, or are due indirectly from Borrower to Lender by reason of Borrower acting as endorser, guarantor, or obligor or indebtedness, liabilities, or obligatins to Lender of any third party), absolute or contingent, due or to become due, and all obligations to perform acts or refrain from taking any action. Obligations also include all interest and other charges chargeable to Borrower or due from Borrower to Lender from time to time and all costs and expenses referred to in 13 and 14 hereof.

1.6   *Event of Default* means any event described in 10 hereof.

2.   *Loans and Interest*

2.1   Lender proposes to make loans to Borrower in an aggregate amount of up to ___% of the outstanding amount of Eligible Receivables. All such loans are hereinafter collectively called the "Loans". All Loans will be made from time to time in the absolute discretion of Lender, and neither this Agreement nor any Loans or other action by Lender shall obligate Lender to make further Loans to Borrower. The Loans may be made in excess of the percentage stated above in the sole discretion of Lender. All Loans are payable on demand.

2.2   The Loans shall bear interest at ___% per annum. Accrued interest shall be payable to Lender on the _____ day of each calendar month (Monthly Payment Date) beginning _____, 19__. All interest shall be computed on a 365-day year and paid for the actual number of days elapsed.

2.3   All Obligations shall be payable by Borrower to Lender on demand and bear interest as provided above. Loans may or may not (at Lender's sole and absolute discretion) be evidenced by notes or other instruments issued and made by Borrower to Lender. When Loans are not so evidenced, the Loans shall be evidenced solely by entries in certain books and records designated by Lender.

2.4   All payments of Obligations, including interest, shall be made by Borrower to Lender in immediately available funds at its principal office or at such other place as Lender may designate in writing.

3.   *Grant of Security Interest* To secure payment and performance of all Obligations, Borrower hereby grants Lender a continuing security interest in and assigns Lender (a) all the Collateral and (b) all Borrower's books of account and records, ledger sheets, files, and documents relating to Collateral which shall, until delivered to or removed by Lender, be held by Borrower in trust for the Lender.

4.   *Representations and Warranties* Borrower represents and warrants:

4.1   (a) Borrower is and at all times hereafter shall be a corporation duly organized, validly existing and in good standing under the laws of the State of _____ and has the corporate power and authority to conduct business now conducted and as proposed while this Agreement is in effect; (b) execution and delivery of this Agreement and performance of the transactions contemplated are within the corporate authority of Borrower and have been duly authorized by all proper and necessary corporate action, and will not violate or contravene any provisions of law or the articles of incorporation or bylaws of Borrower, or result in a breach or default in respect of the terms of any other agreement to which Borrower is a party or by which it is bound, which breach or default would result in the creation, imposition, or enforcement of any lien against any Collateral, or would have a material adverse affect on the conduct of Borrower's business as it is now being conducted or proposed or otherwise impair the value of the security interest granted to Lender hereunder; and (c) Borrower is duly qualified as a foreign corporation and in good standing, duly authorized to do business in every jurisdiction where the nature of its properties or business requires the same.

4.2 This Agreement is a legal and binding obligation of Borrower enforceable in accordance with its terms.

4.3 Execution and delivery of this Agreement and performance of the transactions contemplated do not require any approval or consent of any governmental authority, stockholders of Borrower, or of any other person.

4.4 Borrower has delivered to Lender copies of its financial statements as of and for the period ending _____, 19__, prepared by _____. All financial statements are true and correct, in accord with the respective books of account and records of Borrower and have been prepared in accord with generally accepted accounting principles (or IRS requirements) applied consistently with prior periods, and accurately present the financial condition of Borrower and its assets, liabilities, and results of its operations at such date.

4.5 Since the ending date of the financial statements described in 4.4, there has been no change in assets, liabilities, financial condition, or operation of Borrower, other than changes in the ordinary course of business, the effect of which have not, in any way, been materially adverse.

4.6 Except as reflected in financial statements described in 4.4, Borrower, as of the date hereof does not know or have reasonable grounds to know of any basis for assertion against it of any liabilities or obligations of any nature, direct or indirect, accrued, absolute or contingent, including, without limitation, liabilities for taxes of any kind then due or to become due for any period prior to the date hereof or arising out of transactions entered into, or any state of facts existing prior thereto.

4.7 Borrower has filed all federal, state, local, and other tax returns and reports required to be filed and the same are true and correct. Borrower has paid all taxes, assessments, and other governmental charges lawfully levied or imposed other than those presently payable without penalty or interest.

4.8 There is no litigation, proceeding, or investigation pending or, to the knowledge of Borrower, threatened against or relating to Borrower, its properties or business not reflected in the said financial statements.

4.9 Borrower is not in violation or default under any statute, regulation, license, permit, order, or decree of any governmental department of any kind or court, which would have a material adverse effect on business, properties, or condition of Borrower.

4.10 Borrower is not in default under a contract, which default would have a material adverse effect on business, properties, or conditions respecting any of its indebtedness, and no holder of any indebtedness of Borrower has given notice of any asserted default thereunder, and no liquidation or dissolution of Borrower and no receivership, insolvency, bankruptcy, reorganization, or other similar proceedings relative to Borrower or its properties is pending or, to the knowledge of Borrower, is threatened against it.

4.11 Borrower maintains places of business and owns Collateral only at _____ _____ and maintains its books of account and records, including all Receivables, at _____.

4.12 When Collateral becomes subject to Lender's security interest, Borrower is the sole owner, with good and marketable title, of Collateral, free from all liens, encumbrances, and security interests in favor of any person other than Lender, and has full right and power to grant Lender a security interest therein.

4.13 As to each and every Receivable (a) it is a bona fide existing obligation, valid and enforceable against the Debtor for a sum certain for sales of goods shipped or delivered, or goods leased, or services rendered in the ordinary course of business; (b) all supporting documents, instruments, chattel paper, and other evidence of indebtedness, if any, delivered to Lender are complete, correct, valid, and enforceable in accord with their terms, and all signatures and endorsements appearing thereon are genuine, and all signatories and endorsers have full capacity to contract; (c) the Debtor is liable for and will make payment of the amount expressed in such Receivable per its terms; (d) it will be subject to no discount, allowance, or special terms of payment without Lender's prior approval; (e) it is subject to no dispute, defense, or offset, real or claimed; (f) it is not subject to any prohibition or limitation upon assignment; (g) Borrower has full right and power to grant Lender a security interest therein, and the security interest granted in such Receivable to Lender in Section 3 hereof, when perfected, will be a valid first security interest which will inure to Lender's benefit without further action. The warranties set out herein shall be deemed to have been made with respect to each and every Receivable now owned or hereafter acquired by Borrower.

4.14 The foregoing representations and warranties are made by Borrower with the knowledge and intention Lender will rely thereon, and shall survive execution and delivery of this Agreement and the making of all Loans hereunder.

5. *Affirmative Covenants* Until all Obligations have been paid in full, unless Lender shall otherwise consent in writing, Borrower covenants:

5.1 Borrower shall maintain complete and accurate books of account and records pertaining to Collateral and operations of Borrower, and all such books of account and records shall be kept and maintained at _____. Borrower shall not move such books of account and records without giving Lender at least thirty (30) days written notice.

5.2 Borrower shall grant Lender or its representatives full and complete access to all Collateral and all books of account, records, correspondence, and other papers relating to Collateral during normal business hours and the right to inspect, examine, verify, and make abstracts from and copies of all the same and to investigate such other activities and business of Borrower as then deemed necessary or appropriate.

5.3 Borrower shall, upon creation of Receivables, or when Lender may require, deliver to Lender schedules of all outstanding Receivables. Such schedules shall be in form satisfactory to Lender showing the 30-day aging of such Receivables and containing and accompanied by such other information as Lender may prescribe. Borrower shall also deliver to Lender copies of Debtor's invoices, evidences of shipment or delivery and such other schedules and information as Lender may reasonably request. Items to be provided under this Section are to be prepared and delivered to Lender solely for its convenience in maintaining records of Collateral, and Borrower's failure to give any items to Lender shall not affect, terminate, modify, or otherwise limit Lender's security interest.

5.4 Borrower shall deliver to Lender upon Lender's request, and at Borrower's sole expenses, financial statements, including balance sheet and related profit and loss statement, prepared by persons acceptable to Lender, who shall give their unqualified opinion with respect thereto.

5.5 Borrower shall furnish to Lender such other information and reports in form and substance satisfactory to Lender as and when Lender requests.

5.6 Borrower shall, while this Agreement is in effect, and until the Obligations have been paid in full, (a) maintain its corporate existence in good standing, (b) make no change in the nature of its business, and (c) maintain and keep in full force and effect all licenses and permits necessary to the proper conduct of its business.

5.7 Borrower shall maintain and keep all its properties, real and personal, in good working order, condition, and repair, insured against loss or damage from hazards as are customarily insured against in similar circumstances, or as Lender may specify with insurers, in amounts and under policies acceptable to Lender. If Borrower fails to do so, Lender may (but is not required to) obtain such insurance and charge the cost to Borrower's account and add it to the Obligations. Borrower agrees if any loss should occur, the proceeds of all insurance policies may be applied to payment of the Obligations, as Lender may direct. Borrower shall deliver to Lender the original (or certified) copy of each policy of insurance and evidence of payment of all premiums therefor. Such policies of insurance shall contain an endorsement acceptable to Lender, showing loss payable to Lender, and providing insuror shall give Lender at least 10 days written notice of alteration or cancellation and that no act of default of Borrower or any other person shall affect the right of Lender to recover under such policy. Borrower hereby directs all insurors to pay all proceeds thereunder directly to Lender. Borrower irrevocably makes, constitutes, and appoints Lender (and all persons designated by Lender) as Borrower's true and lawful attorney and agent-in-fact for purpose of making, settling, and adjusting all claims under policies of insurance, endorsing Borrower's name on any instrument of payment for proceeds of such insurance and for making all determinations and decisions with respect to such insurance.

5.8 Borrower shall pay all taxes, assessments, and governmental charges lawfully levied or imposed on or against it and its properties when due, unless Borrower shall contest the validity thereof and in good faith posts any security required by applicable law or by Lender for payment thereof.

5.9 Borrower shall deposit when due all payroll and other taxes as Lender may require, and comply with all requirements of law and Lender with respect thereto.

5.10 Borrower shall, at Lender's request, qualify as a foreign corporation and obtain all requisite licenses and permits in each state where Borrower does business.

5.11 Borrower shall take the steps to file and perfect, at its expense, any lien available to Borrower under laws of the applicable jurisdiction if any Receivable is not paid within 60 days of due date.

5.12 Borrower shall, upon learning thereof, report to Lender any reclamation, return, or repossession of goods, claim, or dispute asserted by any Debtor or other obligor, and any other matters affecting value, enforceability, or collectibility of any Collateral. Borrower shall, at its sole cost and expense (including attorney's fees), settle any and all claims and disputes and indemnify and protect Lender against any liability, loss, or expense arising therefrom; however, if Lender elects, Lender shall have the right to settle, compromise, adjust, or litigate all claims or disputes directly with the Debtor or other obligor and charge all costs and expenses thereof (including attorney's fees) to Borrower's account and add them to the Obligations.

5.13 Borrower shall defend Collateral against all claims and demands of all persons at any time claiming the same or any interest therein and pay all costs and expenses (including attorney's fees) incurred in connection with such defense.

5.14 Borrower shall, at Lender's request, execute and deliver such financing statements, documents, and instruments, and perform other acts as Lender deems necessary or desirable, to perfect fully its security interest in Collateral, and pay, upon demand, all expenses (including attorney fees, filing fees, and taxes) incurred by Lender in connection therewith.

6. *Negative Covenants* Until all Obligations have been paid in full, unless Lender shall otherwise consent in writing, Borrower covenants:

6.1   Borrower shall not discontinue its business, sell a material part of its assets, or liquidate, sell, transfer, assign, or otherwise dispose of any of Collateral; however, it may sell in the ordinary course of business and for full consideration any goods or service produced, marketed, or furnished by it.

6.2   Borrower shall not sell, assign, pledge, or grant a security interest in any Collateral to any person other than Lender, or permit any lien, encumbrance, or security interest to attach to any Collateral, except in favor of Lender.

6.3   Borrower shall not endorse, guarantee, or become surety for obligations of any person, firm, or corporation, except Borrower may endorse checks and negotiable instruments for collection or deposit in the ordinary course of business.

6.4   Borrower shall not make loans to or repay existing loans to its officers, directors, or stockholders.

6.5   Borrower shall not declare or pay dividends or make other payments on capital stock, or issue, redeem, repurchase, or retire any capital stock, or grant or issue any warrant, right, or option pertaining thereto or other security convertible into any of the foregoing, or make any distribution to stockholders.

6.6   Borrower shall not compromise or discount any Receivable except for ordinary trade discounts or allowances for prompt payment.

6.7   Borrower shall not consolidate, merge with, or acquire or purchase any equity or interest in any other entity, or acquire or purchase any assets or obligations of any other entity the value of which exceeds 10% of Borrower's Eligible Receivables, except Borrower is permitted to own notes and other receivables acquired in the ordinary course of business.

6.8   Borrower shall not change its name, do business under an assumed or trade name, or move any Collateral to a location not shown in Section 4.11 without giving Lender at least 30 days prior written notice thereof and executing and delivering to Lender financing statements satisfactory to and requested by Lender.

7.   *Collection of Collateral and Notice of Assignment*

7.1   Lender authorizes and permits Borrower to receive all amounts due on Collateral, from the Debtors or otherwise, subject to direction and control of Lender at all times. Lender may, without notice, terminate this authority and permission at any time. All collections on Collateral shall be Lender's property, to be held in trust by Borrower for the sole benefit of Lender, and not to be commingled with Borrower's other funds or deposited in any bank account of Borrower, or used in any manner except to pay Obligations. Borrower shall deliver to Lender on the date of receipt thereof, duly endorsed to Lender or to bearer, or assigned to Lender, all instruments and forms of payment (other cash) or evidences of indebtedness received by Borrower in total or partial payment of the amount due on Collateral.

7.2   Lender shall in no way be liable for any error, omission, or delay of any kind occurring in the settlement, collection, or payment of any Receivables or any instrument received in payment thereof or for any damage resulting therefrom. Lender may, without notice or consent, sue upon or otherwise collect, extend the time of payment, or compromise or settle upon any terms, any of the Receivables or any securities, instruments, or insurance applicable thereto and/or release the obligor thereon. Lender is authorized to accept the return of goods represented by any Receivables, without notice or consent and the same shall not discharge or affect Obligations hereunder.

7.3   Upon receipt of returned or rejected goods, Borrower shall issue and deliver a credit memo to Lender. Lender may require Borrower to set aside such goods in Lender's name and hold them in trust for Lender at Borrower's expense and, upon request, pay Lender the sales price thereof. If Lender so requests and Borrower fails to forthwith do so, Lender may take possession of such goods and sell or cause the goods to be sold, at public or private sale, at such prices, to such purchasers, and upon such terms as Lender deems advisable. Borrower shall remain liable to Lender for any deficiency and shall pay costs and expenses of such sale, including reasonable attorney's fees.

7.4 Lender may at any time notify Debtors of its security interest in Receivables and require payments to be made directly to Lender. to facilitate direct collection, Borrower hereby appoints Lender and any officer or employee of Lender, as Lender may designate, as attorney-in-fact for Borrower to (a) receive, open, and dispose of all mail addressed to Borrower and take therefrom any payments on or proceeds of Receivables; (b) take over Borrower's post office boxes or make other arrangements, in which Borrower shall cooperate, to receive Borrower's mail, including notifying the post office authorities to change the address for delivery of mail addressed to Borrower to such address as Lender shall designate; (c) endorse the name of Borrower in favor of Lender upon all instruments of payment or Collateral that may come into Lender's possession; (d) sign and endorse the name of Borrower on any invoice or bill of lading relating to any of Receivables, on verifications of Receivables sent to any Debtor, to drafts against Debtors, to assignments of Receivables and to notices to Debtors; and (e) do all acts and things necessary to carry out this Agreement, including signing the name of Borrower on any instruments required by law in connection with the transactions contemplated hereby and on financing statements as permitted by the UCC. Borrower ratifies and approves all acts of such attorneys-in-fact, and no attorney-in-fact shall be liable for any acts of commission or omission, or for error of judgment or mistake of fact or law. This power, being coupled with an interest, is irrevocable so long as any Obligations remain unsatisfied.

7.5 Lender is not liable for or prejudiced by loss, depreciation, or other damage to Receivables or other Collateral unless caused by Lender's willful and malicious act, and Lender shall have no duty to take any action to preserve or collect any Receivable or other Collateral.

7.6 If any warranty is breached as to any Receivable, or if any Receivable is not paid by the Debtor within ____ days from the initial invoice date, or if any Debtor disputes liability or claims any defense or offset, or if a petition in bankruptcy or other application for relief under the Bankruptcy Act or other insolvency proceeding is filed by or with respect to any Debtor, or if any Debtor makes an assignment for benefit of creditors, becomes insolvent, or suspends or goes out of business, or if for any other reason, in Lender's sole discretion, any Receivable owing by any Debtor becomes unacceptable to Lender, then Lender may declare ineligible any and all Receivables owing by the Debtor, and Borrower shall pay the Lender, upon demand, the full amount owing on such Receivables. The Lender may, however, elect to charge such amount against Borrower's account and add it to the Obligations.

8. *Monthly Statements* Lender shall render to Borrower a monthly statement of Borrower's account showing all debts and credits, which statement shall be deemed correct and accepted by and conclusively binding upon Borrower unless Borrower notifies Lender in writing specifically as to discrepancies within 10 days from mailing. All amounts received by Lender in payment of Receivables shall, after a period of ____ days for collection, be credited either to payment of any of Borrower's Obligations to Lender or to Borrower's account, at Lender's election.

9. *Conditions for Closing* Prior to the closing of the first Loan hereunder, Borrower shall deliver to Lender the opinion of its counsel in form and substance prescribed by and satisfactory to

Lender's counsel, and all other documents, receipts, certificates, and instruments as Lender's counsel requests.

10. *Events of Default and Remedies*

10.1 The following constitute Events of Default: (a) failure of Borrower to pay when due any Obligations; (b) failure of Borrower to observe or perform any covenant or negative covenant in this Agreement or otherwise between Borrower and Lender; (c) discovery that a representation or warranty made by Borrower to Lender pursuant to this Agreement or any other agreement was materially false when made; (d) acceleration of maturity of any obligations or liabilities of Borrower to other persons; (e) misrepresentation by the Borrower, orally or in writing, to Lender for the purpose of obtaining credit or an extension of credit; (f) failure of Borrower, after request by Lender, to furnish financial information or permit inspection of Collateral or of books of account and records; (g) suspension by Borrower of operation of its present business, insolvency of Borrower, inability of Borrower to meet its debts as they mature, its admission in writing to such effect, calling any meeting of any creditors, committing any act of bankruptcy, the filing by or against the Borrower of any petition under any provision of the Bankruptcy Code, or the entry of any judgment or filing or any lien against the Borrower, (h) change in Borrower's condition or affairs or in that of any endorser, guarantor, or surety for any of the Obligations that, in Lender's opinion, impairs the value of its security interest in Collateral or increases its risks.

10.2 Upon occurrence of an Event of Default, Lender at its option may (a) terminate this Agreement and declare all Obligations of Borrower immediately due and payable and exercise all its rights and remedies against Borrower and Collateral, and (b) exercise all rights granted to a secured paty under the UCC or otherwise or granted to Lender herein. Lender shall have the right to require Borrower to assemble Collateral and make Collateral available at a location or locations designed by Lender. Lender may foreclose its lien and security interest in Collateral in any lawful way. Lender may enter Borrower's premises without legal process and without incurring a liability to Borrower and remove Collateral to such place or places as Lender deems advisable, or Lender may require Borrower to make Collateral available to Lender at a convenient place and, with or without having the Collateral at the time or place of sale, Lender may sell or otherwise dispose of all or any part of Collateral at public or private sale or at any broker's board, in lots or in bulk, for cash or credit, at any time or place, in one or more sales, and upon such terms and conditions as Lender may elect, and Lender may be the purchaser.

10.3 Lender shall have the right to apply the proceeds of any disposition of Collateral to payment of Obligations in such order of applications as Lender may at its option elect. Any deficiency will be paid to Lender upon demand, and any surplus will be paid to Borrower if Borrower is not indebted to Lender under any other Obligation.

10.4 Rights, options, and remedies of Lender are cumulative and no failure or delay by Lender in exercising any right, option, or remedy shall be deemed a waiver of any Event of Default hereunder. To the extent any of Borrower's Obligations to Lender are now or hereafter secured by property other than Collateral or by the guaranty, endorsement, or property of any other person, firm, corporation, or other entity, then Lender shall have the right to proceed against such other property, guaranty, or endorsement upon default in payment of any Obligation or in any of the terms, covenants, or conditions contained herein, and Lender shall have the right to determine which rights, security, liens, security interests, or remedies Lender shall pursue, relinquish, subordinate, modify, or take any other action with respect thereto, without in any way modifying or affecting any of them or any Lender's rights hereunder.

10.5 Borrower hereby waives any right it may have under existing or future law to notice of foreclosure or any other act described herein, to any hearing relating to foreclosure or any other such acts, and to notice that may be required from Lender prior to such hearing. Borrower expressly releases Lender and its agents from any and all liability relating to such foreclosure and any other acts described herein.

11. *Jurisdiction, Venue, and Waiver* The forum having jurisdiction and venue to adjudicate any claim, dispute, or default arising from execution and delivery of this Agreement and performance of transactions contemplated hereby shall be any chosen by the Lender in the jurisdiction where this Agreement is made. Borrower expressly submits and consents to such jurisdiction and venue and specifically waives any and all rights to contest jurisdiction or venue. Borrower waives trial by jury in any litigation between Lender and Borrower.

12. *Waivers* Borrower and each endorser, guarantor, and surety for any Obligations hereby waives notice of nonpayment, demand, presentment, protest, and notice of protest with respect to any Obligations, any Receivables or other Collateral, and notice of acceptance hereof, notice of Loans made, credit extended, Collateral received or delivered, and any other action taken in reliance hereon, and all other demands and notices of any description.

13. *Collection Costs* All costs and expenses incurred in connection with collection of any Receivables, or incurred in obtaining or enforcing payment of any Obligations or foreclosing Lender's security interest in any of Collateral, or in enforcing or protecting Lender's rights and interests under this Agreement or otherwise between Borrower and Lender or in protecting the rights of any holder or holders with respect thereto, or in defending or prosecuting any actions or proceedings arising out of or relating to Lender's transactions with Borrower, including attorney's fees, shall be paid by Borrower to Lender, upon demand, or, at Lender's election, charged to Borrower's account and added to Obligations, and Lender may take judgment against Borrower for all such costs, expense, and fees in addition to all other amounts due from Borrower.

14. *Expenses* Borrower shall reimburse Lender for all costs and expenses of Lender in connection with preparation of this Agreement and any amendment or supplement hereto and the making of Loans hereunder, including attorney fees, and for all filing, recording, and other costs connected with perfection of Lender's security interest.

15. *Miscellaneous*

15.1 *Notices.* All notices and other communications shall be in writing and deemed to have been given when delivered personally or sent by registered or certified mail, addressed to Borrower or Lender, at their respective addresses set forth at the beginning of this Agreement. Notices of changes of address shall be given in the same manner.

15.2 *Termination.* This Agreement shall continue in full force and effect until one year from the date hereof and from year to year thereafter unless either paty gives the other 30 days written notice of termination. Termination shall not affect the rights of either party or Obligations of Borrower and the provisions hereof shall be fully operative until all transactions have been fully disposed of and all Obligations liquidated. Security interests granted to Lender shall continue in full force and effect, notwithstanding termination until all of Obligations of Borrower have been paid in full or Borrower has furnished Lender with satisfactory indemnity. All representations, warranties, covenants, waivers, and agreements shall survive termination unless otherwise provided.

15.3 *Entire Agreement.* This Agreement constitutes the entire agreement of the parties, and no provision, including the provisions of this Section, may be modified, deleted, or amended in any manner except by agreement in writing executed by the parties. All terms are binding upon, inure to the benefit of, and are enforceable by the parties hereto and their respective successors and assigns, provided, however, Borrower shall not assign or transfer rights without Lender's prior written consent.

15.4 *Construction.* This Agreement shall be deemed to be a contract made under seal and is executed and delivered in _____, _____, and shall be construed and enforced in accordance with the laws of the _____ of _____ without regard to its rule with respect to choice the law. All references in this Agreement to the single number and neuter gender shall be deemed to mean and include the plural number and all genders, and vice versa, unless the context shall otherwise require.

15.5 *Headings.* The italicized headings contained herein are for convenience only and shall not affect the interpretation of this Agreement.

15.6 *Counterparts.* This Agreement may be executed in more than one counterpart, each of which shall be deemed an original.

IN WITNESS WHEREOF, the parties have caused this Agreement to be duly executed and delivered and their signatures affixed and attested by proper and duly authorized officers, as of the date first above written.

(Corporate Seal)
Attest—

_____

by _____
Title _____

by _____
Title _____

(Corporate Seal)
Attest—

Lender:

by _____
Title _____

by _____
Title _____

DEED OF TRUST

THIS DEED OF TRUST is made this _____ day of _____, 19____, by and between
_____, party(ies) of the first part (Borrower), and
_____ of _____, _____ Trustee(s), party(ies)
of the second part, and _____ , Noteholder(s).

WITNESSETH:

That the Borrower, for and in consideration of the sum of Ten Dollars ($10.00), cash in hand, paid receipt of which is hereby acknwoledged, does hereby grant, bargain, sell, and convey, with General Warranty of Title, unto the Trustees, in trust, for the purposes and with the power and authority as hereinafter set forth, the following described property.

Legal description:

having address of _____ .

TOGETHER with all improvements now or hereafter erected on the property, and all easements, rights, appurtenances, rents (subject however to the rights and authorities given herein to Lender to collect and apply such rent), royalties, mineral, oil and gas rights and profits, water, water rights and water stock, and all fixtures now or hereafter attached to the property, all of which, including replacements and additions thereto, shall be deemed to be and remain a part of the property covered by this Deed of Trust; and all of the foregoing, together with said property (or the leasehold estate if this Deed of Trust is on a leasehold) are herein referred to as the "Property."

IN TRUST to secure to the Lender the prompt repayment of the indebtedness evidenced by Borrower's Note dated _____, 19____, in the principal sum of _____ dollars ($_____) payable with interest at _____ percent (____%) per annum on terms as therein set forth, due and payable in full on or before _____, 19____.

This Deed of Trust is made under and subject to the laws of the State of _____ as follows: Insurance required $_____, exemptions waived; subject to all upon default; renewal or extension permitted; any Trustee may act; substitution of Trustees permitted.

Should there be a failure to keep and perform the aforesaid covenants, or any of them, or a failure to pay the indebtedness hereby secured, principal or interest, in accordance with the terms and provisions of the laws relating to trusts, then the indebtedness hereby secured, both principal and interest, shall immediately become due and payable, and upon the request of the beneficiary hereunder, the parties of the second part shall proceed to sell the land hereby conveyed, at public auction, at such places that they may deem most advantageous, after having advertised the time, place, and terms of sale by weekly publication, for ____ successive weeks, in some newspaper published or having general circulation in said County or City, the terms of sale to be cash, and out of the proceeds of sale they shall apply the same, first, to discharge the expenses of executing the trust, including a commission to the trustees of five percentum of the gross proceeds of sale and 2 1/2% in case of advertisement without sale; secondly, to discharge all taxes, levies, and assessments, with costs and interest, including the due pro rata thereof for the current year; thirdly, to discharge in the order of their priority, if any, the remaining debts and obligations secured by this

Deed of Trust (*continued*)

Deed of Trust, and any liens of record inferior to this Deed of Trust under which sale is made, with lawful interest; and, fourthly, the residue of the proceeds shall be paid to the party of the first part, their heirs or assigns.

In the event the lien of this Deed of Trust is subordinate to a prior Deed of Trust on the herein described property, Borrower covenants and agrees that all payments, terms, and conditions required by said prior Deed of Trust shall be made and complied with; that upon default under any terms thereof, Lender, at its option, can cure said default, any payments being made by Lender becoming additional indebtedness of Borrower secured hereby, and any such default under this Deed of Trust entitling Lender to declare a default and the Trustees to proceed as provided herein.

Upon failure of Borrower to timely pay any taxes on the herein described propety or which become a lien superior hereto, or timely pay for hazard insurance for the improvements thereon, or pay any applicable condominium or homeowner fees which if unpaid would entitle any association to obtain a lien superior to this Deed of Trust, Lender may, at its option, make such payments and such sums shall become additional indebtedness of Borrower secured hereby.

Any forebearance by Lender in exercising any right or remedy hereunder, or otherwise afforded by applicable law, shall not be a waiver of or preclude exercise of any such right or remedy. Payment of taxes, insurance premiums, or other obligations of Borrower as herein permitted shall not be a waiver of any other right of Lender.

This Deed of Trust is not assumable without the written consent of the Lender. Any sale, transfer, or conveyance of the propety described herein shall cause acceleration of the note secured by this trust, and constitute a default hereunder.

The covenants and agreements herein contained shall bind, and the rights hereunder inure to the respective successors and assigns of the parties. All rights and obligations herein and hereunder are joint and several.

This Deed of Trust is also subject to the following additional terms:

_____

_____

_____

_____

WITNESS the following signature and seal:

_____(Seal)
(Borrower)

_____(Seal)
(Borrower)

State of _____

_____of _____, to wit

The foregoing Deed of Trust was subscribed, sworn to and acknowledged before me by _____on _____, 19____.

_____

Notary Public

(Notary Seal)

My commission expires _____

FINANCING STATEMENT (UCC)

This financing statement is presented to a filing officer pursuant to the Uniform Commercial Code (UCC) as adopted in the jurisdiction of filing:
This space used for filing officer. Date, time, number of filing office:

_____

_____

Type: Original __ Continuation __ Amendment __ Assignment __ Termination __

1. Name(s) of Debtor(s) _____

2. Address(es) of Debtor(s) _____

    _____

3. Name of Secured Party _____

4. Address of Secured Party _____

    _____

5. This financing statement covers the following items of property:

    _____

    _____

6. Proceeds of collateral __ (are/are not) also covered.

7. This financing statement secures a debt instrument described as:
    Dated _____, _____   Titled _____
    Face Amount $_____.__ Maturity Date _____, _____
    Other related charges, additional terms of default, and other terms are included in such debt instrument and documents referenced therein.

8. Real estate affected _____

9. Other data _____

    _____

Debtors:
_____(Seal)   Date _____, 19____

_____(Seal)   Date _____, 19____

RECEIPT FOR COLLATERAL

Referencing and in connection with both that certain Note made by
_____ ("Borrower") on date of _____, 19____, in favor of
_____ ("Noteholder"), and the related Security Agreement dated
_____, 19__, also made by Borrower in favor of Noteholder, this Receipt for Collateral is hereby
made by Noteholder to record delivery to Noteholder in accord with Borrower's obligations thereunder to Noteholder of the following described Collateral:

All of which Collateral is and remains subject to the lien of the aforesaid Security Agreement and
may be disposed of by Noteholder toward Borrower's obligations under the said Note and Security
Agreement according to their terms and as allowed by law.

Notwithstanding Noteholder's possession of the Collateral, Borrower shall pay all costs and expenses relating to such collateral, including, but not limited, to maintenance, storage, insurance,
taxation, and the like to assure retention of value as provided in the Security Agreement.

This Receipt does not constitute any assurance or acknowledgement of physical condition or
value of the collateral upon possession by Noteholder.

All of Noteholder's rights are cumulatively reserved.

Date _____

_____
Noteholder

COLLATERAL SUBSTITUTION AGREEMENT

_____

ACCOUNT NUMBER

It is understood and agreed by and between_____
(Purchaser/Borrower)

and _____ that the following described property:
(Bank)

New or Used	Year	Make	No. Cyl.	Type of Body	Identification or Motor Number

☐ Automatic Transmission   ☐ 4 Speed Transmission   ☐ Power Steering   ☐ Air Conditioning

Other Collateral_____

_____

is hereby substituted in the place of the property described and covered in and under that certain instalment sale/security agreement

dated _____, 19 ____ between _____
(Purchaser/Borrower)

and _____ and, if applicable, assigned to
(Dealer/Bank)

_____ in the original amount of $_____,
(Bank)

and is subject to the same terms, covenants, conditions and provisions thereof, and all of which shall continue in full force and effect as

therein provided.

Signed by the parties hereto this _____day of _____, 19 ____ .

_____ (Seal)
(Purchaser/Borrower)

_____ (Seal)
(Purchaser/Borrower)

_____
(Bank)

By_____
(Name)   (Title)

The substitution of property is satisfactory to me (us) as assignor of the above mentioned instalment sale agreement and I (we) consent to same, understanding that such substitution in no way alters my (our) obligations under the instalment sale.

_____ (Seal)
(Dealer)

WAREHOUSING AGREEMENT

THIS AGREEMENT, Made and entered into this _____ day of _____ , 19____ , by and between _____
(Company, City, State)
hereinafter referred to as "DEPOSITOR," and _____
hereinafter referred to as "WAREHOUSEMAN."

WITNESSETH

WHEREAS, DEPOSITOR is desirous of obtaining and utilizing certain warehouse facilities and services in the _____ area; and

WHEREAS, WAREHOUSEMAN has certain warehousing facilities and services of the type and kind desired by DEPOSITOR located at _____ ; and

WHEREAS, WAREHOUSEMAN desires to make said facilities and services commercially available to DEPOSITOR subject to the terms and conditions herein specified;

NOW, THEREFORE, for and in consideration of the mutual agreements, covenants and promises herein contained, it is hereby mutually agreed, covenanted and promised as follows:

ARTICLE I. TERM OF AGREEMENT

The term of this Agreement shall commence on the date of its execution by the parties thereto and shall continue thereafter in full force and effect for a period of _____ and shall thereafter automatically renew on a month-to-month basis subject only to either party's right to terminate at any time by serving not less than thirty (30) days prior written notice to that effect upon the other party, said notice to be effective upon receipt. This Agreement shall be deemed cancelled if DEPOSITOR does not store goods with WAREHOUSE-MAN for any period exceeding one hundred and eighty (180) days.

ARTICLE II. ACCEPTANCE OF GOODS, RATES AND CHARGES

During the term of this Agreement, and any extensions or renewals thereof, WAREHOUSEMAN agrees to provide for DEPOSITOR certain warehousing facilities and services described in this Agreement and the attached Schedules "A" and "B" which are made a part hereof, and to accept and keep in a neat and orderly condition such goods described in Schedule "A" as from time to time may be tendered by DEPOSITOR. WARE-HOUSEMAN further agrees to furnish sufficient personnel, equipment, and other accessories necessary to perform efficiently and with safety the services herein described. Rates and charges for public warehousing services are set forth in Schedule "A" and for extra services and conditions in Schedule "B". For any services not specified in Schedule "A" or Schedule "B", DEPOSITOR shall pay to WAREHOUSEMAN such consideration and compensation as may mutually be agreed upon. Consideration for WAREHOUSEMAN'S performance of this Agreement shall be paid to WAREHOUSEMAN by DEPOSITOR within _____ days after receipt by DE-POSITOR of WAREHOUSEMAN'S statement.

ARTICLE III. SHIPPING

DEPOSITOR agrees not to ship goods to WAREHOUSEMAN as the named consignee. If, in violation of this Agreement, goods are shipped to WAREHOUSEMAN as named consignee, DEPOSITOR agrees to notify carrier in writing prior to such shipment, with a copy of such notice to WAREHOUSEMAN, that WAREHOUSE-MAN named as consignee is a warehouseman under law and has no beneficial title or interest in such property. DEPOSITOR further agrees to indemnify and hold harmless WAREHOUSEMAN from any and all claims for unpaid transportation charges, including undercharges, demurrage, detention, or charges of any nature, in connection with goods so shipped.

ARTICLE IV. TENDER FOR STORAGE

All goods tendered for storage shall be delivered at the warehouse in a segregated manner, properly marked and packaged for handling. DEPOSITOR shall furnish or cause to be furnished at or prior to such delivery, a manifest showing the goods to be kept and accounted for separately, and the class or type of storage and other services desired.

ARTICLE V. STORAGE PERIOD AND CHARGES

(A) Storage charges become applicable upon the date that WAREHOUSEMAN accepts care, custody and control of the goods, regardless of unloading date or date of issue of warehouse receipt.

(B) Unless otherwise stated in Schedule "A" hereof, storage rates and charges shall be computed and are due and payable as follows:

1. Goods received on or after the first (1st) day of the month up to and including the fifteenth (15th) day of the month shall be assessed the full monthly storage charge;

2. Goods received after the fifteenth (15th) day of the month up to and including the last day of the month shall be assessed one-half (½) of the full monthly storage charge; and

3. A full month's storage charge will apply to all goods in storage on the first day of the next and succeeding calendar months. All storage charges are due and payable on the first day of storage for the initial month and thereafter on the first day of the calendar month.

ARTICLE VI. TRANSFER, TERMINATION OF STORAGE, REMOVAL OF GOODS

(A) Instructions to transfer goods on the books of WAREHOUSEMAN shall not be effective until said instructions are delivered to and accepted by WAREHOUSEMAN, and all charges up to the time transfer is made shall be chargeable to DEPOSITOR. If a transfer involves the rehandling of goods, it will be subject to rates and charges shown in the attached Schedule "A" or Schedule "B" or as otherwise mutually agreed upon. When goods in storage are transferred from one party to another through issuance of a new warehouse receipt, a new storage date is established on the date of such transfer.

(B) WAREHOUSEMAN may, without notice, move goods within the warehouse in which they are stored; but shall not, except as provided in VI (C), move goods to another location without prior consent of DEPOSITOR.

(C) If, as a result of a quality or condition of the goods of which WAREHOUSEMAN had no notice at the time of deposit, the goods are a hazard to other property or to the warehouse or to persons, WAREHOUSEMAN shall immediately notify DEPOSITOR and DEPOSITOR shall thereupon claim its interest in the said goods and remove them from the warehouse. Pending such disposition, the WAREHOUSEMAN may remove the goods from the warehouse and shall incur no liability by reason of such removal.

ARTICLE VII. HANDLING

(A) Handling rates and charges as shown in the attached Schedules shall, unless otherwise agreed, cover the ordinary labor involved in receiving goods at warehouse door or dock, placing goods in storage, and returning goods to warehouse door or dock. Additional expenses incurred by the warehouseman in loading or unloading cars or vehicles shall be at rates shown in attached Schedules or as otherwise mutually agreed upon.

(B) WAREHOUSEMAN shall not be liable for demurrage, detention or delays in unloading inbound cars or vehicles, or detention or delays in obtaining and loading cars or vehicles for outbound shipment unless WAREHOUSEMAN has failed to exercise reasonable care and judgment as determined by industry practice.

(C) If detention occurs for which WAREHOUSEMAN is liable under Paragraph (B) of this Article, payment of such detention shall be made by DEPOSITOR to the carrier and WAREHOUSEMAN shall reimburse DEPOSITOR for such payment. WAREHOUSEMAN shall keep records concerning the detention of vehicles to assist DEPOSITOR in processing any objection to carrier's imposition of detention charges.

(D) DEPOSITOR shall be responsible for payment of all demurrage charges resulting from receipt by WAREHOUSEMAN of more than _____ carloads of DEPOSITOR'S goods received in any regular working day.

ARTICLE VIII. DELIVERY REQUIREMENTS

(A) No goods shall be delivered or transferred except upon receipt by WAREHOUSEMAN of complete instructions properly signed by DEPOSITOR. However, when no negotiable receipt is outstanding, goods may be delivered or transferred upon instructions received by telephone, TWX, Dataphone or other agreed upon method of communication, but WAREHOUSEMAN shall not be responsible for loss or error occasioned thereby except as caused by WAREHOUSEMAN'S negligence.

(B) When goods are ordered out, a reasonable time shall be given WAREHOUSEMAN to carry out instructions, and if he is unable to because of acts of God, war, public enemies, seizure under legal process, strikes, lockout, riots and civil commotions, or any other reason beyond WAREHOUSEMAN'S reasonable control, or because of loss or destruction of goods for which WAREHOUSEMAN is not liable, or because of any other excuse provided by law, WAREHOUSEMAN shall not be liable for failure to carry out such instructions provided, however, that goods remaining in storage will continue to be subject to regular storage charges as provided for herein.

ARTICLE IX. EXTRA AND SPECIAL SERVICES

(A) Warehouse labor required for services other than ordinary handling and storage must be authorized by DEPOSITOR in advance. Rates and charges will be provided for herein or as mutually agreed by the parties hereto.

(B) Special services requested by DEPOSITOR will be subject to such charges as are provided herein or as mutually agreed upon in advance.

(C) Dunnage, bracing, packing materials or other special supplies used in cars or vehicles are chargeable to DEPOSITOR and may be provided at a mutually agreed upon charge in addition to WAREHOUSEMAN'S cost.

(D) By prior arrangement, goods may be received or delivered during other than usual business hours, subject to a reasonable charge.

(E) Communication expense including postage, teletype, telegram or telephone will be charged to DEPOSITOR if such expense is the result of more than normal inventory reporting or if, at the request of DEPOSITOR, communications are made by other than regular First Class United States Mail.

ARTICLE X. BONDED STORAGE

(A) A charge in addition to regular rates will be made for merchandise in bond.

(B) Where a warehouse receipt covers goods in U.S. Customs bond, such receipt shall be void upon the termination of the storage period fixed by law.

ARTICLE XI. INBOUND SHIPMENTS

(A) WAREHOUSEMAN shall immediately notify DEPOSITOR of any known discrepancy on inbound shipments and shall protect DEPOSITOR'S interest by placing an appropriate notation on the delivering carrier's shipping document.

(B) WAREHOUSEMAN may refuse to accept any goods that, because of infestation, contamination or damage, might cause infestation, contamination or damage to WAREHOUSEMAN'S premises or to other goods in the custody of WAREHOUSEMAN and shall immediately notify DEPOSITOR of such refusal and shall have no liability for any demurrage, detention, transportation or other charges by virtue of such refusal.

(C) All notices required under paragraphs A or B of this Article shall be directed to the attention of _____

ARTICLE XII. LIABILITY AND LIMITATION OF DAMAGES

(A) WAREHOUSEMAN shall be liable for loss of or injury to all goods while under his care, custody and control when caused by his failure to exercise such care in regard to them as a reasonably careful man would exercise under like circumstances. He shall not be liable for damages which could not have been avoided by the exercise of such care.

(B) In consideration of the rates herein, DEPOSITOR declares that said damages will be limited to _____

ARTICLE XIII. LEGAL LIABILITY INSURANCE

WAREHOUSEMAN shall maintain at its sole expense and at all times during the life of this Agreement a policy or policies of legal liability insurance covering any loss, destruction or damage for which WAREHOUSEMAN has assumed responsibility under the terms of Article XII. WAREHOUSEMAN further agrees to provide satisfactory evidence of such insurance upon request by DEPOSITOR.

ARTICLE XIV. NOTICE OF LOSS AND DAMAGE, CLAIM AND FILING OF SUIT

(A) WAREHOUSEMAN agrees to notify DEPOSITOR promptly of any loss or damage, howsoever caused, to goods stored or handled under the terms of this Agreement. All such notices shall be directed to the

attention of _____

_____

_____

(B) Claims by DEPOSITOR must be presented in writing to WAREHOUSEMAN not longer than either sixty (60) days after delivery of the goods by WAREHOUSEMAN or sixty (60) days after DEPOSITOR is notified by WAREHOUSEMAN that loss or injury to part or all of the goods has occurred, whichever time is shorter.

(C) No action may be maintained by DEPOSITOR against WAREHOUSEMAN for loss or injury to the goods stored unless timely written claim has been given as provided in paragraph (B) of this Article and unless such action is commenced either within nine (9) months after the date of delivery by WAREHOUSEMAN or within nine (9) months after DEPOSITOR is notified that loss or injury to part or all of the goods has occurred, whichever time is shorter.

(D) When goods have not been delivered, notice may be given of known loss or injury to the goods by the mailing of a registered or certified letter to DEPOSITOR. All such notices shall be directed to the at-

tention of _____

_____

Time limitations for presentation of claim in writing and maintaining of action after notice begin on the date of receipt of such notice by DEPOSITOR.

ARTICLE XV. RECORDS

DEPOSITOR reserves the right upon reasonable request to enter WAREHOUSEMAN'S premises during normal working hours to examine and count all or any of the goods stored under the terms of this Agreement. WAREHOUSEMAN shall at all reasonable times permit DEPOSITOR to examine its books, records and accounts for the purpose of reconciling quantities and determining with WAREHOUSEMAN whether certain amounts are payable within the meaning of the Agreement.

ARTICLE XVI. INDEPENDENT CONTRACTOR

It is hereby agreed and understood that WAREHOUSEMAN is entering into this Agreement as an independent contractor and that all of WAREHOUSEMAN'S personnel engaged in work to be done under the terms of this Agreement are to be considered as employees of WAREHOUSEMAN and under no circumstances shall they be construed or considered to be employees of DEPOSITOR.

ARTICLE XVII. COMPLIANCE WITH LAWS, ORDINANCES, RULES AND REGULATIONS

(A) WAREHOUSEMAN shall comply with all laws, ordinances, rules and regulations of Federal, State, municipal and other governmental authorities and the like in connection with the safeguarding, receiving, storing and handling of goods.

(B) DEPOSITOR shall be responsible for advising WAREHOUSEMAN of all laws, ordinances, rules and regulations of Federal, State, municipal and other governmental authorities and the like relating specifically to the safeguarding, receiving, storing and handling of DEPOSITOR'S products.

ARTICLE XVIII. NOTIFICATION OF PRODUCT CHARACTERISTICS

DEPOSITOR shall notify WAREHOUSEMAN of the characteristics of any of DEPOSITOR'S products that may in any way be likely to cause damage to WAREHOUSEMAN'S premises or to other products that may be stored by WAREHOUSEMAN.

ARTICLE XIX. ASSIGNMENT

This Warehousing Agreement shall inure to the benefit of and be binding upon the successors and assigns of the parties hereto, provided neither party to this Agreement shall assign or sublet its interest or obligations herein, including but not limited to the assignment of any monies due and payable, without the prior written consent of the other party.

Warehousing Agreement (*continued*)

ARTICLE XX. APPLICABLE STATUTES

The parties understand and agree that the provisions of Article 7 of the Uniform Commercial Code as enacted by the State law governing this Warehousing Agreement shall apply to this Warehousing Agreement. (In the State of Louisiana the provisions of the Uniform Warehouse Receipts Act shall apply.)

ARTICLE XXI. ADDITIONAL TERMS AND CONDITIONS

(Nothing entered hereon shall be construed to extend WAREHOUSEMAN'S liability beyond the standard of care specified in Article XII (A) above.)

ARTICLE XXII.

This Agreement constitutes the entire understanding between DEPOSITOR and WAREHOUSEMAN, and no working arrangements, instructions, or operating manuals intended to facilitate the effective carrying out of this Agreement shall in any way affect the liabilities of either party as set forth herein.

IN WITNESS WHEREOF, the parties hereto have duly executed this Agreement in duplicate the day and year first above written.

WAREHOUSEMAN

By:_____

_____

DEPOSITOR

By:_____

SCHEDULE A
STORAGE AND HANDLING RATES AND CHARGES

Attached to and made a part of Agreement dated the _____ day of

_____ , 19 _____ , by and between _____

_____and_____

DEPOSITOR

_____.

WAREHOUSEMAN

SCHEDULE B
ACCESSORIAL RATES AND CHARGES

Attached to and made a part of Agreement dated the _____ day of _____ , 19 _____ ,

by and between _____ and

DEPOSITOR

_____ .

WAREHOUSEMAN

AMERICAN WAREHOUSE COMPANY
STREET ADDRESS • CITY & AMERICA 00000
TELEPHONE: (312) – 123-4567

ORIGINAL

NON-NEGOTIABLE WAREHOUSE RECEIPT

AMERICAN WAREHOUSE COMPANY claims a lien for all lawful charges for storage and preservation of the goods; also for all lawful claims for money advanced, interest, insurance, transportation, labor, weighing, coopering and other charges and expenses in relation to such goods, and for the balance on any other accounts that may be due. The property covered by this receipt has NOT been insured by this Company for the benefit of the depositor against fire or any other casualty.

RECEIVED FROM

FOR ACCOUNT OF

THIS IS TO CERTIFY THAT WE HAVE RECEIVED the goods listed hereon in apparent good order, except as noted herein (contents, condition and quality unknown), SUBJECT TO ALL TERMS AND CONDITIONS INCLUDING LIMITATION OF LIABILITY HEREIN AND ON THE REVERSE HEREOF. Such property to be delivered to THE DEPOSITOR upon the payment of all storage, handling and other charges. Advances have been made and liability incurred on these goods as follows:

DOCUMENT NUMBER

DATE

CUSTOMER NUMBER

CUSTOMER ORDER NO.

WAREHOUSE NO.

DELIVERING CARRIER	CARRIER NUMBER	PREPAID/COLLECT	SHIPPERS NUMBER

QUANTITY	SAID TO BE OR CONTAIN (CUSTOMER ITEM NO., WAREHOUSE ITEM NO., LOT NUMBER, DESCRIPTION, ETC.)	WEIGHT	RATE CODE	STORAGE RATE / HANDLING RATE	DAMAGE & EXCEPTIONS
	TOTALS				

NO DELIVERY WILL BE MADE ON THIS RECEIPT EXCEPT ON WRITTEN ORDER.

AMERICAN WAREHOUSE COMPANY

BY

AUTHORIZED SIGNATURE

FORM 2 3/70

STANDARD CONTRACT TERMS AND CONDITIONS FOR MERCHANDISE WAREHOUSEMEN

AMERICAN WAREHOUSEMEN'S ASSOCIATION · AWA · Seal of Security · OUR INTEGRITY IS YOUR SECURITY

(APPROVED AND PROMULGATED BY THE AMERICAN WAREHOUSEMEN'S ASSOCIATION, OCTOBER 1968)

ACCEPTANCE — Sec. 1

(a) This contract and rate quotation including accessorial charges endorsed on or attached hereto must be accepted within 30 days from the proposal date by signature of depositor on the reverse side of the contract. In the absence of written acceptance, the act of tendering goods described herein for storage or other services by warehouseman within 30 days from the proposal date shall constitute such acceptance by depositor.

(b) In the event that goods tendered for storage or other services do not conform to the description contained herein, or conforming goods are tendered after 30 days from the proposal date without prior written acceptance by depositor as provided in paragraph (a) of this section, warehouseman may refuse to accept such goods. If warehouseman accepts such goods, depositor agrees to rates and charges as may be assigned and invoiced by warehouseman and to all terms of this contract.

(c) This contract may be cancelled by either party upon 30 days written notice and is cancelled if no storage or other services are performed under this contract for a period of 180 days.

SHIPPING — Sec. 2

Depositor agrees not to ship goods to warehouseman as the named consignee. If, in violation of this agreement, goods are shipped to warehouseman as named consignee, depositor agrees to notify carrier in writing prior to such shipment, with copy of such notice to the warehouseman, that warehouseman named as consignee is a warehouseman and has no beneficial title or interest in such property and depositor further agrees to indemnify and hold harmless warehouseman from any and all claims for unpaid transportation charges, including undercharges, demurrage, detention or charges of any nature, in connection with goods so shipped. Depositor further agrees that, if it fails to notify carrier as required by the next preceding sentence, warehouseman shall have the right to refuse such goods and shall not be liable or responsible for any loss, injury or damage of any nature to, or related to, such goods. Depositor agrees that all promises contained in this section will be binding on depositor's heirs, successors and assigns.

TENDER FOR STORAGE — Sec. 3

All goods for storage shall be delivered at the warehouse properly marked and packaged for handling. The depositor shall furnish at or prior to such delivery, a manifest showing marks, brands, or sizes to be kept and accounted for separately, and the class of storage and other services desired.

STORAGE PERIOD AND CHARGES — Sec. 4

(a) All charges for storage are per package or other agreed unit per month.

(b) Storage charges become applicable upon the date that warehouseman accepts care, custody and control of the goods, regardless of unloading date or date of issue of warehouse receipt.

(c) Except as provided in paragraph (d) of this section, a full month's storage charge will apply on all goods received between the first and the 15th, inclusive, of a calendar month; one-half month's storage charge will apply on all goods received between the 16th and last day, inclusive, of a calendar month, and a full month's storage charge will apply to all goods in storage on the first day of the next and succeeding calendar months. All storage charges are due and payable on the first day of storage for the initial month and thereafter on the first day of the calendar month.

(d) When mutually agreed by the warehouseman and the depositor, a storage month shall extend from a date in one calendar month to, but not including, the same date of the next and all succeeding months. All storage charges are due and payable on the first day of the storage month.

TRANSFER, TERMINATION OF STORAGE, REMOVAL OF GOODS — Sec. 5

(a) Instructions to transfer goods on the books of the warehouseman are not effective until delivered to and accepted by warehouseman, and all charges up to the time transfer is made are chargeable to the depositor of record. If a transfer involves rehandling the goods, such will be subject to a charge. When goods in storage are transferred from one party to another through issuance of a new warehouse receipt, a new storage date is established on the date of transfer.

(b) The warehouseman reserves the right to move, at his expense, 14 days after notice is sent by certified or registered mail to the depositor of record or to the last known holder of the negotiable warehouse receipt, any goods in storage from the warehouse in which they may be stored to any other of his warehouses; but if such depositor or holder takes delivery of his goods in lieu of transfer, no storage charge shall be made for the current storage month. The warehouseman may, without notice, move goods within the warehouse in which they are stored.

(c) The warehouseman may, upon written notice to the depositor of record and any other person known by the warehouseman to claim an interest in the goods, require the removal of any goods by the end of the next succeeding storage month. Such notice shall be given to the last known place of business or abode of the person to be notified. If goods are not removed before the end of the next succeeding storage month, the warehouseman may sell them in accordance with applicable law.

(d) If warehouseman in good faith believes that the goods are about to deteriorate or decline in value to less than the amount of warehouseman's lien before the end of the next succeeding storage month, the warehouseman may specify in the notification any reasonable shorter time for removal of the goods and in case the goods are not removed, may sell them at public sale held one week after a single advertisement or posting as provided by law.

(e) If as a result of a quality or condition of the goods of which the warehouseman had no notice at the time of deposit the goods are a hazard to other property or to the warehouse or to persons, the warehouseman may sell the goods at public or private sale without advertisement on reasonable notification to all persons known to claim an interest in the goods. If the warehouseman after a reasonable effort is unable to sell the goods he may dispose of them in any lawful manner and shall incur no liability by reason of such disposition. Pending such disposition, sale or return of the goods, the warehouseman may remove the goods from the warehouse and shall incur no liability by reason of such removal.

HANDLING — Sec. 6

(a) The handling charge covers the ordinary labor involved in receiving goods at warehouse door, placing goods in storage, and returning goods to warehouse door. Handling charges are due and payable on receipt of goods.

(b) Unless otherwise agreed, labor for unloading and loading goods will be subect to a charge. Additional expenses incurred by the warehouseman in receiving and handling damaged goods, and additional expense in unloading from or loading into cars or other vehicles not at warehouse door will be charged to the depositor.

(c) Labor and materials used in loading rail cars or other vehicles are chargeable to the depositor.

(d) When goods are ordered out in quantities less than in which received, the warehouseman may make an additional charge for each order or each item of an order.

(e) The warehouseman shall not be liable for demurrage, delays in unloading inbound cars, or delays in obtaining and loading cars for outbound shipment unless warehouseman has failed to exercise reasonable care.

DELIVERY REQUIREMENTS — Sec. 7

(a) No goods shall be delivered or transferred except upon receipt by the warehouseman of complete instructions properly signed by the depositor. However, when no negotiable receipt is outstanding, goods may be delivered upon instructions by telephone in accordance with a prior written authorization, but the warehouseman shall not be responsible for loss or error occasioned thereby.

(b) When a negotiable receipt has been issued no goods covered by that receipt shall be delivered, or transferred on the books of the warehouseman, unless the receipt, properly indorsed, is surrendered for cancellation, or for indorsement of partial delivery thereon. If a negotiable receipt is lost or destroyed, delivery of goods may be made only upon order of a court of competent jurisdiction and the posting of security approved by the court as provided by law.

(c) When goods are ordered out a reasonable time shall be given the warehouseman to carry out instructions, and if he is unable because of acts of God, war, public enemies, seizure under legal process, strikes, lockouts, riots and civil commotions, or any reason beyond the warehouseman's control, or because of loss or destruction of goods for which warehouseman is not liable, or because of any other excuse provided by law, the warehouseman shall not be liable for failure to carry out such instructions and goods remaining in storage will continue to be subject to regular storage charges.

EXTRA SERVICES (SPECIAL SERVICES) — Sec. 8

(a) Warehouse labor required for services other than ordinary handling and storage will be charged to the depositor.

(b) Special services requested by depositor including but not limited to compiling of special stock statements; reporting marked weights, serial numbers or other data from packages; physical check of goods; and handling transit billing will be subject to a charge.

(c) Dunnage, bracing, packing materials or other special supplies, may be provided for the depositor at a charge in addition to the warehouseman's cost.

(d) By prior arrangement, goods may be received or delivered during other than usual business hours, subect to a charge.

(e) Communication expense including postage, teletype, telegram, or telephone, will be charged to the depositor if such concern more than normal inventory reporting or if, at the request of the depositor, communications are made by other than regular United States Mail.

BONDED STORAGE — Sec. 9

(a) A charge in addition to regular rates will be made for merchandise in bond.

(b) Where a warehouse receipt covers goods in U. S. Customs bond, such receipt shall be void upon the termination of the storage period fixed by law.

MINIMUM CHARGES — Sec. 10

(a) A minimum handling charge per lot and a minimum storage charge per lot per month will be made. When a warehouse receipt covers more than one lot or when a lot is in assortment, a minimum charge per mark, brand, or variety will be made.

(b) A minimum monthly charge to one account for storage and/or handling will be made. This charge will apply also to each account when one customer has several accounts, each requiring separate records and billing.

LIABILITY AND LIMITATION OF DAMAGES — Sec. 11

(A) THE WAREHOUSEMAN SHALL NOT BE LIABLE FOR ANY LOSS OR INJURY TO GOODS STORED HOWEVER CAUSED UNLESS SUCH LOSS OR INJURY RESULTED FROM THE FAILURE BY THE WAREHOUSEMAN TO EXERCISE SUCH CARE IN REGARD TO THEM AS A REASONABLY CAREFUL MAN WOULD EXERCISE UNDER LIKE CIRCUMSTANCES AND WAREHOUSEMAN IS NOT LIABLE FOR DAMAGES WHICH COULD NOT HAVE BEEN AVOIDED BY THE EXERCISE OF SUCH CARE.

(B) GOODS ARE NOT INSURED BY WAREHOUSEMAN AGAINST LOSS OR INJURY HOWEVER CAUSED.

(C) THE DEPOSITOR DECLARES THAT DAMAGES ARE LIMITED TO ______________________________, PROVIDED, HOWEVER, THAT SUCH LIABILITY MAY AT THE TIME OF ACCEPTANCE OF THIS CONTRACT AS PROVIDED IN SECTION 1 BE INCREASED ON PART OR ALL OF THE GOODS HEREUNDER IN WHICH EVENT A MONTHLY CHARGE OF ______________________________ WILL BE MADE IN ADDITION TO THE REGULAR MONTHLY STORAGE CHARGE.

NOTICE OF CLAIM AND FILING OF SUIT — Sec. 12

(a) Claims by the depositor and all other persons must be presented in writing to the warehouseman within a reasonable time, and in no event longer than either 60 days after delivery of the goods by the warehouseman or 60 days after depositor of record or the last known holder of a negotiable warehouse receipt is notified by the warehouseman that loss or injury to part or all of the goods has occurred, whichever time is shorter.

(b) No action may be maintained by the depositor or others against the warehouseman for loss or injury to the goods stored unless timely written claim has been given as provided in paragraph (a) of this section and unless such action is commenced either within nine months after date of delivery by warehouseman or within nine months after depositor of record or the last known holder of a negotiable warehouse receipt is notified that loss or injury to part or all of the goods has occurred, whichever time is shorter.

(c) When goods have not been delivered, notice may be given of known loss or injury to the goods by mailing of a registered or certified letter to the depositor of record or to the last known holder of a negotiable warehouse receipt. Time limitations for presentation of claim in writing and maintaining of action after notice begin on the date of mailing of such notice by warehouseman.

Module VII

Payments and Releases

INTRODUCTION

The forms in this Module deal generally with the conclusion of transactions and the avoidance of post-transaction liability. They have three principal purposes:

1. To reflect completion of performance
2. To disclaim liability, either as not applicable in the first place or as discharged by consideration
3. To document closeout of the transaction

MODULE FORMS

The 10 forms in this Module are

Waiver and Assumption of Risk
Receipt for Deposit
Receipt for Payment
Payment Advice
Release of Claims
Release of Note

Release of UCC Financing Statement
Certificate of Satisfaction
Waiver and Release of Liens
Mutual Release

Also see the Early Termination and Mutual Release for contracts in Module II.

Waiver and Assumption of Risk

Definition

The waiver and assumption of risk is signed by an individual to waive claims against the provider of a service, activity, or facility in which the individual may encounter specific notable risks.

Comments

a. The kinds of situations in which the form is commonly found are leisure activities, such as boat rentals and skydiving.

b. The risks must be fully disclosed for the waiver to be a good defense.

c. The form is not a substitute for insurance, but a supplement, and may be required as a condition of insurability.

d. The form will not be valid if signed by a minor, or any other person suffering a lack of competence (e.g., drunkard).

Distribution

Original to sales department
Copy to customer

Receipt for Deposit

Definition

The receipt for deposit acknowledges that a deposit, subject to refund, has been made with the holder.

Comments

a. This form is an adjunct to other documents, such as contracts or leases requiring a deposit (e.g., see Modules V and X).

b. Certain types of deposits (e.g., consumer rental security deposits) may in fact require interest. Check with counsel.

Distribution

Same as for governing instrument

Receipt for Payment

Definition

The receipt for payment is used as evidence of performance on a payment obligation.

Comments

a. The principal benefit of this form to the payee is that it provides clear rights in the event the check bounces.

b. The principal benefit to payor is proof that payment has been received.

c. Even if the payor's check will prove payment, obtaining a receipt is wise in case proof is needed before the check is available in the payor's bank statement.

Distribution

Original signature to each party

Payment Advice

Definition

The payment advice is used to tell the payee what payment applies to, so as to assure proper accounting.

Comments

a. In the absence of a payment advice, the law presumes payments apply to the oldest bills first, which can be very troublesome if a dispute arises regarding an older transaction.

b. The payment advice by itself may not necessarily be binding on the payee, depending on the nature of the transaction and state law, but to assure validity, the payor should place an endorsement on the back of the check: "Accepted per payment advice submitted herewith."

c. The other advantage of the payment advice is to protect the payor's rights in the event of later discovered defects.

Distribution

Original, sent with payment instrument, to payee

Copy, with invoice paid, to accounting department

Release of Claims

Definition

The release of claims is used to release liability claimed or existing against a person or company.

Comments

a. This form is primarily used where tort (e.g., accident) claims arise, but also can be used in settlement of a contract dispute, especially after the contract has ended (e.g., warranty claim).

b. The form will not be valid unless some consideration is received by the person granting the release. Such consideration may be nominal, as long as the grantor is not misled.

c. Signing such a release is a significant action, which should not be undertaken without advice of counsel.

Distribution

Original to party released

Copy to signer

Release of Note

Definition

The release of note is a document showing release of a note for full payment.

Comments

a. Return of the original note, marked "paid in full," to the borrower can accomplish the same purpose. This form is most useful when the original cannot be located, or when more formal proof is desired, such as when a new lender makes the new loan conditional on release of the old.

b. The form can also be used when the note is released for reasons other than full payment (e.g., gift, release of a claim), but such reason should be stated in place of "full payment."

c. This form will not release liens from the land or chattel records in most jurisdictions.

Distribution

Original to borrower

Copy to noteholder

Release of UCC Financing Statement

Definition

The release of UCC financing statement is used for releasing a lien of a recorded financing statement.

Comments

a. Payment releases the obligation; this form clears the lien.

b. The form is also known as a "termination."

c. The lien will not be cleared until the document is both signed and recorded.

d. Notarization is technically not required, but is recommended for the protection of the secured party as a regular procedure in order to prevent forgery.

Distribution

Original signature plus copy to place of recording

Original signature to borrower

Copy to secured party

Certificate of Satisfaction

Definition

The certificate of satisfaction is used to release a lien against real estate.

Comments

a. Comments regarding the release of UCC financing statement are applicable to the certificate of satisfaction, as well.

b. As this will be recorded in land records, it must be notarized.

c. Other release forms may apply in some jurisdictions. Consult with counsel.

Distribution

Original to land records

Copy to borrower

Copy to noteholder

Waiver and Release of Liens

Definition

The waiver and release of liens is used to reflect payment to a person who would have mechanic's lien rights, so as to waive such rights.

Comments

a. Not all jurisdictions allow mechanic's liens, but use of the form is recommended in any event to show payment.

b. A variant of the form also can be used to avoid other types of liens (e.g., serviceman's, warehouseman's), which would also be signed on payment.

c. Notarization allows the form to be recorded if the payee claims lack of payment and records a mechanic's lien.

d. A form should be used each time a payment is made, and should be required in actual hand-to-hand exchange for the check.

Distribution

Original to payor

Copy to payee

Mutual Release

Definition

The mutual release is used to settle claims and disputes between parties, and which releases both from further liability.

Comments

a. The early termination (see Module II) contains a release for contracts awaiting performance up to that point. This form is designed primarily for settlement of postperformance disputes.

b. It could also be used for tort claims, particularly where both parties are claiming against one another.

c. Like all releases, there must not be concealment or fraud used to induce signature, or the release may be invalidated.

Distribution

Original signature to each party

WAIVER AND ASSUMPTION OF RISK

I, _____ (hereinafter called "Customer"), voluntarily make and grant this Waiver and Assumption of Risk in favor of _____ (hereinafter called "Seller") as partial consideration (in addition to moneys paid to Seller) for the opportunity to use the facilities, equipment, materials, and/or other assets of Seller; and/or to receive assistance, training, guidance, tutelage, and/or instruction from the personnel of Seller; and/or to engage in the activities, events, sports, festivities, and/or gathering sponsored by Seller; I do hereby waive and release any and all claims of personal injury, bodily injury, property damage, damages, losses, and/or death that may arise from my aforesaid use or receipt, as I understand and recognize that there are certain risks, dangers, and perils connected with such use and/or receipt, which I acknowledge have been fully explained to me and which I fully understand, and which I nevertheless accept, assume, and undertake after inquiry and investigation of extent, duration, and completeness wholly satisfactory and acceptable to me. I further agree to use my best judgment in undertaking these activities, use, and/or receipt and to faithfully adhere to all safety instructions and recommendations, whether oral or written. I certify that I am a competent adult assuming these risks of my own free will, being under no compulsion or duress. This Waiver and Assumption of Risk is effective from _____, 19____, to _____, 19____, inclusive, and may not be revoked, altered, amended, rescinded, or voided without the express prior written consent of Seller.

_____ (Seal)   _____

Customer's Signature   Date

_____   _____

Print Name   Age

Address _____

155

RECEIPT FOR DEPOSIT

Received this date from _____ ("Depositor"), whose address is

_____ and whose ___Social Security

Number ___Employer ID Number is _____, the sum of

_____ dollars ($_____) in form of

____Cash   ____Personal Check   ____Travelers Checks   ____Cashier's Check

____Certified Check   ____Bank Wire   ____Other: _____

received by _____ ("Holder") as a ____full____partial deposit on____lease

____invoice ____purchase order   ____contract   ____other: _____ (hereinafter "Instru-

ment"), which Instrument is dated _____, 19____, and numbered _____ , relative to

_____

_____

The Deposit shall be held by the undersigned according to the terms of the Instrument under which said Deposit has been paid, and, unless provided for therein or required by law, said Deposit shall not bear interest. The Deposit shall be repaid when such repayment is due under the terms of the Instrument, unless the same has been used, charged against, or expended as required by or allowed according to the terms of the Instrument. Depositor and the undersigned acknowledge that the terms of the Instrument govern this Deposit, and any conflict between these terms and the terms of the Instrument shall be governed by the Instrument.

Date _____, 19____

_____   _____
Depositor   Holder

156

RECEIPT FOR PAYMENT

Received this date from _____ ("Payor"), whose address is

_____ and whose ___Social Security

Number ___Employer ID Number is _____, the sum of

_____ dollars ($_____) in form of

____Cash ____Personal Check ____Travelers Checks ____Cashier's Check

____Certified Check ____Bank Wire ____Other: _____

received by _____ ("Payee") as a ____full____partial payment

of____invoice____statement____sales slip____note____other: _____, which is dated

_____, 19____, and numbered _____.

    Payor guarantees the instrument(s) of payment hereby receipted to be Payor's own, which is (are) free of encumbrance, lien, or claims of others. Payor further certifies all funds hereby receipted to be good and collectible without delay in full, without deduction, charge, or offset. Payor agrees to pay all costs of collection, including, but not limited to, bank charges, court costs, and attorney fees, in the event any enforcement action is necessary for Payee to receive full collected funds for such instrument(s). Payor agrees that this receipt waives no rights of Payee to collect nor any other rights of Payee under any other agreements or instruments between Payor and Payee, and acknowledges that Payee has fully and cumulatively reserved all rights.

Date _____, 19____

Payor:

_____

Payee:

_____

PAYMENT ADVICE

Enclosed herewith is our Check No. _____ dated _____, 19____, in full/partial payment of your Invoice/Statement No. _____, dated _____, 19____.

Payment does not constitute unconditional acceptance of goods or services, nor does it constitute waiver of any rights, all of which rights are hereby reserved, including, but not limited to, the rights to claims, refunds, exercises or warranties, rescission, further performance, credits, and offset as may be appropriate.

Thank you.

Date _____   _____
                                                Signature

RELEASE OF CLAIMS

I, _____ , an adult, in consideration of payment of _____ dollars ($_____), received by me prior to my signing below, hereby, for myself and my heirs, executors, successors, assigns, and administrators, do release, acquit, and forever discharge the Releasee, who is _____ , and all agents, servants, successors, heirs, executors, administrators, and assigns of Releasee, and all other persons and entities, natural and unnatural, of and from any and all claims, actions, causes of actions, demands, rights, damages, costs, loss of service, expenses, and compensation whatsoever, which I have or may in the future have on account of or in any way growing out of any and all known and unknown, forseen and unforseen, bodily and personal injuries and property damage and all consequences thereof, resulting from the accident, casualty, or event occurring on _____, 19____, at _____, _____ and described as _____ ("Incident").

I agree this settlement is the compromise of a disputed claim. Payment to me is not an admission of liability by any party, and is made strictly to avoid litigation and the costs thereof and to buy peace.

I agree my injuries are or may be permanent and progressive, and recovery is uncertain and indefinite. I further agree there may be unknown, undiscovered, or unanticipated injuries resulting from the Incident, and this Release specifically includes all the same. I have made my own judgment and decision with regard to the Incident and to this settlement uninfluenced by and without reliance on Releasee or any agent of or person employed by Releasee, and without any consideration except as recited above and without any outside inducement, duress, or influence. This Release's terms are contractual and not a mere recital. This Release contains the entire agreement between myself and the Releasee, superseding all prior agreements, expressly reserving all rights of Releasee and all claiming through or on account of Releasee, including, but not limited to, claims for contribution, property damage, and personal injury.

I have read, understand, and agree to all of the foregoing.

Date _____, ____   _____ (Seal)
                                       Signature

_____ of _____
_____ of _____ , to wit

On _____, 19____, _____ personally appeared before me who swore to and acknowledged the foregoing Release of Claims as a voluntary act and deed.

                                       _____
                                       Notary Public

My commission expires _____, 19____   (Seal)

RELEASE OF NOTE

KNOW ALL MEN BY THESE PRESENTS:

That the undersigned Noteholder, for and in consideration of full payment made in accord with the terms of a Note dated _____, 19____, in the face amount of _____ dollars ($_____), full payment of which has been made to said Noteholder by or on behalf of the Borrower(s), _____, the receipt of which is hereby acknowledged, does hereby remise, release, and forever discharge said Borrower(s), their heirs, executors, administrators, successors, assigns, and transferees, of and from any and all manner of action and actions, cause and causes of action, suits, debts, dues, sums of money, or accounts due under or on account of the said Note.

In witness whereof, _____ , Noteholder, has set his/her hand and seal this _____ day of _____, 19____.

_____ (Seal)
Noteholder

State of _____
_____ of _____

The foregoing Release of Note was signed, sworn to, and acknowledged before me on _____, 19____, by the Noteholder, _____.

_____
Notary Public

(Notary Seal)

My commission expires _____

RELEASE OF UCC FINANCING STATEMENT

This Release of a financing statement is presented to a filing officer per the Uniform Commercial Code as adopted in the jurisdiction of filing.

1. Name of Debtor _____

2. Address of Debtor _____

   _____

3. Name of Secured Party _____

4. Address of Secured Party _____

   _____

5. Personalty securing _____

6. File number of financing statement _____

7. Place financing statement was filed _____

Secured party _____

By _____
Duly Authorized Signatory

State of _____
_____ of _____
The foregoing Release of UCC Financing Statement was signed, sworn to, and acknowledged before me on _____, 19__, by the duly authorized Signatory, _____, of and on behalf of the Secured Party, _____.

_____
Notary Public

(Notary Seal)

My commission expires _____

CERTIFICATE OF SATISFACTION

Place of record: County/City of _____, State of _____

Deed of Trust/Mortgage dated _____, 19____   Deed Book ____ Page ____

Note amount secured $_____   Note dated _____, 19____

Name(s) of Beneficiary(ies)/Noteholder(s) _____

Name(s) of Grantor(s)/Borrower(s) _____

Name(s) of Trustee(s) _____

Brief description of property encumbered _____

_____

    The undersigned Holder(s) of the above-mentioned obligation, secured by the above-mentioned Deed of Trust/Mortgage hereby certify(ies) the same has/have been paid in full and the lien created therein is hereby released. The undersigned makes oath the undersigned was the creditor under said Deed of Trust/Mortgage; the debt secured thereby is fully paid; the creditor was, when the debt was satisfied, entitled and authorized to receive same; and the undersigned subscribes this instrument in further testimony of full payment.

Date _____, 19____   Holder _____

Date _____, 19____   Holder _____

_____ of _____

_____ of _____ , to wit

    Subscribed, sworn to, and acknowledged before me by the Noteholder(s),
_____, on _____, 19____.

                                   _____
                                   Notary Public

                                           (Notary Seal)

My commission expires _____

State of _____
        In the clerk's office of the _____
                County/City of _____

This Certificate was presented and admitted to record on _____, 19____, at ____ o'clock ____. M. Clerk's fee of $_____ has been paid.
                        Attest _____
                               Clerk

WAIVER AND RELEASE OF LIENS

THE UNDERSIGNED, for and in consideration of the sum of $_____ paid by _____ ("Payor") and other good and valuable consideration, the receipt of which is hereby acknowledged, does hereby waive and release any and all liens, lien rights, and claims of right of lien under the statutes of the State of _____ or otherwise relating to mechanics' liens on the following described property and improvements thereon

_____

_____

_____

and on the monies or other consideration due or to become due from the general contractor on account of labor or services, material, fixtures, or apparatus heretofore furnished prior to the date of _____ .

As a condition for rendering the check payable to your order, the Lender and title insurance company do or may require your execution of this Waiver and Release of Liens without modification thereto.

Please return completed form to

_____

_____

_____

The Undersigned acknowledges future payments are contingent upon prompt return of this executed release form, and that this payment and future payments by the Payor do not waive or limit any rights of Payor.

_____

Date: _____   By _____
                              An Authorized Signatory

_____ of _____

_____ of _____ , to wit

On _____, 19____, personally appeared before me in my jurisdiction _____, authorized Signatory for _____, on whose authority and on whose behalf the foregoing Waiver and Release of Liens was sworn to, signed, and acknowledged.

_____
Notary Public
                                      (Seal)

My commission expires _____

MUTUAL RELEASE

We the undersigned, _____ and _____, binding and inuring to the benefit of each and each's representatives, assigns, affiliates, and successors-in-interest of every kind and character, and do hereby mutually release, remise, and forever discharge each other from any and all claims, demands, and causes of action arising or claimed as arising between us prior to this date, including, but not limited to, the matter of
_____.

The reciprocal forebearances and covenants stated above, together with
_____, constitute the entire consideration for this Release, and such consideration is contractual and not a mere recital. All agreements and understandings between us are reflected in this Release. We understand this Release does not admit liability, and the consideration is exchanged in compromise of disputed issues in order to avoid the expenses of further investigation and litigation.

We further state that we have carefully read this document, know and understand its content, and sign the same as each's free act and deed, which shall become effective only upon all signatures being affixed.

Date _____   _____ (Seal)

Date _____   _____ (Seal)

State of _____

_____ of _____

The foregoing Mutual Release was signed and acknowledged before me on _____, 19____, by _____ and _____.

_____

Notary Public

(Notary Seal)

My commission expires _____

Module VIII

Safety

INTRODUCTION

Safety usually requires customized forms (e.g., checklists, instructions, warnings) particularized to the location and circumstances at the prevention end of the spectrum. The forms in this Module are useful in the damage control mode at the other end of the spectrum. Nonetheless, familiarization may help to alert personnel to be prepared to execute damage control as efficiently as possible.

The purposes of safety forms are

1. To record the event to facilitate investigation
2. To provide information for taking remedial measures to prevent repetition
3. To use in determining liability or exoneration

On this last point, personnel, especially those dealing with outsiders, should be trained in how to avoid making admissions against interest, especially erroneously, when preparing these reports, while, of course, reporting truthfully. Insurors and counsel can be of assistance.

MODULE FORMS

The five forms in this module are

Injury Report and Investigation Form
Preliminary Report of Accident or Loss
Security Incident Report
Insurance Incident Report
Report of OSHA Inspection

Employee Injury Report and Investigation Form

Definition

The injury report and investigation form is used for reporting bodily injury of an employee, for which the company may be alleged responsible.

Comments

a. A variant of the form can also be used for nonemployee injuries (e.g., visitors, customers).

b. Any injury on premises should be written up on the form. Off-premises injuries should be written up if the employee is on duty or if the injury involves any employer interest.

c. Employee injuries will usually be covered by workman's compensation insurance. Be sure the insuror approves of the form.

Distribution

Original to personnel department
Copy to insurance department
Copy to workman's compensation insurance carrier
Copy to department head
Copy to employee (if requested)

Preliminary Report of Accident or Loss

Definition

The preliminary report of accident or loss is used to report a motor vehicle collision or incident.

Comments

a. This form is recommended by American Trucking Associations as a supplement to police reports or those of other officials.

b. As nearly every business uses vehicles, the form has wide applicability, and all drivers for the business should carry the form when on business.

c. It is called "preliminary" as follow-up investigation may reveal different facts or conclusions.

Distribution

Original to insurance department

Copy to personnel department

Copy to counsel

Copy retained by employee

Security Incident Report

Definition

The security incident report is used for reporting crimes or suspicious incidents affecting company personnel or assets.

Comments

a. Make these forms widely available, and familiarize employees with them so that there is no confusion if and when an incident occurs, as rapid response may help to limit costs and, where a crime is involved, may make the difference in catching the criminal.

b. Values listed may well be approximate. If known to be exact, footnote the fact.

c. Note the critical tie-in to the insurance incident report, which follows.

Distribution

Original to security department

Copy to insurance department

Copy to insurance carrier

Copy to department head

Copy to reporting employee

Insurance Incident Report

Definition

The insurance incident report is used for collecting critical information on incidents where insurance claims may be made.

Comments

a. This form may be used to supplement any of the foregoing forms in this Module.

b. Check acceptability for the various insurance companies that are providing coverage.

Distribution

Original to insurance department

Copy to insurance carrier

Copy to department head

Copy to employee (if requested)

Other copies if due per distribution of attachment

Report of OSHA Inspection

Definition

The report of OSHA inspection is for use in on-the-spot reporting on OSHA (U.S. Occupational Safety and Health Administration) inspections, which are controlled by federal law.

Comments

a. This form is also provided by American Trucking Associations.

b. The form serves, in part, as a checklist for conduct during the course of the inspection.

c. By monitoring the inspector's activities and writing up a counterreport, the business has evidence that may protect it against inaccurate inspection.

d. Variations of the form may be applicable and desirable for other types of regulatory inspections.

Distribution

Original to personnel department

Copy to affected departments

Employee Injury Report and Investigation Form   UNIT: _____

INJURY REPORT AND INVESTIGATION FORM

1

EMPLOYEE'S NAME _____ MARITAL STATUS _____ SEX: M _____ F _____

ADDRESS: _____ SOC. SEC. NO: _____

DATE OF BIRTH: _____ TELEPHONE NO: _____ STATE: _____ COUNTY: _____

DATE OF INJURY: _____ TIME: _____ DATE INJURY REPORTED _____

DEPARTMENT ASSIGNED: _____ SHIFT: AM/PM _____ DEPARTMENT HEAD: _____

DATE HIRED: _____ WAGE/SALARY # _____ DAYS WORK PER WEEK: S☐ M☐ T☐ W☐ T☐ F☐ S☐

2

DID YOU HAVE AN ACCIDENT ON COMPANY PREMISES: YES:☐ NO:☐

TO WHOM WAS ACCIDENT REPORTED? _____

SPECIFY WORK AREA WHERE ACCIDENT OCCURRED: _____

DESCRIBE HOW ACCIDENT OCCURED: (WHAT, HOW, OBJECT OR SUBSTANCE INVOLVED) _____

_____

_____

_____

_____ EMPLOYEE'S SIGNATURE: _____ DATE: _____

3

DISPOSITION

	YES	NO
DISABLING INJURY:		
SENT TO HOSPITAL		
SENT TO COMPANY DOCTOR OR NURSE		
RETURN TO REGULAR JOB		
RETURN TO LIGHT DUTY JOB		
RECORDABLE ON OSHA FORM 200		

EST. DAYS OF DISABILITY: _____

DATE TO RETURN TO WORK: _____

INITIAL MEDICAL DIAGNOSIS: _____

_____

IF HOSPITALIZED, NAME & ADDRESS OF HOSPITAL:

_____

_____

BODY PART INJURED

☐ EYE
☐ HEAD
☐ CHEST
☐ BACK
☐ ABDOMEN
☐ ARM
☐ HAND - FINGER
☐ LEG
☐ FOOT - TOE
☐ RESPIRATORY SYSTEM
☐ _____

TYPE OF INJURY

☐ LACERATION
☐ ABRASION
☐ PUNCTURE
☐ BURN
☐ FRACTURE
☐ STRAIN - SPRAIN
☐ AMPUTATION
☐ FOREIGN BODY
☐ HERNIA
☐ CONTUSION
☐ _____

ATTENDING PHYSICIAN OR MEDICAL ATTENTION: _____

5

SUPERVISOR'S DESCRIPTION OF ACCIDENT AFTER INVESTIGATION: (NOTE IF EMPLOYEE WAS WEARING PERSONAL PROTECTIVE EQUIPMENT)

_____

_____

_____

DEPARTMENT HEAD SIGNATURE: _____ DATE: _____

3/85

PRELIMINARY REPORT OF ACCIDENT OR LOSS

Form C0820, Reorder from
American Trucking Associations, Inc.
2200 Mill Road
Alexandria, VA 22314

Exact Date
of Accident _____ Time _____   ☐ A.M.
☐ P.M.   Day of Week _____

HOW MANY VEHICLES WERE INVOLVED IN ACCIDENT?

Company Employee_____ Tractor No. _____ Trailer No. _____

Can you be reached by phone, if necessary to call back?

Area Code_____ Phone No. _____ City _____

Accident Within City or Village Limits	Accident Occurred	In_____ _____ (City or Village) (County) On _____(Street) At or Near_____(Cross Street)

Accident Outside City Or Village Limits	Accident Occurred On_____ Near _____ In_____ (Route Number and road name) (Town) (County) At _____ Width_____ Were Lanes (Name intersection or state distance and of Road Marked? Yes ☐ No ☐ direction from nearest community, highway (2-3-4 or more lanes) junction, crossroad, railroad crossing or bridge) Were Opposing Lanes Separated by a Curb or Mall?_____Yes ☐ No ☐

TYPE OF TRAFFIC CONTROL AT PLACE OF ACCIDENT

1—Police Officer ☐   2—Signal Light ☐   3—Stop Sign ☐   4—Caution Sign ☐   5—Other Control ☐   6—No Control ☐

Cause of Accident or Loss	Weather_____ Condition of Road _____ Description of accident:_____ _____ _____ _____ _____ _____

Driver of Other Vehicle	Name_____ Make of Vehicle _____ Address _____ Model_____ (Street or R.D.) (City & State) Operator's License No. _____ Registration_____ (No.) (State) (No.) (State)

	Yes	No		Yes	No
Was Anyone Injured? (indicate fatalities) _____	☐	☐	Have you secured witnesses-names & addresses?____	☐	☐
Company Employee_____	☐	☐	Did accident involve fire or explosion? _____	☐	☐
Occupations other vehicles_____	☐	☐	Can your unit proceed safely under own power?_____	☐	☐
Pedestrians_____	☐	☐	Do you need mechanic or wrecker or another unit?____	☐	☐
Have you called Police? _____	☐	☐	Have you properly set emergency warning devices? ___	☐	☐
Have you called doctor and/or ambulance? _____	☐	☐			

Where have injured persons been taken?

Hospital _____

City _____

Was unit transporting hazardous materials? _____ substances _____ waste _____

Give name(s) and class(es) of hazardous materials_____

Were there any leaks or spills of the above materials?_____

Is there any fuel leakage from your unit?_____

Notes on instructions to Company Employee: *(Use other side of this form for additional information)*

Person Notified _____ Time _____   A.M.
 P.M.

Date _____   Signature _____

SECURITY INCIDENT REPORT

Description and value of item(s) damaged/missing:

Number	Description	Value Each	% of Damage	Total Damage

Name, address, and phone number of person(s) involved and/or injured:

	Person #1	Person #2
Name	_____	_____
Address	_____	_____
	_____	_____
Phone	_____	_____
Injury Claimed	_____	_____
	_____	_____

Names and addresses of witnesses (if any):

	Witness #1	Witness #2
Name	_____	_____
Address	_____	_____
	_____	_____
Phone	_____	_____

Description of incident:
(Give location, times, events, etc. Use reverse if more space is needed.)

Prepared by _____   _____

                                       Signature

Date _____   Time _____   Phone _____

If insurance applies, notify insuror and attach insurance incident report

171

INSURANCE INCIDENT REPORT

Report time ____:__ __M   Report date ___/___/___

Insuror _____   Telephone _____

Insuror address _____

Policy type _____   Policy No. _____

Person reported to _____

Nature of incident:
(Give date, times, location, events, etc. Use reverse if more space is needed.)

If police notified:
Officer name and rank _____   Badge No. _____

Police force _____   Station _____

Persons claiming injuries:

	Person #1	Person #2
Name	_____	_____
Address	_____	_____
	_____	_____
Telephone	_____	_____
Injury Claimed	_____	_____

Witnesses:

	Witness #1	Witness #2
Name	_____	_____
Address	_____	_____
	_____	_____
Telephone	_____	_____

I swear the foregoing is true and complete to the best of my knowledge.

Print name: _____   _____
                                              Signature

If motor vehicles involved, attach report of accident or loss. If security involved, attach to security incident report.

ATA Form C0770
Reorder from:
American Trucking Associations
2200 Mill Road
Alexandria, Virginia 22314

Report of OSHA Inspection

This report is to be completed during and following a state or federal OSHA inspection by the company official who meets with and accompanies the inspector. A copy of the report and notes made by the company official are to be sent by mail to the safety director, and other specified company officials.

Location: _____

Inspection Date:_____ Time Began:_____ Time Ended:_____

Company official & Title: _____

1. PRE-INSPECTION

A. The OSHA inspector must present credentials. Make note of:

Inspector's full name: _____

Agency: _____

Office address and phone # of inspector: _____

_____

B. The inspector must explain nature, purpose and scope of inspection. Determine why inspection is being made
☐ Complaint   ☐ Accident   ☐ General

Explain nature of complaint or circumstances of accident that brought about inspection. (Include name of complainant, if any)

_____

_____

C. Explain to the inspector the nature and extent of safety program activities conducted at the terminal such as safety meetings, etc.

D. Names of employee representatives on inspection _____

_____

_____

2. INSPECTION

A. Inspector can confer privately with any employee during inspection. Do not attempt to interfere or determine from the employee what was discussed.

B. Make notes of any items, hazards, violations mentioned by the inspector. Take immediate action to correct minor problems such as obstruction in an aisle, poor housekeeping, fire extinguisher not accessible, etc.

_____

_____

_____

_____

_____

(Continued on back)

Report of OSHA Inspection (*continued*)

_____

_____

_____

_____

_____

_____

_____

_____

3. POST INSPECTION CONFERENCE

A. Inspector will advise of violations, and each rule that was violated. Make a list of these and determine if each is considered serious, non-serious or de minimis and why. Be certain you understand what the violation is and why. Be polite, point out any efforts during the inspection to correct conditions noted by the inspector.

VIOLATIONS

(1) Rule # _____ Considered: ☐ Serious   ☐ Non-serious   ☐ de minimis   ☐ other

Hazard or violation (Explain) _____

_____

_____

Corrective Action Taken:_____

(2) Rule #_____ Considered: ☐ Serious   ☐ Non-serious   ☐ de minimis   ☐ other

Hazard or violation (Explain) _____

_____

_____

Corrective Action Taken:_____

(3) Rule #_____ Considered: ☐ Serious   ☐ Non-serious   ☐ de minimis   ☐ other

Hazard or violation (Explain) _____

_____

_____

Corrective Action Taken:_____

(NOTE: Use space below or additional pages for listing violations and any corrective action taken by company or recommended by inspector. Send copy of notes and other information to safety director within 24 hours.)

Module IX

Sale of Business Assets

INTRODUCTION

Sales outside the ordinary course of business, which include sales of the entire business, have their own pecularities. Where the business is principally engaged in the sale of goods, such sales are subject to the Bulk Transfers Act under Article 6 of the Uniform Commercial Code. The Internal Revenue Code has many provisions dealing with such transfers, and the tax effects may be substantial. Local license laws and other regulations are also likely to bear on the transaction.

The purposes of these forms are

1. To control the transaction so each party receives what's intended
2. To comply with the many laws that affect business transfers
3. To protect against competitive pressure at a time when the business is likely to be more vulnerable because of the transfer

MODULE FORMS

The nine forms in this Module are

Potential Acquirer's Covenant of Confidentiality
Invention Confidentiality Agreement
Business Sale Agreement
Bulk Transfers Notice
Bulk Transfer Tax Authorities Notice
Bulk Transfer Affidavit

Bulk Sales Compliance Affidavit
Affidavit of Title
Bill of Sale

Potential Acquirer's Covenant of Confidentiality

Definition

The potential acquirer's covenant of confidentiality is a nondisclosure form provided prior to release of sensitive information to a potential buyer.

Comments

a. If the business wishes to keep its very identity a secret, have the form presented by a business broker, attorney, banker, or other trusted party.

b. Some acquirers may want a reciprocal agreement of confidentiality, as the fact they are searching the market may be sensitive.

Distribution

Original to seller

Copy to acquirer

Invention Confidentiality Agreement

Definition

The invention confidentiality agreement is a nondisclosure document for use by an inventor in seeking to market the invention for production, licensing, or sale.

Comments

a. Because of the importance of patent protection and the danger of infringement, no technical disclosure should be made until the signed agreement is in hand.

b. Disclosure of an invention prior to the filing of a patent application may result in disqualification of the application. Check with a patent lawyer before undertaking any marketing or disclosure.

c. The evaluator may desire a further statement that no guarantee of acceptance is implied by reason of evaluation.

Distribution

Original signature to each party

Business Sale Agreement

Definition

The business sale agreement is a contract for sale of a business.

Comments

a. This agreement is for sale of business assets, as opposed to sale of the shares in the business. It is designed to highlight the typical topics of consideration, but any such transaction obviously requires assistance of counsel and other professionals regarding taxes, operating contracts, insurance, and other phases of the business.

b. The type of business entity (corporation, partnership, proprietorship, other) will usually play an important role in contract development.

c. State laws, particularly where corporations are involved, may also weigh heavily, further inviting counsel assistance.

Distribution

Original signature to each party and to each of their professionals designated as providing assistance

Bulk Transfers Notice

Definition

The bulk transfers notice, used by businesses subject to the Bulk Transfer Act, is to be sent to all creditors for compliance.

Comments

a. The purpose of the Bulk Transfers Act is to prevent sale of the business, especially its inventory, while the buyer absconds owing creditors who provided the inventory but were not paid for it.

b. Failure to comply with the act will mean the creditors will have a lien on the assets transferred to the buyer.

c. Check the technical requirements in each state where the business has assets being sold, as the Uniform Commercial Code has been adopted with differences in some jurisdictions.

Distribution

Original to buyer

Copy to each creditor

Copy retained by seller

Bulk Transfer Tax Authorities Notice

Definition

The bulk transfer tax authorities notice is similar to the bulk transfer notice, but may also be required to satisfy state tax authorities.

Comments

a. In some states, such notification is required of *all* businesses, and is for the purpose of resolving all tax liabilities.

b. If not complied with, the buyer may be responsible for seller's tax liabilities, at least to the extent of assets transferred.

c. Before proceeding with marketing and sale, an evaluation of tax compliance may be wise, as such notices may provoke an audit of local taxes.

Distribution

Original to state tax authorities

Copy to buyer

Copy retained by seller

Bulk Transfer Affidavit

Definition

The bulk transfer affidavit is a closing document for buyer's comfort regarding possible liabilities under the Bulk Transfer Act.

Comments

a. The listed creditors will normally be those for liabilities the buyer has agreed to pay. Otherwise, the list will say "none."

b. The form may be used even when the Bulk Transfer Act (also known as the Bulk Sales Act in some jurisdictions) does not apply, to protect the buyer against a later finding it should have applied.

Distribution

Original to buyer

Copy retained by seller

Bulk Sales Compliance Affidavit

Definition

The bulk sales compliance affidavit is a seller's covenant that the Bulk Transfer Act does not apply to the transaction.

Comments

a. This document should be delivered by seller to buyer at the closing of the sale.

b. Copies of all bulk transfer notices to creditors and tax authorities should also be delivered at the same time if not already provided to buyer.

Distribution

Same as for Bulk Transfer Affidavit

Affidavit of Title

Definition

The affidavit of title is a seller's covenant of good title to assets being transferred to buyer.

Comments

a. Title to most business assets is not registered with any governmental authority. The affidavit of title is intended to compensate for nonregistration, giving comfort to the buyer that the seller indeed owns and has the power to transfer the assets being sold.

b. If the assets are being accepted subject to a lien, the buyer should also be provided with a statement from the lienholder detailing and confirming the amount and terms of payment.

c. This form should be made and delivered at closing.

Distribution

Original to buyer

Copy to seller

Bill of Sale

Definition

The bill of sale is a document of title, proving ownership, especially for assets for which title is not registered with any authority.

Comments

a. Note that the warranties in the body are strict and necessary to pass unclouded title. If there is any doubt as to any asset, the issue should be investigated and determined.

b. A bill of sale is useful as proof for insurance coverage, warranty claims, collateralized borrowing, and tax calculations.

c. Notarization is technically not a necessity, but such authentication tends to be useful in supporting proof value.

Distribution

Original to buyer

Copy to seller

POTENTIAL ACQUIRER'S COVENANT OF CONFIDENTIALITY

_____ ("Company"), a company engaged in the business of _____ in the City and State of _____, _____, makes this Covenant in consideration for the disclosure to it of Confidential Information from and about the "Disclosing Party" which is also engaged in a similar business. Such Confidential Information may include, but is not limited to, customer lists, price lists, financial statements, inventory data, equipment listings, tax returns, processes, patents, intellectual property, research, and other trade secrets. The purpose of disclosure is to allow evaluation of such Confidential Information for consideration of possible acquisition. Company hereby agrees to the following:

1. Company will not disclose any such information to any third parties nor disclose the same to any persons outside of its executive officers and their immediate staff charged with analytical duties, other than to its Board Members, CPA, Attorney, Lender and/or Insuror, all of whom Company guarantees will adhere to this Covenant.

2. Company will not use any of such Confidential Information in unfair competition against the Disclosing Party, whose identity is to be disclosed upon execution hereof.

3. If Company ceases to pursue acquisition of the Disclosing Party, all written materials provided by Disclosing Party shall be returned to Disclosing Party without retention by Company or anyone on its behalf of any copy, abstract or write-up of such material.

4. This Covenant is binding upon all successors and assigns of Company.

Company _____

by _____   Date _____
    An Authorized Officer

INVENTION CONFIDENTIALITY AGREEMENT

In consideration of the mutual promises herein contained, this Agreement is made by and between _____("Inventor") and
_____("Evaluator") regarding
_____("Invention") invented by the Inventor, as follows:

Whereas Inventor has invented the Invention, filed for patent protection, and solicited (subsequent to filing) Evaluator as a potential licensee for rights to manufacture and sell the Invention; and

Whereas Evaluator has responded to Inventor's solicitation with a request for disclosure by Inventor of data about the Invention; and

Whereas, by receiving disclosure of such data Evaluator will learn valuable, secret, confidential, and proprietary data about the Invention, developed at great cost over a long time by Inventor;

Inventor agrees to provide data to Evaluator for the strictly limited purpose of permitting Evaluator to form an opinion about becoming a licensee or entering into additional contracts with Inventor, and Evaluator agrees to receive and evaluate such data in strictest confidence only for the purpose described above, and further agrees to the following:

1. Evaluator will keep absolutely secret all data provided by Inventor, will use all data only in accord herewith, and will not permit data to be used for any other purpose, be infringed upon, or disclosed to any third party.

2. No copies or photos will be made or retained of any materials or written data supplied. At the conclusion of communications, or upon demand by the Inventor, all data, including documents, instructions, prototypes, photographs, memoranda, and notes taken by the Evaluator shall be promptly returned.

3. No disclosure shall be made by Evaluator to any consultant or third party without Inventor's prior express written consent.

4. Evaluator will not infringe, distribute, reproduce, manufacture, sell, copy, or utilize the Invention, any facsimile based thereupon, or any of the valuable, secret, confidential, or proprietary data provided by Inventor about the Invention, without the express prior written consent of Inventor.

5. Evaluator shall have no obligation with respect to data recorded as known by Evaluator prior to date of this agreement.

Evaluator _____   Inventor _____

by _____   by _____

Address _____   Address _____

_____   _____

Date _____   Date _____

BUSINESS SALE AGREEMENT

THIS BUSINESS SALE AGREEMENT is made this _____, 19____, by and between
_____ ("Buyer") and _____
("Seller") as follows:

1. SUBJECT Seller is selling and Buyer is buying the assets listed on attached Schedule A, for the price listed below, comprising all the business assets located in leased premises at _____. The allocation of the Purchase Price to the assets as shown therein shall control, and the parties certify that the same complies with the Internal Revenue Code.

2. DEPOSIT Buyer has given an earnest money deposit in the form of check, in amount of $_____. Deposit to be held in escrow by _____, subject to the terms of this Sale Agreement. Said deposit is to be applied at settlement toward the closing price.

3. PRICE and PAYMENT The total price of the aforesaid assets is _____ dollars ($_____) payable as follows:

Initial Cash Payment (including Deposit)	$_____
Promissory Note Payable (see below)	$_____
Total Price	$_____

4. NOTE The $_____ Note is to bear interest at _____ percent (___%) per year, payable monthly for _____ years at $_____ per month with first payment due one (1) month after settlement. The Note will be secured by a First Lien UCC Financing Statement and by a Purchase Money Security Agreement, all of which documents shall be in customary commercial form. The Note is to be prepayable without limitation and without penalty.

5. SETTLEMENT Settlement shall be held on _____, 19_____, at a mutually convenient time (or as soon thereafter as all necessary arrangements are completed in accord with this Contract) at the offices of _____ at _____. Recording fees to be paid by Buyer. Each party shall be responsible for its own attorney fees. All recurring charges, such as rental payments, utilities, property taxes and the like shall be prorated to settlement, Seller paying for settlement date.

6. INDEMNITIES Seller shall indemnify and hold harmless Buyer from any undisclosed liabilities, lawsuits, claims, charges and encumbrances, Buyer retaining a right to offset therefor. Seller further warrants at the time of settlement there will be no liabilities, lawsuits, claims, charges, or encumbrances outstanding against the assets, and any then existing shall reduce the purchase price accordingly. Seller further agrees to indemnify Buyer in and from all liabilities and damages of every kind and character arising from ownership of the assets prior to the time of settlement. Buyer similarly agrees to indemnify Seller in and from all liabilities and damages of every kind and character arising from ownership of the assets after the time of settlement.

7. TAXES Seller shall indemnify Buyer against adjustment to property taxes for any period before settlement. Seller warrants all property tax returns have been prepared in good faith and properly filed.

8. INSURANCE Buyer will carry hazard and liability insurance in prudent amounts with Seller named in and provided with Certificates of Insurance.

9. PURCHASER REPRESENTATIONS Buyer represents Buyer is financially capable of completing this transaction; this transaction will not be in violation of any obligation of Buyer; Buyer has had, to the extent desired, sufficient counsel, and Buyer has full capacity to make this Contract.

10. SELLER REPRESENTATIONS Seller warrants
    a. To provide Buyer with good and marketable title to the assets, free and clear of all liens and encumbrances
    b. All assets to be in working order and in all respects in no worse physical condition as when viewed by Buyer on _____, 19____
    c. No judgments are outstanding or pending against any Seller
    d. Seller has full power to make this Contract and such Contract is not in violation of any obligation of Seller
    e. To indemnify, defend, and save harmless Buyer in and from all claims, liabilities, and damages, resulting from requirements of the Bulk Sales Act
    f. Full compliance through the time of settlement with the Lease on the Premises and shall indemnify, defend, and save harmless Buyer from all claims under said Lease for events prior to settlement
    g. Full disclosure of all material facts without misrepresentation
    h. No municipal, health, or other orders or violations, whether or not already charged, will be outstanding or pending at settlement.

11. POSSESSION Possession and control will be transferred at or before settlement, including all manufacturer warranties (if any) and lease rights. All assets shall be delivered at the leased premises.

12. TIME Time is of the essence of this Agreement.

13. BROKERAGE There are no brokers to this transaction, and no commission or other payment is due to any third party on account of this transaction.

14. RESTRICTIVE COVENANT Seller agrees that during the time the Note is outstanding, but for at least three (3) years, Seller will not directly or indirectly engage in, invest in, own, be employed by, employ others in, support, consult with, or otherwise promote or assist any business within a radius of _____ miles of the Premises, in competition with the business of Buyer. Seller also agrees to refrain from disclosing any confidential information about the business, including, but not limited to, price lists, customer lists, financial statements, processes, operations, employees, facilities, equipment, or any other confidential data to any third person without the express written prior consent of Buyer. If Seller shall breach this covenant, Seller may be both enjoined and liable for all damages caused by such breach, Buyer's remedies being cumulative.

15. EMPLOYEES Buyer shall have the right, but not the duty, to hire any of the employees of Seller employed at the Premises. All employment taxes shall be current and prorated as of settlement. Seller shall cooperate in providing employment data for the evaluation for employment by Buyer.

16. ASSIGN INSURANCE Buyer may elect to receive assignment of Seller's hazard insurance policy covering the assets. If Buyer shall so elect, Buyer shall reimburse Seller for the pro-rata prepaid premium.

17. PERMITS This Contract is further contingent on Buyer obtainment of Permits for operation required by law for a _____ business at the aforesaid leased premises, to be obtained by settlement.

18. LEASE This Contract is also conntingent on Landlord's approval of assignment of the Lease on the said Premises to Buyer, without additional consideration from Buyer to Landlord, other than obligating themselves under the Lease. The parties shall cooperate to obtain such consent.

19. BANK FINANCING Seller acknowledges Buyer has applied for bank financing of $_____ at commercially reasonable rates to be used toward operations and/or fulfillment of this Agreement. In addition to all other contingencies, this Agreement is fully contingent on Buyer being granted a loan of not less than the said amount for such purposes.

Business Sale Agreement (*continued*)

20. UNFULFILLED CONTINGENCIES If any contingency in this Agreement is not fulfilled by the time required for settlement, then either party may declare this Agreement null and void, whereupon the deposit shall be returned to Buyer and the parties shall thereby stand fully released from this transaction.

21. ENTITIES Buyer may assign part or all of their interests in this Agreement to one or more corporations or other entities, or among themselves, all without limitation, except that no such assignment shall relieve Buyer of obligations to Seller hereunder.

22. MISCELLANEOUS All covenants, warranties, and promises contained herein are made jointly and severally by the respective parties, and all such covenants, conditions, and warranties shall survive settlement and delivery and not be merged therein. If any portion of this Agreement is or becomes invalid by operation of law or rule of court, the same shall not invalidate the entire contract, which shall continue in full force and effect as if the invalid portion had never been a part hereof. This Contract shall fully bind and inure to the benefit of all successors of both parties, as if each successor were an original party. This Contract (including attachments) is the entire agreement between the parties and may be modified only in writing signed by all parties. This Contract is made under the laws of _____.

Buyer: Seller:

_____(Seal)   _____(Seal)

_____(Seal)   _____(Seal)

BULK TRANSFERS NOTICE

THIS NOTICE is made to you under the Uniform Commercial Code regarding Bulk Transfers, as you have been identified as a creditor or claimholder of

_____ ("Company")

Address _____

which has committed to transfer certain business personalty assets outside the ordinary course of business to

_____ ("Transferee")

Address _____

Please note that during the last three (3) years the Company has also been known by or used the following additional names and trade names:

_____

The Company's debts ____ (are/are not) to be paid in full as they fall due. If NOT, please be further advised:

1. The location and general description of property being transferred is

_____

_____

2. The estimated total of the Company's debts equals $_____.

3. The schedule of property and list of creditors may be inspected at the following address during normal business hours on business days.

_____

4. The Transfer ____ (is/is not) being engaged in to pay existing debts. If so engaged in, also be further advised:

    The amount of such debts and the creditor(s) intended for payment are

    $_____ owed to _____

    $_____ owed to _____

    $_____ owed to _____

5. The transfer ____ (is/is not) made for new consideration. If so made, the amount thereof and the time and place set for transfer are $_____ on _____, 19____, at ____:__ __M at the address of _____.

Bulk Transfers Notice (*continued*)

6. A copy of this Notice is being sent to all listed creditors and claimholders and to all tax authorities having jurisdiction over Company or any of the business personalty assets intended for transfer.

7. This Notice is required by law for the comfort of the Transferee and Creditors. Neither inclusion on the list nor mailing or receipt validates any disputed claim nor waives any rights to dispute, correct, adjust, offset, contest, or deny any claim or debt, and all rights of Company and of Transferee with regard to any and all such claims and debts are hereby cumulatively reserved, without limitation.

Dated _____, 19____

Company _____   Transferee _____

by _____   _____
Authorized Signatory   Authorized Signatory

To _____

_____

_____

BULK TRANSFER TAX AUTHORITIES NOTICE

Re: Request for certification that no tax, penalties, or interest are due from

_____ Federal ID No. _____

Type of Tax(es) _____   Tax Account No. _____

Address _____

Contact Person _____   Phone _____

Dear Tax Authority:

_____ ("Company") registered with you as listed above intends to transfer certain business assets outside the ordinary course of business to _____ ("Transferee"), with a business address of _____, which transfer is scheduled for closing on _____, 19____, at ____:__ __M.

   Please issue a certificate showing no taxes, penalties, or interest are due from the Company, or if any are due, please issue a statement to such effect to the Company's address (Attn: the Contact Person) as shown above.

   Any outstanding tax liability owed to you by the Company _____ (is/is not) expected to be paid in full at the time of closing. Please forward subsequent invoices and notices, if any, to the following:

_____.

   Thank you for your attention to this matter.

Date _____, 19____   Company _____

                                 by _____
                                 Authorized Signatory

BULK TRANSFER AFFIDAVIT

In accordance with the Bulk Sales Act of the Uniform Commercial Code as adopted in the State of _____, the undersigned Signatory, by and on behalf of _____("Seller"), and with full power and capacity to do so, hereby executes this Affidavit for the benefit of _____("Buyer").

The following constitutes a full and complete list of all creditors of Seller's business known as _____as of this date, and includes all persons known to Seller to assert claims against Seller even though such claims may be disputed by Seller. Seller is not an obligor of outstanding bonds, notes, or the like to which there is an indenture trustee.

Name of Creditor	Business Address	Amount Owed

Date _____, 19____   Seller _____

                                   by _____
                                   An Authorized Signatory

State of _____

_____of _____

The foregoing Bulk Transfer Affidavit was signed, sworn to, and acknowledged on _____, 19____, by _____the _____, of and on behalf of _____(Seller).

_____
Notary Public

                         (Notary Seal)

My commission expires _____

BULK SALES COMPLIANCE AFFIDAVIT

_____, duly authorized Signatory of and on behalf of
_____ ("Seller"), hereby makes Affidavit under oath that:

a. Seller is the sole owner of certain assets being contemporaneously sold to
    _____

b. Such assets comprise all or substantially all assets of a business operated heretofore by Seller
    under the name _____

c. Seller is not and has not been engaged in a business subject to the Bulk Sales Act of the State of
    _____

d. No further compliance with said State's Bulk Sales Act is required

e. Seller knows of no creditors who may assert a claim, disputed or otherwise, against the assets or
    business, nor is Seller an obligor, jointly or severally, of outstanding bonds, notes, or the like to
    which there is an indenture trustee.

f. The sale of the said assets is a bona fide sale, made for good and valid consideration had and
    received, and is not made for the purpose or with the intent of defrauding, delaying, hindering,
    or avoiding Seller's creditors nor for the purpose of hiding or wrongfully converting said assets.

g. Signatory has full power and capacity to make this Affidavit, doing so intentionally, voluntarily,
    and with advice of Counsel, hereby swearing under oath all the foregoing to be true statements
    made for and on behalf of Seller.

Seller _____

Date _____, 19____   by _____(Seal)
                                       An Authorized Signatory

State of _____

_____ of _____

    The foregoing Bulk Sales Compliance Affidavit was signed, sworn to, and acknowledged before
me by _____, authorized Signatory, for and on behalf of
_____(Seller) on _____, 19____.

_____
Notary Public

(Notary Seal)

My commission expires _____

AFFIDAVIT OF TITLE

_____("Seller") hereby makes this Affidavit of Title on _____ , 19____,
for the benefit and comfort of and in favor of _____ ("Buyer"), certifying
as follows:

1. Seller is now in possession of and is the absolute owner of the following described asset(s)
   about to be conveyed to Buyer, who is relying hereon, and has been the absolute owner at least
   since the date indicated as to each such asset.

   _____

   _____

   _____

2. Possession and ownership has been unchallenged, unquestioned, and undisputed, except
   heretofore by _____ , which claim was disposed of as follows on the
   date indicated.

   _____

   _____

3. Seller knows of no fact, claim, reason, challenge, dispute, or circumstance that reasonably may
   threaten or prevent conveyance to Buyer of any asset listed above, or threaten or prevent
   Buyer's peaceable enjoyment, ownership, and rights in and to any such asset.

4. No contract, option, or other right to acquire, contingent or otherwise, exists with respect to any
   such asset other than to Buyer.

5. No lien, encumbrance, financing statement, security interest, or other secured creditor claim
   affects any such asset, except the following, subject to which Buyer takes and accepts such
   asset(s).

   _____

   _____

6. No lawsuit, administrative proceeding, arbitration, or other dispute is pending against Seller or
   in rem against any such asset, that may or would affect Buyer's acquisition or rights in any such
   asset.

7. No bankruptcy court action of any kind is now pending against Seller, nor has Seller made any
   assignment for the benefit of creditors, nor committed any act of bankruptcy, nor is Seller
   insolvent, nor does Seller have the intent of seeking and is not seeking protection of any bankruptcy court.

8. Seller is a valid entity as represented to Buyer in good standing in every jurisdiction where
   doing business and where such asset(s) is(are) located, if required by law to be qualified in such
   jurisdiction(s).

9. Seller's ownership and possession, and the conveyance to Buyer, will not be in violation of any law affecting or binding Seller.

10. Seller has full power and authority to make the conveyance to Buyer and to make this Affidavit, all corporate formalities having been strictly observed and all laws having been fully complied with.

11. Seller's signatory has been duly authorized to sign on behalf of Seller, and such authority is in force.

Date _____, 19____   Seller _____

                                      by _____
                                         Authorized Signatory

State of _____

_____ of _____, to wit

The foregoing Affidavit of Title was sworn to and acknowledged before me on _____, 19____, by _____ for and on behalf of the Seller, _____.

_____
Notary Public

                                       (Seal)

My commission expires _____

BILL OF SALE

FOR AND IN CONSIDERATION of the sum of _____dollars ($_____)
and other valuable consideration, the undersigned Seller, _____, hereby
sells, transfers, conveys, and assigns to the Buyer, _____, all right, title, and
interest in and to the following listed assets:

_____

_____

And which assets are located at the following address:

_____

_____

Seller hereby covenants and warrants:

a. Seller has the right to sell, transfer, convey, and assign the said assets.

b. Seller has done no act to encumber same.

c. Seller warrants specially and generally the said assets.

d. Seller will execute such further assurances as may be necessary respecting same and will
    warrant and defend the same against claim of any and all other persons, entities, and claimants.

e. The said assets are not subject to the lien of any debt, tax, claim, or legal proceeding.

WITNESS our hands and seals this _____ day of _____, 19____.

Made by Seller   Accepted—Buyer

by _____(Seal)   by _____(Seal)
   An Authorized Signatory   An Authorized Signatory

State of _____
_____of _____

The foregoing Bill of Sale was signed, sworn to, and acknowledged on _____, 19____, by
_____, the _____of and on behalf of
_____(Seller) and by _____, the _____ of and on
behalf of _____(Buyer).

_____
Notary Public

(Notary Seal)

My commission expires _____

Module X

Sale of Goods and Services

INTRODUCTION

These documents form the lifeblood of every business and should therefore receive special attention. For too many businesses, familiarity seems to breed contempt, as little real attention is paid to the system of operation they foster, even if inadvertently.

The purposes of these forms are

1. To protect the rights of the sender and to limit the rights of the recipient against the sender
2. To provide an adequate audit trail on transactions for operational efficiency
3. To provide a database easily analyzed for management decision making
4. To promote fulfillment of the economic mission of yielding profits by increasing sales and controlling costs

MODULE FORMS

The 13 forms in this module are

Catalogue Disclaimer

Federal Bidder's Mailing List Application

Request for Quotation

Quotation

Purchase Order

Order Acknowledgment

Blanket Purchase Order Requisition

Consignment Agreement

Maintenance Agreement

Services Agreement

Contract for Sale of Goods

Notice of Warranty Claim

Disclaimer of Warranty

Catalogue Disclaimer

Definition

The catalogue disclaimer is to be included with a catalogue or similar promotional material to disclaim liability and protect pricing rights.

Comments

a. If the catalogue were to constitute an offer, and a buyer sent notice of acceptance, refusal or failure to fulfill it would subject the seller to liability for breach of contract.

b. Businesses in highly competitive markets may not want to take the chance of offending customers by including such a statement.

c. The disclaimer can be placed at the end of the catalogue or included in small print.

Distribution

Included in each catalogue

Federal Bidder's Mailing List Application

Definition

The federal bidder's mailing list application is a U.S. government form used by businesses wishing to be notifed of upcoming contracts available for bid.

Comments

a. Each agency of the government usually has its own purchasing arm, so the form may be filed in several places.

b. The third page is the supplement for defense contracts.

c. Sales to the U.S. government are subject to an incredible number of regulations and requirements. Investigate carefully before proceeding.

Distribution

Original to each agency of interest
Copy retained by sales department

Request for Quotation

Definition

The request for quotation is an inquiry to a potential seller for price and availability of products or services.

Comments

a. The terms of the quotation on the second page should match to those that would be issued as part of the purchase order (to be defined later).

b. Ignore the "Quantity" and "Price/Unit" columns if not applicable on service contracts. Spec sheets can be included as attachments.

Distribution

Original plus copy to proposed vendor
Copy to purchasing department
Copy to requisitioning department

Quotation

Definition

The quotation is an offer to sell goods or services, subject to specific terms.

Comments

a. The terms of the quotation should match those of the order acknowledgment (to be defined later).

b. Quotations should be sent in response to phone or other verbal inquiries, even if confirming a verbal offer, in order to assert the other controlling terms.

c. Note that the form can be used as an order form by the recipient.

Distribution

Original to potential customer
Copy retained by sales department

Purchase Order

Definition

The purchase order is an offer to purchase goods or services subject to specific terms.

Comments

a. Comments regarding the request for quotation are applicable to the purchase order, as well.

b. Shipment without any preceding documentation accepts the terms of the purchase order.

c. If documentation is received that varies the terms, the variations will apply to the contract formed, unless some protest is made and a compromise negotiated.

Distribution

Original to vendor

Copy to receiving/traffic department

Copy to accounting department

Copy retained by purchasing department

Order Acknowledgment

Definition

The order acknowledgment is an acceptance of an offer to buy goods and services.

Comments

a. The order acknowledgment is the reciprocal to the purchase order and the very document to be used to assert more favorable terms, correct errors, or notice price changes.

b. Comments regarding both the quotation and the purchase order are applicable to the order acknowledgment, as well.

Distribution

Original to buyer

Copy to shipping/operations department

Copy to accounting department

Copy retained by sales department

Blanket Purchase Order Requisition

Definition

The blanket purchase order requisition is used to draw more deliveries from vendor when a blanket contract for multiple deliveries has been made.

Comments

a. This form may apply to a purchase order or to a contract for sale of goods (to be defined later).

b. See the comments regarding both those forms.

Distribution

Same as for purchase order

Consignment Agreement

Definition

The consignment agreement is a contract entrusting another with goods for sale to third parties.

Comments

a. Consignment agreements are relatively rare outside the retail field.

b. Obviously this is a relationship requiring a high degree of trust, communication, and coordination between the contract parties.

c. Counsel assistance in developing consignment arrangements, especially across state lines, is recommended.

Distribution

Original signature to each party

Maintenance Agreement

Definition

The maintenance agreement is a contract for services under which the service provider takes custody over assets of the buyer.

Comments

a. The custody issue is the principal difference between a maintenance agreement and a simple services agreement (to be defined later).

b. Because of custody, the nature of liability exposure and rights of the party, including that of the repairer to a mechanic's lien in some jurisdictions, are somewhat particularized.

c. A blanket agreement of this kind also may facilitate scheduling of equipment downtime for maintenance needs.

Distribution

Original signature to each party

Services Agreement

Definition

The services agreement is a contract for the provision of services from vendor to customer.

Comments

a. Most service contracts will require customization.

b. The example provided is designed for consultants and similar service providers.

Distribution

Original signature to each party

Contract for Sale of Goods

Definition

The contract for sale of goods is used for the provision of goods by vendor to customer.

Comments

a. These kinds of contracts, in place of purchase orders and order acknowledgments, are more common where some customization of the product, such as manufacture to specifications, is involved.

b. As these are sale of goods transactions, they will be subject to the Uniform Commercial Code.

Distribution

Original signature to each party

Notice of Warranty Claim

Definition

The notice of warranty claim is a claim by a buyer that warranted goods or services have been found defective and require correction.

Comments

a. If warranties have been implied by law (e.g., UCC), this notice will be effective for claiming them, providing it is sent within a reasonable time.

b. If the contract warranty requires a specific procedure for making claims, the procedure must be followed to validate the claim.

c. The claim must be asserted before the warranty expires.

Distribution

Original to vendor

Copy to purchasing department

Copy to accounting department

Copy retained by initiating department

Disclaimer of Warranty

Definition

The disclaimer of warranty eliminates the buyer's warranty rights.

Comments

a. Especially for sales to consumers, such a disclaimer may not be valid in all jurisdictions, or may be limited in effect.

b. The disclaimer should be signed at the time of purchase.

c. While the terms of the disclaimer can be included in a contract of sale (and should be for the vendor), a separate document draws attention to the disclaimer to avoid a fraud claim.

Distribution

Original signature to each party

CATALOGUE DISCLAIMER

Thank you for your interest in our company!

Because the products and prices in this catalogue are continually updated, we cannot always guarantee that they will be available or in effect at the time of order placement, so we ask you to contact us for verification.

The catalogue and its contents are a solicitation for offers and do not constitute an offer. All orders are subject to acceptance.

Again our thanks for your interest.

Catalogue Contents: Copyright 19____, by _____

SOLICITATION MAILING LIST APPLICATION

1. TYPE OF APPLICATION	2. DATE	FORM APPROVED OMB NO.
☐ INITIAL ☐ REVISION		**3090-0009**

NOTE—Please complete all items on this form. Insert N/A in items not applicable. See reverse for Instructions.

3. NAME AND ADDRESS OF FEDERAL AGENCY TO WHICH FORM IS SUBMITTED *(Include ZIP code)*	4. NAME AND ADDRESS OF APPLICANT *(Include county and ZIP code)*

5. TYPE OF ORGANIZATION *(Check one)*

☐ INDIVIDUAL   ☐ NON-PROFIT ORGANIZATION

☐ PARTNERSHIP   ☐ CORPORATION, INCORPORATED UNDER THE LAWS OF THE STATE OF:

6. ADDRESS TO WHICH SOLICITATIONS ARE TO BE MAILED *(If different than Item 4)*

7. NAMES OF OFFICERS, OWNERS, OR PARTNERS

A. PRESIDENT	B. VICE PRESIDENT	C. SECRETARY
D. TREASURER	E. OWNERS OR PARTNERS	

8. AFFILIATES OF APPLICANT *(Names, locations and nature of affiliation. See definition on reverse.)*

9. PERSONS AUTHORIZED TO SIGN OFFERS AND CONTRACTS IN YOUR NAME *(Indicate if agent)*

NAME	OFFICIAL CAPACITY	TELE. NO. *(Include area code)*

10. IDENTIFY EQUIPMENT, SUPPLIES, AND/OR SERVICES ON WHICH YOU DESIRE TO MAKE AN OFFER *(See attached Federal agency's supplemental listing and instructions, if any)*

11A. SIZE OF BUSINESS *(See definitions on reverse)*	11B. AVERAGE NUMBER OF EMPLOYEES *(Including affiliates)* FOR FOUR PRECEDING CALENDAR QUARTERS	11C. AVERAGE ANNUAL SALES OR RECEIPTS FOR PRECEDING THREE FISCAL YEARS
☐ SMALL BUSINESS *(If checked, complete items 11B and 11C)* ☐ OTHER THAN SMALL BUSINESS		$

12. TYPE OF OWNERSHIP *(See definitions on reverse) (Not applicable for other than small businesses)*	13. TYPE OF BUSINESS *(See definitions on reverse)*			
☐ DISADVANTAGED BUSINESS ☐ WOMAN-OWNED BUSINESS	☐ MANUFACTURER OR PRODUCER ☐ SERVICE ESTABLISHMENT	☐ REGULAR DEALER *(Type 1)* ☐ REGULAR DEALER *(Type 2)*	☐ CONSTRUCTION CONCERN ☐ RESEARCH AND DEVELOPMENT	☐ SURPLUS DEALER

14. DUNS NO. *(If available)*	15. HOW LONG IN PRESENT BUSINESS?

16. FLOOR SPACE *(Square feet)*		17. NET WORTH	
A. MANUFACTURING	B. WAREHOUSE	A. DATE	B. AMOUNT $

18. SECURITY CLEARANCE *(If applicable, check highest clearance authorized)*

FOR	TOP SECRET	SECRET	CONFIDENTIAL	C. NAMES OF AGENCIES WHICH GRANTED SECURITY CLEARANCES *(Include dates)*
A. KEY PERSONNEL				
B. PLANT ONLY				

CERTIFICATION — I certify that information supplied herein *(Including all pages attached)* is correct and that neither the applicant nor any person *(Or concern)* in any connection with the applicant as a principal or officer, so far as is known, is now debarred or otherwise declared ineligible by any agency of the Federal Government from making offers for furnishing materials, supplies, or services to the Government or any agency thereof.

19. NAME AND TITLE OF PERSON AUTHORIZED TO SIGN *(Type or print)*	20. SIGNATURE	21. DATE SIGNED

NSN 7540-01-152-8086
PREVIOUS EDITIONS UNUSABLE

129-106

STANDARD FORM 129 (REV. 10-83)
Prescribed by GSA
FAR (48 CFR) 53.214(c)

Solicitation Mailing List Application (*continued*)

INSTRUCTIONS

Persons or concerns wishing to be added to a particular agency's bidder's mailing list for supplies or services shall file this properly completed and certified Solicitation Mailing List Application, together with such other lists as may be attached to this application form, with each procurement office of the Federal agency with which they desire to do business. If a Federal agency has attached a Supplemental Commodity list with instructions, complete the application as instructed. Otherwise, identify in Item 10 the equipment supplies and/or services on which you desire to bid. (Provide Federal Supply Class or Standard Industrial Classification Codes if available.) The application shall be submitted and signed by the principal as distinguished from an agent, however constituted.

After placement on the bidder's mailing list of an agency, your failure to respond (submission of bid, or notice in writing, that you are unable to bid on that particular transaction but wish to remain on the active bidder's mailing list for that particular item) to solicitations will be understood by the agency to indicate lack of interest and concurrence in the removal of your name from the purchasing activity's solicitation mailing list for the items concerned.

SIZE OF BUSINESS DEFINITIONS
(See Item 11A.)

a. Small business concern—A small business concern for the purpose of Government procurement is a concern, including its affiliates, which is independently owned and operated, is not dominant in the field of operation in which it is competing for Government contracts and can further qualify under the criteria concerning number of employees, average annual receipts, or other criteria, as prescribed by the Small Business Administration. (See Code of Federal Regulations, Title 13, Part 121, as amended, which contains detailed industry definitions and related procedures.)

b. Affiliates—Business concerns are affiliates of each other when either directly or indirectly (i) one concern controls or has the power to control the other, or (ii) a third party controls or has the power to control both. In determining whether concerns are independently owned and operated and whether or not affiliation exists, consideration is given to all appropriate factors including common ownership, common management, and contractual relationship. (See Items 8 and 11A.)

c. Number of employees—(Item 11B) In connection with the determination of small business status, "number of employees" means the average employment of any concern, including the employees of its domestic and foreign affiliates, based on the number of persons employed on a full-time, part-time, temporary, or other basis during each of the pay periods of the preceding 12 months. If a concern has not been in existence for 12 months, "number of employees" means the average employment of such concern and its affiliates during the period that such concern has been in existence based on the number of persons employed during each of the pay periods of the period that such concern has been in business.

TYPE OF OWNERSHIP DEFINITIONS
(See Item 12.)

a. "Disadvantaged business concern"—means any business concern (1) which is at least 51 percent owned by one or more socially and economically disadvantaged individuals; or, in the case of any publicly owned business, at least 51 percent of the stock of which is owned by one or more socially and economically disadvantaged individuals; and (2) whose management and daily business operations are controlled by one or more of such individuals.

b. "Women-owned business"—means a business that is at least 51 percent owned by a woman or women who are U.S. citizens and who also control and operate the business.

TYPE OF BUSINESS DEFINITIONS
(See Item 13.)

a. Manufacturer or producer—means a person (or concern) owning, operating, or maintaining a store, warehouse, or other establishment that produces, on the premises, the materials, supplies, articles, or equipment of the general character of those listed in Item 10, or in the Federal Agency's Supplemental Commodity List, if attached.

b. Service establishment—means a concern (or person) which owns, operates, or maintains any type of business which is principally engaged in the furnishing of nonpersonal services, such as (but not limited to) repairing, cleaning, redecorating, or rental of personal property, including the furnishing of necessary repair parts or other supplies as part of the services performed.

c. Regular dealer (Type 1)—means a person (or concern) who owns, operates, or maintains a store, warehouse, or other establishment in which the materials, supplies, articles, or equipment of the general character listed in Item 10, or in the Federal Agency's Supplemental Commodity List, if attached, are bought, kept in stock, and sold to the public in the usual course of business.

d. Regular dealer (Type 2)—In the case of supplies of particular kinds (at present, petroleum, lumber and timber products, machine tools, raw cotton, green coffee, hay, grain, feed, or straw, agricultural liming materials, tea, raw or unmanufactured cotton linters and used ADPE), Regular dealer means a person (or concern) satisfying the requirements of the regulations (Code of Federal Regulations, Title 41, 50-201.101(a)(2)) as amended from time to time, prescribed by the Secretary of Labor under the Walsh-Healey Public Contracts Act (Title 41 U.S. Code 35-45). For coal dealers see Code of Federal Regulations, Title 41, 50-201.604(a).

● COMMERCE BUSINESS DAILY—The Commerce Business Daily, published by the Department of Commerce, contains information concerning proposed procurements, sales, and contract awards. For further information concerning this publication, contact your local Commerce Field Office.

✿ GPO : 1983 O – 381-526 (9041)   **STANDARD FORM 129 BACK** (REV. 10-83)

BIDDER'S MAILING LIST APPLICATION SUPPLEMENT

FORM APPROVED
OMB NO. 0704-0011

IF ADDITIONAL SPACE IS REQUIRED, ATTACH SEPARATE SHEET AND REFER TO ITEM NUMBER

1. NUMBER OF EMPLOYEES	OPERATIONS AT	ENGINEERING	PRODUCTION	OTHERS	TOTAL
	MAXIMUM LEVEL				
	MINIMUM *(During last 2 yrs.)*				
	PRESENT LEVEL				

2. CONTRACTS HELD WITH ARMED SERVICES DURING PAST 3 YEARS *(List separately)*

CONTRACT NUMBER	DESCRIPTION OF ITEMS	DOLLAR VALUE

3. TYPES OF EQUIPMENT COMPONENTS, MATERIAL OR SERVICES NOW BEING MANUFACTURED, PERFORMED, OR DEVELOPED *(Commercial and Military)*

4. FLOOR SPACE *(Sq. ft.)*	ENGINEERING	LABORATORY	TOTAL FLOOR SPACE *(Including warehouse and manufacturing space)*

5. BRIEF DESCRIPTION OF BUILDINGS *(Type of construction and use)*

6. MACHINERY AND EQUIPMENT

7. TESTING AND/OR LABORATORY FACILITIES

8. ADDRESSES *(Including counties)* **OF FACTORIES, FOUNDRIES, MINES, OR YARDS, IF ANY** *(Specify)* *(Include Zip Code)*

9. SECURITY CLEARANCE *(If applicable, check highest clearance authorized by clearing agency)*

FOR KEY PERSONNEL		FOR PLANT ONLY	
TOP SECRET	CONFIDENTIAL	SECRET	CONFIDENTIAL
SECRET			

LIST DEPARTMENTS WHICH HAVE GRANTED SECURITY CLEARANCE AND DATES GRANTED

10. INCLOSURES *(Check)*
☐ FINANCIAL STATEMENTS, INCLUDING OPERATING STATEMENTS   ☐ DESCRIPTIVE LITERATURE
☐ ADDITIONAL INFORMATION ATTACHED   ☐ BROCHURE   ☐ CATALOG   ☐ PHOTOGRAPHS

11. I CERTIFY THAT THE INFORMATION SUPPLIED HEREIN *(Including any attachments)* **IS CORRECT**

DATE	NAME AND ADDRESS OF APPLICANT *(Include Zip Code)*	SIGNATURE

Give brief, representative outline of type and condition of machinery, equipment (6), and facilities (7) available; If not owned by firm, give status in detail.

DD FORM 1 AUG 60 **558-1**   EDITION OF 1 JAN 54 IS OBSOLETE.   GPO : 1983 O - 405-820

REQUEST FOR QUOTATION
— Not An Order —

Request from: Request to:

_____   _____

_____   _____

_____   _____

Delivery address   _____

                        _____

Please quote price and delivery by item and advise of more economical quantities. No charges for extras, deposits, drayage, minimums, or like will be valid unless quoted and accepted. Terms and conditions on reverse apply to all purchase transactions. All rights reserved, including rights to reject any and all bids.

Additional sheets attached? ___Yes   ___No

This request for quotation is genuine.

Date _____, 19____   _____

                              Authorized Buyer Representative

SPECIFICATIONS		Vendor Data		
Quantity	Description	Price/Unit	Total Price	Lead Time

F.O.B. _____   Payment Terms _____

Carrier _____   Shipping Method _____

Vendor Contact _____   Phone _____

_____   Date _____, 19____
Vendor Signature

Title _____   Phone _____

QUOTATION TERMS AND CONDITIONS

All transactions made pursuant to the Quotation shall be made only in accord with these following terms and conditions, which are incorporated in all documentation for such transactions, whether or not specifically referenced.

1. Unless specified, no charge is to be made for containers, boxing, dunning, drayage, marking, storage, or bundling. Only specified charges are allowed.

2. All performance and delivery are subject to Buyer approval. Seller shall promptly correct any defects or deviation from Specification upon Buyer demand.

3. Payment terms are to be calculated from later of delivery or billing date.

4. Delivery is to be when and where specified, or Buyer may order elsewhere and charge Seller for any extra costs, or Buyer may cancel altogether. Buyer may refuse delivery because of strike, act of God, or other uncontrollable cause.

5. Seller warrants all goods and services conform to Specifications, are free of defects, merchantable, fit for Buyer's purposes, and free of encumbrance. Seller further warrants to Buyer all additional warranties required by law and agrees all warranties inure to Buyer's customers, assigns, and all successors-in-interest of Buyer. Seller warrants all goods delivered and services furnished do not infringe on any patent or otherwise violate the right of any person, and Seller has full power, authority, and capability to perform according to specifications. Seller shall indemnify and save harmless Buyer from all claims, damage, loss, expense, liability, cost, attorney fees, and detriment arising from any and all duties of Seller to Buyer without limitation. Seller expressly waives all defenses, including, but not limited to, assumption of risk and contributory negligence. Seller shall reimburse Buyer for all expenses and losses due to Seller failure to conform to Specifications, to misdelivery, or to other breach.

6. Seller warrants insurance coverage for products liability, comprehensive liability, and workman's compensation in commercially reasonable amounts.

7. Buyer may make written changes to any order prior to shipment.

8. Seller warrants all performance to comply with all applicable law.

9. Unless specified, the Specifications do not include taxes collectible from Buyer, which are to be shown separately on Seller's invoice. Seller shall be responsible for all other taxes due on account of the transaction and shall honor exemption evidence, if presented, in lieu of payment for such taxes.

10. No assignment of any order or contract is allowed without Buyer's written consent.

11. No change in terms or Specifications is allowed without Buyer's written consent.

12. This Agreement is made under laws of state of Buyer's "bill to" address.

13. No purchase order is binding upon Buyer until signed by an authorized Buyer representative.

QUOTATION

Quotation by:

    Seller   _____

    Address   _____

                    _____

Quotation to:

    Buyer   _____

    Address   _____

                    _____

Quotation Date _____ Expiration Date _____

We are pleased to quote, subject to prior sale, and further subject to the Terms listed below and on the reverse side of this form, the following:

Quantity	Description	Price/Unit	Total Price

Shipment ___ days from receipt of order   F.O.B. _____

Required Deposit $_____   Payment Terms _____

TO ORDER: Please return a signed and dated copy of this Quotation, with the required Deposit, and advise delivery destination (below). No cancellation is permitted without Seller approval, and may result in certain charges to Buyer.

                          Quotation Validated by _____
                                            Seller Authorized Representative

Accepted and Ordered _____   Date _____
                    Buyer Authorized Representative

Delivery Destination _____

_____

TERMS

The obverse-listed Quotation is made only under all the following Terms:

1. The price(s) for the goods sold shall be the listed prices only if shipment can be made prior to the listed expiration date. Otherwise, prices will be those in effect on the shipment date.

2. All sales taxes and other governmental charges shall be paid by Buyer and are the responsibility of Buyer, except as limited by law.

3. The expected shipping date is for estimation only. Seller is not liable for damages because of variance from the expected shipping date.

4. Seller may, without liability, delay performance or cancel this contract on account of force majeure or other circumstance beyond its control, including, but not limited to, work stoppages, embargoes, acts of God, war, political unrest, failure of source of supply, or casualty.

5. Unless otherwise specified in writing by Seller, Seller warrants goods sold hereunder to be new and free from substantive defects in workmanship and materials. SELLER'S LIABILITY UNDER THE FOREGOING WARRANTY IS ABSOLUTELY LIMITED TO REPLACEMENT OF GOODS, OR REPAIR OF DEFECTS, OR REFUND OF THE PURCHASE PRICE, AT SELLER'S SOLE OPTION. NO OTHER WARRANTY, EXPRESS OR IMPLIED (INCLUDING, BUT NOT LIMITED TO, MERCHANTABILITY OR FITNESS) IS MADE BY SELLER, AND NONE SHALL BE IMPUTED OR PRESUMED, AND IN NO EVENT SHALL SELLER BE LIABLE FOR ANY GENERAL, CONSEQUENTIAL, INCIDENTAL, PUNITIVE, OR OTHER DAMAGES, NOR FOR ANY CLAIMS ARISING FROM BUYER'S USE OR TRANSFER OF THE GOODS.

6. Seller may, at its sole option, withhold shipment, delivery, and performance of all or any part of the order or cancel the order if at any time Buyer's account with Seller is in arrears, or if for any reason Seller believes Buyer to be not creditworthy, or if Buyer fails to comply with Seller's credit requirements, or if any payment instrument of Buyer is not honored, or if Seller shall discontinue sale of the product.

7. If Buyer fails to pay when due per the stated payment terms, Buyer shall pay interest at 1.5% per month (or maximum allowed by law, if less) plus a 4% late charge (or maximum allowed by law, if less) plus all collection costs including, but not limited to, attorney fees.

8. If the goods are not substantively defective and Buyer rejects delivery or returns the goods or cancels the order without Seller's approval, Buyer shall pay Seller (per the stated payment terms) a restocking charge of 15% of price per item, plus all costs of redelivery to Seller, which shall not be obligated to accept nondefective returns beyond 30 days after shipment by Seller.

9. These Terms will govern any purchase under the Quotation between Buyer and Seller. Seller shall not be bound by any terms not written herein, unless written amendment is signed by an authorized Seller representative. If any portion hereof is found invalid by operation of law or rule of court, the same shall not invalidate the entire contract, the balance of which shall remain in full force and effect. This agreement is governed by _____law.

PURCHASE ORDER

Account No. _____   P.O. No. _____

From Buyer _____

To Seller _____

Ship to: Bill to:

_____   _____

_____   _____

_____   _____

F.O.B. _____   Ship Date _____   Terms _____

Contact Person _____   Phone _____

SPECIFICATIONS

ID No.	Quantity	Description	Price/Unit	Total Price

Subject to terms on reverse. Additional sheets attached? ___Yes   ___No

Date _____, 19____   _____

                                            Authorized Buyer Representative

PURCHASE ORDER TERMS AND CONDITIONS

1. Unless specified, no charge is to be made for containers, boxing, dunning, drayage, marking, storage, or bundling. Only specified charges are allowed.

2. All performance and delivery are subject to Buyer approval. Seller shall promptly correct any defects or deviation from Specification upon Buyer demand.

3. Payment terms are to be calculated from later of delivery or billing date.

4. Delivery is to be when and where specified, or Buyer may order elsewhere and charge Seller for any extra costs, or Buyer may cancel altogether. Buyer may refuse delivery because of strike, act of God, or other uncontrollable cause.

5. Seller warrants all goods and services conform to Specifications, are free of defects, merchantable, fit for Buyer's purposes, and free of encumbrance. Seller further warrants to Buyer all additional warranties required by law and agrees all warranties inure to Buyer's customers, assigns, and all successors-in-interest of Buyer. Seller warrants all goods delivered and services furnished do not infringe on any patent or otherwise violate the right of any person, and Seller has full power, authority, and capability to perform according to specifications. Seller shall indemnify and save harmless Buyer from all claims, damage, loss, expense, liability, cost, attorney fees, and detriment arising from any and all duties of Seller under this Purchase Order, without limitation. Seller expressly waives all defenses, including, but not limited to, assumption of risk and contributory negligence. Seller shall reimburse Buyer for all expenses and losses due to Seller failure to conform to Specifications, to misdelivery, or to other breach.

6. Seller warrants insurance coverage for products liability, comprehensive liability, and workman's compensation in commercially reasonable amounts.

7. Buyer may make written changes to this Purchase Order prior to shipment.

8. Seller warrants all performance to comply with all applicable law.

9. Unless specified, the Purchase Order does not include taxes collectible from Buyer, which are to be shown separately on Seller's invoice. Seller shall be responsible for all other taxes due on account of the transaction and shall honor exemption evidence, if presented, in lieu of payment for such taxes.

10. No assignment of this Purchase Order is allowed without Buyer's written consent.

11. No change in terms or Specifications is allowed without Buyer's written consent. Shipment of any portion of the order or furnishing of any portion of the services by Seller shall constitute absolute acceptance of these terms and the entire Purchase Order.

12. This Agreement is made under laws of state of Buyer's "bill to" address.

13. This Purchase Order is not binding upon Buyer until signed by an authorized Buyer representative.

ORDER ACKNOWLEDGMENT

Seller _____

Address _____

_____

Contact _____   Phone _____   Fax _____

Acknowledgment Date _____   Cust. Acct. No. _____   Trace No. _____

Buyer _____   Order by _____   Rec'd by _____

Bill to _____   Ship to _____

_____   _____

_____   _____

P.O. Date _____   P.O. No. _____   Tax Exemp. No. _____

Deposit _____   Terms _____   F.O.B. _____

Expected Ship Date _____   Carrier _____

Quantity	Description	Code	Price	Per	Extension

Total Order _____

Comments:

Thank you for your order!

Please Immediately verify we have PROCESSED IT CORRECTLY. Notify the above-listed Contact of any discrepancy without delay. Your order is ACCEPTED SUBJECT TO ALL TERMS ON THE REVERSE side of this ORDER ACKNOWLEDGMENT, which supersede all prior agreements regarding this transaction. We appreciate your business.

_____
Authorized Representative

ACKNOWLEDGMENT TERMS

The obverse-listed Order is accepted only under all the following Terms:

1. The price(s) for the goods sold shall be Seller's prices in effect on the shipment date. Prices listed (if any) are the latest, but are not guaranteed and may be altered without prior notice.

2. All sales taxes and other governmental charges shall be paid by Buyer and are the responsibility of Buyer, except as limited by law.

3. The expected shipping date is for estimation only. Seller is not liable for damages because of variance from the expected shipping date.

4. Seller may, without liability, delay performance or cancel this contract on account of force majeure or other circumstance beyond its control, including, but not limited to, work stoppages, embargoes, acts of God, war, political unrest, failure of source of supply, or casualty.

5. Unless otherwise specified in writing by Seller, Seller warrants goods sold hereunder to be new and free from substantive defects in workmanship and materials. SELLER'S LIABILITY UNDER THE FOREGOING WARRANTY IS ABSOLUTELY LIMITED TO REPLACEMENT OF GOODS, OR REPAIR OF DEFECTS, OR REFUND OF THE PURCHASE PRICE, AT SELLER'S SOLE OPTION. NO OTHER WARRANTY, EXPRESS OR IMPLIED (INCLUDING, BUT NOT LIMITED TO, MERCHANTABILITY OR FITNESS) IS MADE BY SELLER, AND NONE SHALL BE IMPUTED OR PRESUMED, AND IN NO EVENT SHALL SELLER BE LIABLE FOR ANY GENERAL, CONSEQUENTIAL, INCIDENTAL, PUNITIVE, OR OTHER DAMAGES, NOR FOR ANY CLAIMS ARISING FROM BUYER'S USE OR TRANSFER OF THE GOODS.

6. Seller may, at its sole option, withhold shipment and delivery of all or any part of the order or cancel the order if at any time Buyer's account with Seller is in arrears, or if for any reason Seller believes Buyer to be not creditworthy, or if Buyer fails to comply with Seller's credit requirements, or if any payment instrument of Buyer is not honored, or if Seller shall discontinue sale of the product.

7. If Buyer fails to pay for the goods when due per the stated payment terms, Buyer shall pay interest at 1.5% per month (or maximum allowed by law, if less) plus a 4% late charge (or maximum allowed by law, if less) plus all collection costs including, but not limited to, attorney fees.

8. If the goods are not substantively defective and Buyer rejects delivery or returns the goods, Buyer shall pay Seller (per the stated payment terms) a restocking charge of 15% of price per item, plus all costs of redelivery to Seller, which shall not be obligated to accept nondefective returns beyond 30 days after shipment by Seller.

9. These Terms encompass the entire agreement between Buyer and Seller, superseding all other terms and conditions. Seller shall not be bound by any terms not written herein, unless written amendment is signed by an authorized Seller representative. If any portion hereof is found invalid by operation of law or rule of court, the same shall not invalidate the entire contract, the balance of which shall remain in full force and effect. This agreement is governed by
_____law.

BLANKET PURCHASE ORDER REQUISITION

To _____

P.O. Reg. No. _____ P.O. Reg. Date _____

Orig. P.O. No. _____ Orig. P.O. Date _____

Bill to Address: Ship to Address:

_____   _____

_____   _____

_____   _____

Requested Delivery Date _____ Ship by _____

Requisition is hereby made of the following under the referenced blanket purchase order:
_____

Ser. No.	Number	Description	Price Each	Total

All terms of the blanket purchase order are hereby ratified, confirmed, and reserved.

_____
Authorized Signature

CONSIGNMENT AGREEMENT

This Agreement is made between _____ ("Consignee") and
_____ ("Seller") as follows:

1. *MERCHANDISE* Seller hereby consigns to Consignee the following described merchandise, to be displayed at Consignee's Premises and offered for sale at the price set forth, of which the designated percentage shall be deducted out of proceeds by Consignee for its compensation.

MERCHANDISE DESCRIPTION	PRICE	CONSIGNEE %

2. *TIME* Said merchandise shall be displayed until the earlier of sale or the time when ____ days have elapsed, at which time Seller may remove the same from Consignee's premises, or the parties shall agree on an extension with such different terms as they mutually agree in writing.

3. *RETURN* If Seller shall fail to remove any unsold merchandise after ____ days, then Consignee may thereafter send written notice to Seller demanding removal within ____ days, and if not sooner removed, Consignee may reship the merchandise to Seller, deducting the costs of shipment from any proceeds then due Seller, and Consignee shall thereafter have no further liability to Seller for such merchandise. However, if Consignee shall maintain the merchandise on display and shall later sell it, then Consignee shall be entitled to an ADDITIONAL ___ percent of the proceeds, though Consignee shall be under no obligation to further display or sell such unsold-after-____-days merchandise.

4. *ADDITIONAL MERCHANDISE* On ten (10) days advance notice, without written objection from Consignee, Seller may further deliver other additional merchandise to Consignee for consignment sale, all of which shall be governed by the same terms and conditions. Such notice shall contain the same information on the additional merchandise as is provided above in Paragraph 1.

5. *TAXES* Appropriate sales tax shall be collected and paid by Consignee and shall not be considered part of the price nor subject to percentage allocation. Property taxes on merchandise consigned shall be the sole responsibility of Seller, but Consignee may deduct and pay such property taxes if assessed to Consignee, provided Consignee accounts therefor to Seller.

6. *CONDITION* Merchandise is to be delivered by Seller in good and salable condition and free of defects. Seller hereby agrees to indemnify Consignee for all costs and liabilities arising from defective merchandise. Consignee shall maintain the merchandise with care, shall keep it insured, and shall make all reasonable efforts to comply with Seller's instructions for the care of the merchandise. In the event Consignee fails to do so, Consignee shall be liable for the price for said merchandise set forth above, less the percentage thereof allocated to Consignee.

Consignment Agreement (*continued*)

7. *PROCEEDS* Consignee shall sell only at the price listed herein, unless authorized by Seller to sell at a different price. At the end of each month, Consignee shall account for and pay to Seller all proceeds of sales of the merchandise consigned by Seller.

8. *SPECIAL ORDERS* If Consignee obtains any special orders for merchandise and/or service to be provided by Seller, then Consignee shall be entitled to receive a compensation percentage thereon equal to the highest compensation above listed, unless a different percentage is agreed in writing.

9. *INSURANCE* Each party certifies itself to carry and warrants to keep in force comprehensive liability, casualty, and product liability insurance. Such liability insurances shall be in the amount of not less than one million dollars ($1,000,000). Either party shall provide certificates of insurance naming the other as an insured upon the request of the other party.

10. *PROMOTIONAL MATERIAL* Seller may, but is not required to, provide to Consignee advertising or other promotional materials, including literature, displays, decorations, or other forms thereof, and, if so provided, Consignee shall use the same in good faith and for their intended purpose, shall keep the same safe and free from damage as if it were merchandise, and shall return any unused portion after all merchandise is sold, or this Agreement is terminated, or upon demand of Seller.

11. *TERMINATION* This Agreement may be terminated by either party upon sixty (60) days written notice. If Consignee shall have no merchandise of Seller on hand for sale for more than sixty (60) consecutive days, this Agreement shall also stand as terminated, notwithstanding the failure of either party to give written notice. All promises and warranties shall survive termination.

12. *CHOICE OF LAW* This Agreement is made under and shall be construed under the laws of the State of _____.

Dated _____, 19____

SELLER _____

by _____

Address _____

_____

_____

CONSIGNEE _____

by _____

Address _____

_____

_____

MAINTENANCE AGREEMENT

Under the following Terms and Conditions, _____ ("Servicer") agrees for the stated fees to perform preventive maintenance service for one (1) year from the effective date for _____ ("Customer") on the equipment listed by model and serial number.

1. Each regularly scheduled preventive maintenance call shall include a complete inspection during which cleaning, lubrication, and mechanical adjustments determined as due by Servicer will be performed.

2. If this Agreement includes parts coverage, those parts found to be faulty by Servicer will be replaced or repaired at no additional charges, unless due to casualty, act of God, low or high voltage, negligence, or abuse. This Agreement includes ____/excludes ____ parts coverage.

3. No additional charge will be levied for legitimate interim Customer trouble calls on listed equipment if performed during Servicer's regular hours.

4. Customer warrants the listed equipment is in good condition on the effective date of this Agreement.

5. All service covered by this Agreement will be performed during Servicer's regular hours of ___A.M. to ___P.M. weekdays. If service is requested outside such regular hours, the Servicer's overtime hourly rates prevail. Availability of overtime personnel is on a man-available basis and not guaranteed.

6. Repairs necessitated by casualty, act of God, voltage aberrations, abuse, or negligence, are not covered by this Agreement, but will be provided at Servicer's hourly rate(s) plus parts.

7. Cost of supply items are not included herein, and will be charged to Customer as used at Servicer's standard prices.

8. No additional charge for travel will be made unless Customer's location is more than twenty (20) miles from Servicer's closest office, or service is requested outside Servicer's normal business hours.

9. Costs of equipment installation, refurbishing, alteration, and disassembly and reassembly when moving machine are not included herein.

10. Customer agrees Servicer shall not be liable to Customer for lost profits, business opportunities, consequential damages, or any other damages. Servicer's maximum liability hereunder is strictly limited to no more than the revenue collected by Servicer under this Agreement.

11. Either party may terminate this Agreement on thirty (30) days written notice. Servicer will refund to Customer the time-prorated amount less all outstanding invoices, interest, and adjustments. Termination shall not relieve Customer of payment for all charges incurred through the date of termination.

Customer Initials _____   Servicer Initials _____

12. All Servicer invoices carry terms of Net 10. If Customer fails to make any payments on any invoices of any kind from Servicer, at Servicer's option, unamortized prepaid amounts may be credited against such invoices and the term of coverage under this Agreement reduced accordingly. Past due balances shall bear interest at the rate of one and one half percent (1.5%) per month. If collection action of any kind is necessary, Customer shall pay all costs of collection including, but not limited to, a twenty-five (25%) attorney fee.

Maintenance Agreement (*continued*)

Customer _____   Signature Date _____

by _____   Effective Date _____

Title _____   Deposit Amount _____

Customer Address _____

Agreement not binding upon Servicer until ratified below by Servicer.

Servicer _____   Date _____

by _____   Title _____

EQUIPMENT LISTING

No. Units	Model Nos.	Serial Nos.	Location Address/Dept./etc.	Maint. Freq.	Annual Fee/Unit	Total Fees

(Attach additional sheets for listing if needed.)

SERVICES AGREEMENT

THIS AGREEMENT is made between _____ ("Servicer") and
_____ ("Client") on _____, 19____, as follows:

1. *PURPOSE* Client engages Servicer to provide and perform certain consultative services described and defined as follows:

   _____

   _____

   _____

2. *PERFORMANCE* Servicer shall perform such services using due diligence, best efforts, and commercially reasonable judgment, but unless specifically delineated in writing, guarantees no specific outcome to Client. Servicer shall provide adequate personnel time to fulfill the service requirements, and may perform services at times at Client's location(s) as the parties may agree.

3. *COOPERATION* Client agrees to furnish Servicer with accurate data on a timely basis as reasonably requested by Servicer. Client shall provide Servicer access to personnel, records, facilities, and assets as reasonably necessary to facilitate Servicer performance. If requested, Client shall designate "Contact Persons" to whom Servicer's communications shall be primarily channeled.

4. *EXPENSES* Client shall advance $_____ to Servicer, upon signing, in addition to deposit (see Paragraph 6), toward reimburseable Servicer expenses, to be accounted for on a vouchered basis. Reimburseable expenses are estimated at

   _____ $_____

   _____ $_____

   _____ $_____

   If Servicer expects any such expense to exceed the estimate by 10% or anticipates the need for other expenses, Client's advance written approval is required for reimbursement.

5. *CHARGES* Client shall pay Servicer according to the following:

   _____

   _____

   _____

6. *DEPOSIT* At signing of this Agreement, Client shall pay Servicer a deposit of $_____ toward the Charges as a precondition for Servicer's performance, to be credited to the last payment due.

Services Agreement (*continued*)

7. *PAYMENTS* Client shall pay Servicer the Charges plus expenses then due for reimbursement within five (5) days of billing. Overdue payments shall bear a five percent (5%) late charge. If Servicer undertakes collection or enforcement efforts, Client shall be liable for all costs thereof, including attorney fees.

8. *TERM* This Agreement shall commence on _____ and terminate on _____, unless the parties agree otherwise.

9. *INDEMNITY* Client shall hold Servicer harmless in and from all claims, liabilities, damages, and detriments not arising from Servicer's actual negligence or malfeasance.

10. *MISCELLANEOUS* This Agreement establishes strictly an independent contractor relationship and contains the entire recitation of legal terms governing the relationship. Operational directions and requests shall not amend such terms, which may only be amended by writing signed by both parties. This Agreement is binding on all successors of the parties. All provisions hereof are severable. This Agreement is governed by _____ law.

Client _____   Servicer _____

by _____   by _____

Date _____   Date _____

CONTRACT FOR SALE OF GOODS

THIS CONTRACT is made between _____ ("Seller") and
_____ ("Buyer") on _____, 19____, as follows:

1. *PURPOSE* Buyer hereby agrees to purchase from Seller and Seller hereby agrees to vend to Buyer the following described goods.

   ID No.   Quantity   Description & Specifications   Price/Unit   Total Price

2. *DELIVERY* Buyer shall requisition so much of the total for delivery as Buyer desires, by giving Seller ____ days advance notice of quantity. Upon receipt of requisition, Seller shall arrange for delivery by carrier chosen by Seller, the costs of which shall be F.O.B. _____. All goods shall conform to specifications, but Buyer may not reject any deliveries, but shall have the right to return any materially nonconforming goods for replacement by Seller, with costs of redelivery to be borne by Seller.

3. *CHARGES* Seller shall invoice Buyer upon and for each shipment. Buyer shall pay all charges on terms of _____. Any late payment shall bear a late charge of ____%. Overdue invoices shall also bear interest at the rate of ____% per _____. If Seller undertakes collection or enforcement efforts, Buyer shall be liable for all costs thereof, including attorney fees. If Buyer is in arrears on any invoice, Seller may, on notice to Buyer, apply the deposit thereto and withhold further delivery until the deposit and all arrearages are brought current.

4. *DEPOSIT* At signing of this Contract, Buyer shall pay Seller a deposit of $_____ toward the total price as a precondition for Seller's performance, which deposit is to be credited to the last shipment.

5. *TERM* This Contract shall commence on _____ and terminate upon the last delivery, which shall be shipped, with or without requisition for the balance of goods then unshipped by _____, unless the parties agree otherwise. However, if as of such date, Buyer is in arrears on the account, Seller may then cancel this Contract and sue for its damages, including lost profits, offsetting the deposit thereagainst, and further recover its cost of suit including attorney fees.

6. *WARRANTY* Seller warrants goods sold hereunder to be new and free from substantive defects in workmanship and materials. Seller's liability under the foregoing warranty is limited to replacement of goods or repair of defects or refund of the purchase price at Seller's sole option. No other warranty, express or implied, is made by Seller, and none shall be imputed or presumed.

7. *TAXES* All sales taxes, tarriffs, and other governmental charges shall be paid by Buyer and are Buyer's responsibility except as limited by law.

8. *FORCE MAJEURE* Seller may, without liability, delay performance or cancel this Contract on account of force majeure or other circumstances beyond its control, including, but not limited to, strikes, acts of God, political unrest, embargo, failure of source of supply, or casualty.

Contract for Sale of Goods (*continued*)

9. *MISCELLANEOUS* This Contract is binding on all successors of the parties. This Contract contains the entire Agreement between the parties to which no modification shall be made except in writing signed by both parties. All provisions hereof are severable. This Contract is governed by _____law.

Buyer _____   Seller _____

by _____   by _____

Date _____   Date _____

NOTICE OF WARRANTY CLAIM

Under the Terms of Warranty obtained from you we hereby requisition repair to good operating condition or replacement of the following:

Serial No. _____

Product Description:

_____

_____

Delivery/Installation Date _____

Problem Description:

_____

_____

_____

_____

_____

_____

Exercise of warranty rights does not constitute waiver of any other rights, all of which are hereby reserved.
Your prompt attention is appreciated.

Date _____   _____
                          Signature

DISCLAIMER OF WARRANTY

The Buyer(s), _____, hereby acknowledge(s) to the Vendor, _____, the following:

1. This Disclaimer relates to the transaction described as follows:

   _____

   _____

2. Buyer acknowledges that the goods and/or services provided under the aforesaid transaction are without any warranties of any kind.

3. Buyer acknowledges all goods (including, but not limited to, parts, supplies, and all other tangible items, whether central to or incidental to the transaction, if any) are sold strictly "as is."

4. Buyer knowingly and intentionally waives all statutory warranties capable of waiver, including, if permissible under law, warranties of merchantability, fitness for a particular purpose, and title.

5. Buyer acknowledges that no portion of the consideration paid to Vendor or otherwise provided to Vendor is offered or intended to purchase or receive in exchange from Vendor any kind of warranty, and any and every kind of warranty for the above-described transaction is hereby absolutely and irrevocably waived to the fullest extent allowed by law.

6. Buyer(s) acknowledge(s) being at least 18 years of age and making this disclaimer voluntarily, intentionally, and without duress or undue influence.

Date _____, 19____

_____ (Seal)   _____ (Seal)
Buyer   Buyer

Module XI

Shipment and Delivery

INTRODUCTION

This, the concluding Module, deals with the final acts of vendor performance, shipment, and delivery. Where goods are involved, the Uniform Commercial Code (UCC) sets out specific procedures for dealing with problem deliveries. A party who is unfamiliar with those rules stands at a great legal disadvantage.

The forms in this Module are designed to accomplish three purposes:

1. To verify shipment and delivery in accord with the agreement of the parties
2. To safeguard and preserve rights in the event of defects in shipment, delivery, or the goods themselves
3. To provide an audit trail, especially for tracing the whereabouts of the fruits of the transaction

MODULE FORMS

The eight forms in this Module are

Straight Bill of Lading
Packing Slip
Delivery Receipt
Notice of Rejection

Claim for Damage
Notice of Return of Goods
Receipt and Conditional Credit
Receipt for Completed Services

Straight Bill of Lading

Definition

The straight bill of lading is issued by a carrier, acknowledging receipt of the cargo and defining the terms of transporting the cargo.

Comments

a. The bill of lading makes the carrier the possessory agent of the party paying the freight, and also gives the carrier a possessory lien on the goods if the freight bill is not paid.

b. This bill of lading is non-negotiable. If the bill of lading is deliverable to "bearer," or to "the order of" a party, it becomes a negotiable document of title. Most transactions for goods other than commodities (which use both) are delivered under straight bills.

c. A shipper has the duty to disclose to the carrier any particulars about the goods that may create a hazard, either to the carrier or to the welfare of the goods.

d. Descriptions of the goods in the bill of lading should match those in the order acknowledgment, etc., especially as the consignee (i.e., the recipient) will want to be sure the goods shipped are those ordered.

Distribution

Original to carrier
Copies to shipper's accounting and shipping departments
Copies to consignee's accounting and receiving departments

Packing Slip

Definition

The packing slip accompanies the goods, identifying their source and cause of shipment.

Comments

a. Although not a document of title and not normally thought of as a legal document, the packing slip nevertheless should be consistent with other documents exchanged (e.g., order acknowledgment), as it will be in the hands of a potentially adverse party if any claim arises relative to the transaction.

b. Note that the packing slip can be used to fill an order or to return goods.

Distribution

Original with goods to destination party

Copy to accounting department

Copy retained by shipping department

Delivery Receipt

Definition

The delivery receipt is used as an acknowledgment of receiving a delivery.

Comments

a. The bill of lading will serve to acknowledge delivery, but the delivery receipt is for use when no bill of lading is involved, such as for packages sent through ordinary mail, by courier, or delivered directly by the seller.

b. The important point about the delivery receipt is the reservation of rights against later discovered defects.

c. Once again the description of goods should match other transaction documents.

Distribution

Original to shipper

Copy to carrier

Copy to accounting department

Copy retained by receiving department

Notice of Rejection

Definition

The notice of rejection, under the UCC, is a notice to a vendor that goods are not accepted as conforming to the contract.

Comments

a. If the buyer does not notify the seller within a reasonable time of the rejection, the buyer will be liable for the whole order, subject, of course, to contractual agreement otherwise.

b. Under the UCC, in the absence of contract language to the contrary, a buyer can accept part of a shipment and reject the balance.

c. The cause of rejection must be contemplated in the contract, or it will not excuse the buyer from liability for payment.

d. If the goods are perishable, the buyer will be liable unless the vendor is given the chance to seasonably instruct on the disposition of the goods *and* guarantees all costs to the buyer.

e. See Article 2 of the UCC, and consult counsel in the event a rejection seems appropriate.

Distribution

Original to vendor

Copy to carrier

Copy to accounting department

Copy to purchasing department

Copy retained by receiving department

Claim for Damage

Definition

The claim for damage is a notice to a carrier of a claim that the carrier is liable for damage in transit to the goods.

Comments

a. Ordinarily, the party employing the carrier will use this form. If the goods have been taken by the buyer's carrier from the seller, damage in transit is the buyer's problem. If the seller's carrier is the cause, the buyer's claim is direct against the seller. (Again presuming no variation is contained in the contract.)

b. Reservation of rights to all other parties in the transaction is also critical, as sometimes it is discovered that the carrier is not responsible for the damage.

c. Check your own insurance coverage, as it may be possible to claim with your own insuror and let the insuror subrogate for recovery.

Distribution

Original to carrier

Copies to vendor's accounting, sales, and shipping departments

Copies to buyer's accounting, purchasing, and receiving departments

Notice of Return of Goods

Definition

The notice of return of goods gives notice that goods are being sent back after having been previously accepted.

Comments

a. Comments regarding the notice of breach (Module II) are applicable to the notice of return of goods, as well.

b. A contractual right (e.g., automatic return) must exist to base a return upon, although the right may be implied (e.g., implied warranty).

c. If the attempted return is not provided for by contract, acceptance of the goods by the vendor will ordinarily be deemed to modify the contract, so the vendor should refuse delivery if the return is not permitted.

Distribution

Original by certified mail to vendor

Copy returned with goods to vendor

Copy to purchasing department

Copy to accounting department

Receipt and Conditional Credit

Definition

The receipt and conditional credit is used to accept returned or rejected goods and to allow credit to the buyer for return.

Comments

a. The receipt is made conditionally, in order to preserve the rights of the vendor if the return is found to violate the contract (e.g., only unopened goods could be returned, but some were open).

b. If a restocking charge is permissible under the contract, it should be deducted from the amount of the credit.

c. The effect of the customer's waiver also limits the liability of the vendor for any claim of consequential or other damages.

Distribution

Original to buyer

Copy to sales department

Copy to accounting department

Receipt for Completed Services

Definition

The receipt for completed services is used as an acknowledgment by the customer that service work has been performed and provided to specification.

Comments

a.   Services are not UCC-governed.

b.   The receipt acknowledges that payment is due and essentially waives all defenses to payment, except perhaps later-discovered defects, depending on contractual terms and local law.

Distribution

Original to billing department

Copy to service department

Copy to customer

STRAIGHT BILL OF LADING—SHORT FORM—Original—Not Negotiable

SHIPPER'S NO.

CARRIER'S NO.

CARRIER

RECEIVED, subject to the classifications and tariffs in effect on the date of the issue of this Bill of Lading,

AT _____ 19 ___ FROM _____

the property described below, in apparent good order, except as noted (contents and condition of contents of packages unknown), marked, consigned and destined as indicated below, which said carrier (the word carrier being understood throughout this contract as meaning any person or corporation in possession of the property under the contract) agrees to carry to its usual place of delivery at said destination, if on its route, otherwise to deliver to another carrier on the route to said destination. It is mutually agreed, as to each carrier of all or any of said property over all or any portion of said route to destination, and as to each party at any time interested in all or any of said property, that every service to be performed hereunder shall be subject to all the terms and conditions of the Uniform Domestic Straight Bill of Lading set forth (1) in Uniform Freight Classification in effect on the date hereof, if this is a rail or a rail-water shipment, or (2) in the applicable motor carrier classification or tariff if this is a motor carrier shipment. Shipper hereby certifies that he is familiar with all the terms and conditions of the said bill of lading, including those on the back thereof, set forth in the classification or tariff which governs the transportation of this shipment, and the said terms and conditions are hereby agreed to by the shipper and accepted for himself and his assigns. **(Mail or street address of consignee — For purposes of notification only.)**

CONSIGNED TO

DESTINATION   STATE   COUNTY

DELIVERY ADDRESS ★

(★To be filled in only when shipper desires and governing tariffs provide for delivery thereat.)

ROUTE

DELIVERING CARRIER   CAR OR VEHICLE INITIALS   NO.

NO. PKGS	KIND OF PACKAGE, DESCRIPTION OF ARTICLES, SPECIAL MARKS AND EXCEPTIONS	* WEIGHT (SUB TO COR)	CLASS OR RATE	CK COL	
					Subject to Section 7 of conditions of applicable bill of lading, if this shipment is to be delivered to the consignee without recourse on the consignor, the consignor shall sign the following statement:
					The carrier shall not make delivery of this shipment without payment of freight and all other lawful charges.
					_____ (Signature of Consignor)
					If charges are to be prepaid, write or stamp here, "To be Prepaid."
					Received $_____ to apply in prepayment of the charges on the property described hereon.
					_____ Agent or Cashier
					_____ PER (The signature here acknowledges only the amount prepaid.)
					Charges Advanced $_____

* If the shipment moves between two ports by a carrier by water, the law requires that the bill of lading shall state whether it is "carrier's or shipper's weight."

NOTE — Where the rate is dependent on value, shippers are required to state specifically in writing the agreed or declared value of the property.   The agreed or declared value of the property is hereby specifically stated by the shipper to be not exceeding

_____ per _____

† The fibre boxes used for this shipment conform to the specifications set forth in the box maker's certificate thereon, and all other requirements of Uniform Freight Classification.

† Shipper's imprint in lieu of stamp, not a part of bill of lading approved by the Interstate Commerce Commission.

SHIPPER, PER _____   AGENT, _____

Permanent post-office address of shipper, _____

(This Bill of Lading is to be signed by the shipper and agent of the carrier issuing same.)

ORIGINAL BILL OF LADING - CUSTOMER'S COPY

PACKING SLIP

Date _____, 19____

To Destination Party: From Shipper:

_____   _____

_____   _____

_____   _____

Reference Purchase Order No. _____   Account No. _____   Invoice No. _____

Carrier _____   Shipping Date _____

   Packed herewith for delivery to you are the following described goods in accord with ___Your Order/___Our Return.

Serial No.	Description & Specifications	Quantity Ordered	Quantity Backordered	Quantity Packed

   All goods are shipped at risk of Destination Party. All claims for damage must be made to Carrier. No offset or deduction is allowed against Shipper's invoice. No cancellation or return is permitted without prior authorization from Shipper, and must conform to Shipper instructions, or no credit will be due or issued. All of Shipper's rights are reserved. Nothing contained herein shall alter any terms under documents or instruments issued by Shipper.

DELIVERY RECEIPT

Date _____, 19____

To Shipper: From Recipient:

_____   _____

_____   _____

_____   _____

Reference Purchase Order No. _____   Account No. _____   Invoice No. _____

Carrier _____   Delivery Date _____

    Receipt of delivery from you of the following described goods, in accord with ___Our Order/ ___Your Return, is hereby acknowledged.

Serial No.	Description & Specifications	Quantity Ordered	Quantity Received	Quantity Defective	Quantity Accepted

    All rights to claim and obtain remedies for subsequently discovered damages, defects, misdelivery, nonconformance with specifications, or other defalcations are hereby reserved against Shipper and Carrier, as applicable, as are all other rights, cumulatively and not exclusively. Claim against one or release of one to the exclusion of the other does not waive any rights whatsoever against the other. Nothing contained herein shall alter any terms under documents or instruments issued by Recipient, or subject Recipient to any charges of any kind unless specifically agreed to in writing by Recipient.

NOTICE OF REJECTION

To _____   From _____

_____   _____

_____   _____

TAKE NOTICE that under Contract made _____, 19____, as evidenced by the following documents: _____, we are hereby REJECTING the performance and/or delivery as tendered to us on or about _____, 19____, on account of defects in the goods, services, and/or performance and reasons stated as follows:

If any of the goods delivered are perishable, further Notice is hereby given that instructions and indemnity are immediately demanded from you, in accord with the Uniform Commercial Code, for the disposition of such goods.

This Notice is made under the Uniform Commercial Code (if applicable) and all other applicable laws. All rights are hereby reserved, none of which are waived. Any forebearance or temporary waiver from enforcement shall not constitute permanent waiver or waiver of any other right.

You are urged to cure your Breach forthwith.

Date _____, 19____

Rejecting Party   _____

by   _____
Authorized Signatory

CLAIM FOR DAMAGE

To Carrier: From Claimant:

_____   _____

_____   _____

_____   _____

Reference: Shipment from _____, _____ to _____, _____

Shipped by _____ to _____

Bill of Lading No. _____   Delivery Date _____

As ___/Shipper___/Recipient, we hereby give Notice to you, the Carrier, that goods received through you on the Delivery Date were found to be damaged:

No. Units	Description of Goods Damaged	Description of Damages to Goods	Value Claimed

Total Claimed: _____

Compensation for the aforesaid damages is hereby claimed and demanded. Such claim does not limit our rights to further claims and damages, in the event additional claims or damages are discovered on account of such delivery. Settlement with or release to you does not waive any of our rights against any third party, nor does the same with any third party waive any rights against you. All rights are reserved, cumulatively and not exclusively. Nothing contained herein shall alter any other documentation issued by us, unless specifically so stated.

Date _____, 19____   Claimant _____

by _____
Authorized Signatory

By Certified Mail

NOTICE OF RETURN OF GOODS

To _____   From _____

_____   _____

_____   _____

    TAKE NOTICE that under Contract made _____, 19____, as evidenced by the following documents: _____, we are hereby RETURNING the goods previously delivered to us on or about _____, 19____, on account of defects in the goods and reasons stated:

Serial No.	Description of Goods Returned	Description of Return Defects/Reasons	Quantity Returned	Price Each	Credit Due

Total Credit Due: _____

    Credit for the goods returned is hereby claimed and demanded. Such claim does not limit our rights to further credits or damages in the event that additional credits or damages are discovered to be due or additional returns are made. Settlement with or release to you does not waive any rights against any other party. All rights are reserved cumulatively, and not exclusively. Nothing contained herein shall alter any other documentation issued by us, unless specifically so stated.

    This Notice is made under the Uniform Commercial Code (if applicable) and all other applicable laws.

Date _____, 19____ Returning Party _____

by _____
              Authorized Signatory

RECEIPT AND CONDITIONAL CREDIT

Received this date from _____("Customer") the following goods returned for credit.

Serial No.	Number	Product Description	Condition	Credit Each	Total Credit

Grand Total _____

Reason for Return:

Condition listed is the apparent condition of the goods and is not binding if condition is later discovered to be otherwise. Seller granting credit hereby reserves the right to charge back Customer if it is later discovered that Customer is not entitled to any portion or all of the credit.

Customer is being permitted to return the goods, electing such return as Customer's recourse, waiving all other claims as to such goods.

Date _____

Acknowledged: Validated:

_____   _____
Customer   Authorized Employee

RECEIPT FOR COMPLETED SERVICES

Customer _____   Date _____

Address where services performed:

_____

_____

_____

Contract/P.O. Reference _____

    Customer hereby acknowledges satisfactory completion of the services performed by
_____in accord with Customer's order. Customer agrees to
promptly pay the balance due for such services when invoiced in accord with the terms of the
Contract.

Date _____   _____
                                                                    Authorized Customer Signature

Index

Accident report, 166–167, *170*
Acknowledgment
    attorney-in-fact, 25, 26, *33*
    corporate, 25, 28, *35*
    individual, 24, 25–26, *32*
    notarization, 24–27, *32–35*
    order, 8, 194, 195, 196, *210–211*
    partner's, 25, 26–27, *34*
    Uniform Recognition Act, 26
Advice of payment, 149, 151, *158*
Affidavit
    bulk sale compliance, 176, 178–179, *189*
    bulk transfer, 175–176, 178, *188*
    title, 176, 179, *190*
Agreement. *See* Contract.
Amendment. *See* Contract.
American Arbitration Association, 30, 41
American Trucking Associations, 59, 68–69, 166,
    168, 170, 173–174
American Warehousemen's Association, 106, 140,
    147
Application
    approval of credit, 43, 44, *53*
    business credit, 42, 43, *47–48*
    consumer loan, 42, 43–44, *49–50*
    employment, 57, 58, *64–65*
    federal bidder's mailing list, 193, 194, *201–203*
    rejection of credit, 43, 45, *54*
Appointment of collection agent, 8, 10–11, *19*

Arbitration agreement, 25, 30, *41*
Assignment
    account for collection, 8, 11, *20*
    contract, 25, 28–29, *38*
    insurance, 183
    lease, 82, 84–85, 87, 88, *95–98*
    note, 101
    notice of account, 8, 11–12, *21*
    security agreement, 130
Assumption of risk (waiver of), 149, 150, *155*
Attorney
    bankruptcy, 12, 23
    collection, 10
    employment law, 57, 61
    help from, 5–6
    -in-fact, 25, 26, 33, 36, 115–116
    lease, 83
    note, 101–103
    power of, 25, 26, 36
    right of rescission, 103
    truth-in-lending, 100

Bankruptcy, 8, 22–23, 91
    affidavit of title, 190
    guaranty, 123
    note, 111, 113, 115
    proof of claim, 8, 12, *22*
    reaffirmation of debt, 8, 13, *23*
    security agreement, 120, 127, 131, 132

Note: Italicized page numbers indicate location of the form.

Bill of lading, 223, 224–225, *229*
Bill of sale, 176, 179, *192*
Blanket purchase order requisition, 194, 197, *212*
Blanks in forms, 4, 43
Breach, notice of, 25, 29, *40*, 227
Bulk transfer (bulk sale)
 act, 175, 177, 178, 183
 affidavit, 175–176, 178, *188*
 compliance, 176, 178–179, *189*
 notice to creditors, 175, 177, *185–186*
 tax authorities notice, 175, 177–178, *187*

Catalogue disclaimer, 193, 194, *200*
Certificate of satisfaction, 150, 153, *162*
Certified mail
 bulk transfer tax notice, 187
 guarantor, 124
 notice of breach, 29, 40
 notice of rejection, 232
 notice of return, 227, 234
 security agreement, 133
Claim
 damages, 224, 226, *233*
 release of, 25, 29, *39*, 149, 150, 151–152, 154, *159*
 warranty, 194, 199, *221*
Collateral, 99. *See also* Security.
 guaranty, 122
 receipt, 100, 105, *138*
 substitution, 100, 106, *139*
Collection, 7–23
 agent, 10, 19
Commerce Business Daily, The, 202
Confess judgment note. *See* Note.
Confidentiality
 covenant, 175, 176, *180*, 183
 employee certification, *58, 62,* 73, 75, 77, 78
 invention, 175, 176, *181*
Consent
 account assignment, 28–29, 38
 employment verification, 58–59, 66
 guarantor, 122
 lease assignment, 84, 85
 lessor, 88–89, 183
 medical examination, 59, 67
 medical records, 60, 70
 quotation, 205, 207
 security agreement, 128
Consignment
 agreement, 194, 197, *213–214*
 bill of lading, 224, 229

Consumer price index, 88
Consumer, 5
 loan application, 42, 43, *44–45*
 loan, 100, 112–113
 security agreement, 100, 103, *119–121*
 truth-in-lending, 100
Contract
 administration and formation, 24–41
 amendment, 28, 37
 assignment, 25, 28–29, *38*
 breach, 25, 29, 40
 business sale, 175, 176, *182–184*
 consignment, 194, 197, *213–214*
 deposit receipt, 156
 dispute, 152, 154
 early termination, 25, 29, 39
 employment, 58, 61, *73–74*
 formation and administration, 24–41
 goods, 194, 197, 198, *219–220*
 maintenance, 194, 197–198, *215–216*
 modification, 25, 28, *37*
 services, 194, 197–198, *217–218*
 warranty disclaimer, 199
Corporate acknowledgment, 25, 27, *35*
Counsel. *See* Attorney.
Covenant
 confidentiality, 58, 62, *77*, 175, 176, *180*
 deed of trust, 135–136
 employment, 58, 61, 73–74, *75–76*
 realty lease, 88–89, 92
 security agreement, 128–130
Cover (UCC meaning), 40, 130–131
Cover sheet (letter of intent), 24, 25, *31*
Credit
 conditional, 224, 227, *235*
 extension, 42–56, 99, 104, 122
Cure of breach, 29, 40, 90

Debt. *See also* Note.
 reaffirmation, 8, 13, *23*
Deed of trust, 100, 104, *135–136*
 certificate of satisfaction, 162
 lease subordination, 90
Delivery, 223–236
 consignment, 213
 order acknowledgment, 211
 purchase order, 196, 209
 receipt, 223, 225, *231*
 sale of goods, 219
Demand
 final for payment, 8, 10, *18*

invoice, 9, 17
   payment, 8, 9, *17*
Deposit
   business sale, 182
   quotation, 206
   receipt, 149, 150, *156*
   security, 90, 98
   services, 217
Disclaimer
   catalogue, 193, 194, *200*
   warranty, 194, 199, 207, 211, 215, 219, *222*
Discounter (of receivables), 11
Drug testing, 59

Early termination, 25, 29, *39*, 150, 154
Employment, 57–80
   application, 57, 58, *64–65*
   contract, 58, 61, *73–74*
   eligibility (I-9), 58, 60–61, *71–72*
   injury, 166, 169
   note, 100, 102, *114*
   security, 167
   verification, 57, 58–59, *66*
Endorsement, 151
Equipment lease, 82, *86–87*
   assignment, 82, 84, *95*, *96*
Expense voucher, 5, 58, 63, *80*
Expression of interest, 25

Factor (of receivables), 11
Fax, 5
Federal bidder's mailing list application, 193, 194,
      201–203
Financial statement
   confidentiality, 73, 75, 77, 180
   credit application, 43, 48
   personal, 42, 44, *51–52*
   security agreement, 127–128
Financing statement (UCC), 100, 105, *137*
   affidavit of title, 190
   business sale, 182
   lease, 82, 91
   note, 100, 105
   release, 150, 152–153, *161*
   security agreement, 120, 129
   termination, 150, 152–153, *161*
Forms management, 4, 5

Guaranty
   lease, 82, 83, 86, *92*
   note, 100, 103–104, 113, *122–124*

notice to cosigner, 100, 101, 103, 113, *118*
   security agreement, 132

I-9 (employment eligibility), 58, 60–61, *71–72*
Income tax
   business sale, 175–179
   lease, 81–82
Injury report, 166, *169*
Insurance
   business sale, 182–183
   consignment, 213–214
   damage claim, 226
   incident report, 166–168, *172*
   leases, 87, 89–90
   liability, 59
   quotation, 205, 207
   security agreement, 120, 129
   truth-in-lending, 107
   waiver and assumption of risk, 150
   workman's compensation, 166
Interest
   credit, 47, 53
   deposit, 156
   guaranty, 122–124
   invoice, 14, 15
   maintenance agreement, 215
   note, 109–116
   order acknowledgment, 211
   quotation, 207
   rates, 5, 44
   rescission period, 103
   statement, 16
Invention confidentiality, 175, 176, *181*
Invoice, 5, 7–8
   assignment of account, 11
   demand for payment, 9
   deposit, 156
   goods, *14*
   payment, 157, 158
   services, *15*
   statement, 9
Itemization of amount financed, 108

Jurat. *See* Notary.

Late charges
   credit application, 53
   equipment lease, 87
   note, 110–113, 115
   notice to cosigner, 118
   realty lease, 88

Late charges *(continued)*
truth-in-lending, 107
Lawyer. *See* Attorney.
Lease, 81–89
assignment, 82, 84–85, *95, 96, 97, 98*
deposit, 156
equipment, 81, *86–87*, 95, 96
guaranty, 82, 83, 86, *92*
memorandum, 82, 83–84, 91, *93–94*
realty, 82–83, *88–91*, 97, 98, 182–183
Letter of intent, 24, 25, *31*
Limited partnership, 27
Loans. *See* Note; Security.

Mailing list (federal bidder's), 193, 194, *201–203*
Maintenance agreement, 194, 197–198, *215–216*
Mechanic's lien, 153–154, 163, 198
Medical
exam authorization, 57, 59, *67*
exam form, 58, 59, *68–69*
injury, 169
records request, 58, 60, *70*
Memorandum of lease, 82, 83–84, 91, *93–94*
Modem, 5
Modification agreement, 25, 28, *37*
Mortgage. *See* Deed of trust.

Noncompetition
business sale, 183
employee, 73–76
Notary, 5, 24–25, 153, 154, 179. *See also* Acknowledgment.
Note, 100–148. *See also* Security.
business sale, 182
commercial, 100–101, *110–111*
confess judgment, 100, 102, *115–116*
consumer, 100–102, *112–113*
employee, 100, 102, *114*
payment, 157
promissory, 100–101, *109*
receipt for collateral, 138
release, 149, 152, *160*
Notice
account assignment, 8, 11–12, *21*
breach of contract, 25, 29, *40*
bulk transfer, *185–189*
change credit terms, 43, 45, *55*
confession of judgment, 116
contract assignment, 29
cosigner, 100, 101, 103, 113, *118*
defects, 87

lease assignment, 84, 85, 87
realty lease, 88–90
rejection of goods, 223, 225–226, *232*
return, 224, 226–227, *234*
security agreement, 130, 133
warranty claim, 194, 199, *221*
Numbering forms, 5

Order acknowledgment, 2, 194, 196, *210–211*
bill of lading, 224
invoice, 8
packing slip, 224
quotation, 195
sale contract, 198
OSHA (U.S. Occupational Safety and Health
Administration)
report of inspection, 166, 168, *173–174*

Packing slip, 223, 224–225, *230*
Partner's acknowledgment, 25, 26, *34*
Patent, 176, 181
Payment
advice, 149, 151, *158*
demand, 8, 9, *17*
final demand, 8, 10, *18*
receipt, 149, 151, *157*
Physical examination. *See* Medical.
Power of attorney, 25, 27, *36*
Proof of claim, 8, 11, *22*
Purchase order, 1–3, 194, 196, *208–209*
completed services, 236
deposit receipt, 156
invoice, 8
packing slip, 230
quotation, 195, 205, 207
requisition, 194, 197, *212*
sales contract, 198

Quotation, 194, 195, *206–207*
order acknowledgment, 196
purchase order, 196
request for, 194, 195, *204–205*

Reaffirmation of debt, 8, 13, *23*
Realty
certificate of satisfaction, 153, 162
deed of trust, 135–136
financing statement, 105
lease, 82, 85, *88–91, 92, 93,* 97–98
Receipt
collateral, 100, 105, *138*

completed services, 224, 227–228, *236*
conditional credit, 224, 227, *235*
delivery, 223, 225, *231*
deposit, 149, 150, *156*
documents, 58, 62, *78*
payment, 149, 151, *157*
samples and documents, 58, 62, *78*
warehouse, 100, 106, *147–148*
Regulation Z. *See* Truth-in-lending.
Rejection
   credit application, 43, 45, *54*
   goods, 219
   notice, 223, 225–226, *232*
   order acknowledgment, 211
Release
   claims, 149, 151–152, *159*
   deed of trust, 150, 153, *162*
   financing statement, 150, 152–153, *161*
   liens, 150, 153–154, *163*
   mutual, 25, 29, *39*, 150, 154, *164*
   note, 149, 152, *160*
Request
   employment verification, 57, 58–59, *66*
   medical records, 58, 60, *70*
   quotation, 194, 195, *204–205*
Requisition, 194, 197, *212*, 219
Return of goods
   consignment, 213
   notice, 224, 226–227, *234*
   order acknowledgment, 211
   packing slip, 225
   sale of goods, 219
Right of rescission, 100, 102–103, *117*

Safety, 165–174
Sale
   assets, 175–192
   business, 175–192
   bill of, 176, 179, *192*
   goods and services, 193–222
   invoice, 8
Security
   agreement, 101, 104, 119–121, *125–134*, 182
   consumer, 100, 102, 103, *119–121*
   deed of trust, 104
   incident report, 166, 167, *171*
   lease, 82, 90–91, 92
   loan, 99–148
Services
   agreement, 194, 197, 198, *217–218*
   receipt, 224, 227–228, *236*

Shipment. *See* Delivery.
Signature. *See also* Notary.
   authentication, 26
   authority, 5, 128
   lines, 5
   notarization, 25–27
Statement, 8, 9, *16*, 131
   payment, 157, 158

Termination
   consignment, 214
   contract, 25, 29, *39*
   credit line, 43, 45–46, *56*
   employment, 73–78, 102, 114
   financing statement, 153, 161
   maintenance agreement, 215
   realty lease, 89
Time sheet, 58, 62–63, *79*
Title, 105–106, 120, 222
   affidavit, 176, 179, *190–191*
   bill of lading, 224
   packing slip, 224
Trade secrets, 73, 75, 77
Trustee
   bulk transfer affidavit, 189
   certificate of satisfaction, 162
   deed of trust, 135–136
Truth-in-lending, 100, 101, *107–108*

Uniform Arbitration Act, 30
Uniform Commercial Code (UCC), 4
   bulk transfer, 175, 177, 185–189
   business sale, 182
   financing statement, 105, 137, 152–153, 161
   goods, 198
   invoice, 14, 15
   lease, 81
   notice of breach, 29, 40
   rejection, 225, 232
   return, 234
   sale of goods, 198
   security agreement, 125
   services, 228
   shipment, 223
   warehousing, 106
   warranties, 199
Uniform Recognition of Acknowledgments Act, 26
U.S. Bureau of Labor Statistics, 88
U.S. Department of Transportation (DOT), 59, 68–69
Usury, 5

Verification
   eligibility (I-9), 58, 60–61, *71–72*
   employment, 57, 58, *66*

Waiver
   assumption of risk, 149, 150, *155*
   release of lien, 150, 153–154, *163*
   right of rescission, 100, 102–103, *117*
Warehousing
   agreement, 100, 106, *140–146*
   receipt, 100, 106, *147–148*
Warranty

bill of sale, 179, 192
business sale, 182–183
claim, 152, 194, 199, 221
disclaimer, 194, 199, 207, 211, 215, 219, *222*
equipment lease, 86
goods, 219
notice, 194, 199, *221*
payment advice, 158
purchase order, 209
quotation, 205, 207
return, 227
sale of goods, 219